The Sultan

Also by Joan Haslip

Parnell: A Biography
Lady Hester Stanhope
Lucrezia Borgia
The Lonely Empress: A Biography
of Elizabeth of Austria
The Crown of Mexico
(Imperial Adventurer)

NOVELS

Out of Focus
Grandfather Steps
Portrait of Pamela

The Sultan

The Life of Abdul Hamid II

Joan Haslip

Holt, Rinehart and Winston
NEW YORK   CHICAGO   SAN FRANCISCO

For my favourite story-teller

Copyright © 1958 by Joan Haslip
First published in the United States in 1973
All rights reserved, including the right to
reproduce this book or portions thereof in any form.

Library of Congress Catalog Card Number: 72-91568
ISBN: 0-03-006936-X

Printed in the United States of America

Author's Acknowledgements

I wish to give particular thanks to Lady Wanda Max Muller in letting me have access to the correspondence of the late Sir William Max Muller; to Mr. Brinsley Ford in allowing me to quote from the papers of his grandfather Sir Clare Ford, and to the Curators of the MS. Room of the British Museum in giving me access to the hitherto unpublished Layard Papers.

Among many others to whom I am indebted for help and information are His Excellency the Turkish Ambassador, Nuri Birgi; His Excellency Sherif Pasha; Mr. Sami Gunzberg; Marchese Aldobrandino Malvezzi dei Medici; the Honble. Sir Harold Nicolson, and Mr. Harold Bowen. My thanks are also due to my friends Mr. and Mrs. Williamson Napier and Mr. Donald Riddle for their hospitality during my stay in Istanbul, and their help in putting me into contact with many valuable sources.

J.H.

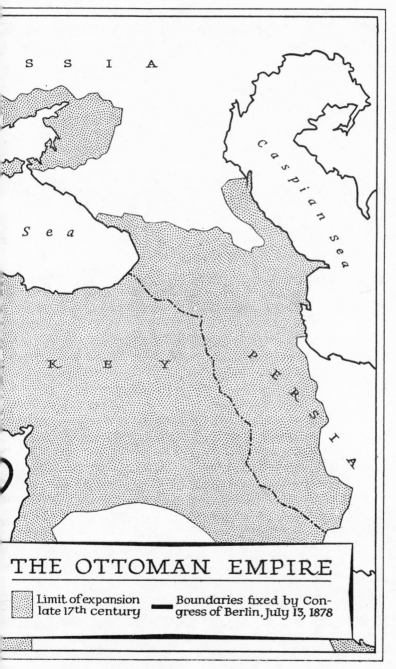

THE OTTOMAN EMPIRE

Limit of expansion
late 17th century ▬ Boundaries fixed by Congress of Berlin, July 13, 1878

I am sure that the historians will vindicate me, and even if the Turkish historians do not do so I am certain that some foreign historian will do me justice.

ABDUL HAMID at Salonika

Chapter I

SULTAN ABDUL MEDJID was at the baths when the Chief Eunuch informed him that a baby boy had been born in the harem. Instinctively the Sultan reached for his purse to reward the messenger who had brought the news, news which was all the more welcome for, of his five children, only one so far had been a boy. Then realising his nakedness, he frowned; it was a bad omen to receive such tidings empty-handed.

Who was the mother? Which of the five hundred women of his harem had been fortunate enough to beget a prince of the sacred race of Osman? Pregnancy in such circumstances was fraught with danger, and there was not a woman in the harem who would hesitate to destroy the chances of a rival who might one day aspire to the most coveted of all positions, that of Valide Sultana, mother to the ruling sovereign. It required both wit and courage to conceal a pregnancy from the prying eyes of frustrated rivals and embittered eunuchs.

On hearing the answer the Sultan was silent—an ominous silence which, throughout the years to come, was to bring discredit to the reputation of his son. It was not that he had forgotten Pirimujgan, the Circassian dancer who had first come to his notice as a slave in his brother-in-law's harem. On the contrary, there had been a time when he had loved her more passionately than any other woman, and the neglect of the past few months originated from the night when she had been seized with a violent fit of coughing and a small spot of blood had appeared on the pillow of the royal bed. Nervous and delicate, frightened for his health, Abdul Medjid had turned away from a woman tainted with an illness of which he suspected he had himself the germ. And now with apprehension he learned that of all the voluptuous beauties of his harem it was this little consumptive dancer who had given him a son.

(1)

Watchful and submissive, the eunuch waited on his master's reactions, trained to detect every change of expression, to anticipate his every passing whim, waiting for the official proclamation with which it was customary to notify the Grand Vizir of the birth of a royal prince, and which it was his privilege to convey to the Sublime Porte. But on this morning of September 22, 1842 (H.1258), Abdul Medjid dismissed His Highness the Kizlar Agasi* without putting his signature to any document, and for three days his son remained nameless and unacknowledged. This delay was all the more strange, for when according to custom the Sultan sent to enquire of Pirimujgan the time and place in which she believed the child had been conceived, the answer appears to have been satisfactory. From his already vast store of amatory experiences the twenty-year-old Abdul Medjid remembered the winter's morning when he had surprised the little dancer on her way to the hammam. It was his habit to wander unannounced into the harem and take some woman unawares, while either at her toilet or at the bath. But water was of bad omen and in his superstitious fear the Sultan hesitated to proclaim a birth under such unfavourable auspices. It was not until three days later that the Kizlar Agasi, wearing his robes of state and attended by a retinue of black and white eunuchs, proceeded by imperial caique from the Cheragan palace on the Bosphorus to the Sublime Porte in Stamboul, bearing the proclamation in which His Imperial Majesty Abdul Medjid announced to his faithful Vizir the birth of a son Abdul Hamid 'bidding him convey the joyful tidings to all ministers and servants of the Porte and to order a salvo of artillery to be fired five times a day for seven days, and all ministries and public buildings to be illuminated at night.'

But despite these official rejoicings, the unaccountable delay gave rise to scandalous rumours and unfounded assertions. And though the little Circassian dancer was recognised as a Haseki-Sultana, mother of a royal prince, and rewarded with the customary present, derogatory stories continued to circu-

---

* The chief eunuch, who at court receptions took precedence immediately after the royal princes.

late in the harem and the lovely Pirimujgan remained lonely and ignored.

Lying in her great gilded bed, one of those beds but lately imported from Vienna to comply with the young Sultan's western tastes, she could hear the guns booming across the water and see by night the torch-lit minarets of Scutari reflected from the Asiatic shore. For three days she had lived in terror, waiting for the first gun-shot to reassure her of the future of her son. All her hopes and ambitions were now centred in this puny baby, third in succession to the Ottoman throne, for the laws of inheritance of the house of Osman decreed that the Sultanate should pass not from father to son, but to the oldest living male member of the family. The present Sultan had not only an elder son, the two-year-old Murad, but also a younger brother, the eleven-year-old Abdul Aziz, as sturdy and as healthy as his mother, the buxom peasant woman of whom the Sultan Mahmud had been so enamoured that he had raised her to the rank of a *kadin**. Yet however remote might be the chances of Abdul Hamid ever coming to the throne, Pirimujgan was sufficiently familiar with the tales of palace revolutions to give free rein to her imagination. From the older eunuchs she had heard tell of the turbulent days at the beginning of the century when the Janissaries made and unmade sultans at their will and the assassination of his brother and his cousin had ended by placing the Sultan Mahmud on the throne.

Ambitious plans for the future were her only consolation as the days passed without bringing a message from the Sultan. At nineteen she refused to admit her life was over, and that all her training in the arts of love was to be wasted. As the mother of a royal prince she would even be denied the last normal outlet of a discarded palace favourite—marriage to a pasha of the Sultan's entourage.

Only a year ago, and she had imagined that the day when she bore Abdul Medjid a son would be the proudest in her life.

It was at the time of the Bairam festival and the Sultan was paying a visit to his newly-married sister at her *yali* at Arnaut-keui. Fate seemed to favour Pirimujgan when from among all

---

* The four principal Sultanas equivalent to the four wives allowed by Moslem law.

her slaves the fourteen-year-old princess singled her out to dance before her brother, and noting his approval, presented her to his Imperial Majesty as a Bairam gift. It had been a long way from a primitive mountain village in the Caucasus, the open slave-market at Trabzon, to a pasha's *yali* on the Bosphorus. But it was a short way from Arnautkeui to the palace of Cheragan and Pirimujgan's future seemed very bright on the day her royal mistress supervised her toilet and adorned her with some of her own jewels, before handing her over to the two black eunuchs who conveyed her to the palace.

In the rigid hierarchy of the Imperial harem she was still only a slave, a *gedikli*, one of those 'on whom the master had cast his eye', and as such she had to submit to the disciplining of the eunuchs, the tuition of the *kalfas*, the older and more experienced women of the harem who initiated the novices in the subtle technique of love. Ardent and ambitious, she proved an apt pupil and when, a few weeks after her arrival, she was summoned to the Sultan's presence she was already sufficiently accomplished to win her way to favour. The Grand Mistress of the Wardrobe had allotted her the finery of an established favourite, the eunuchs had begun to treat her with deference, when one evening, at a time when she was ill with fever, an illness she had not dared to confess for fear of the harem doctors discovering the fact that she was pregnant, she was sent for by the Sultan for the last time. Never had Abdul Medjid appeared to be more passionate and more demanding than on that night, never had she responded more warmly to his embraces, yet in some way she had displeased him, and in displeasing him lost her only foothold on the slippery steps to power.

Time after time in the lonely months that followed she had gone over every word and gesture of that last night, trying to discover where she had failed, refusing to believe that a cough, so quickly, so bravely controlled had been the cause. For how could a simple slave-girl realise that Abdul Medjid avoided her from fear, that 'the Commander of the Faithful, the Lord of the Seven Seas, the Shadow of God on Earth' was so obsessed by a terror of disease, so frightened for his own life, that a small spot of blood on a pillow had been sufficient not only to kill his ardour but to prejudice the future of her unborn child?

When Abdul Medjid, thirty-first Sultan of the House of Osman, ascended the throne at the age of seventeen, he had inherited, together with a vast empire, a legacy of fear. For centuries the Ottoman sultans had ruled by fear—centuries of family feud and fratricide fostered by the unnatural laws of succession—till they ended by becoming themselves the victims of the terror they inspired. Sometimes, as in the case of the Sultan's father Mahmud, a fortuitous revolution brought a young and vigorous ruler to the throne, but all too often some old and senile prince was invested with the sword of Osman* after half a life-time spent in captivity in the so-called princes' 'cages', where their only relaxation was to over-indulge in the erotic pleasures of the harem. And, though heirs to the throne were no longer immured in those luxurious prisons in the seraglio gardens, circumstances were such that even the generous-hearted Abdul Medjid was forced to regard his younger brother with suspicion and distrust.

In Mahmud, Turkey found a ruler worthy of the tradition of Mahomet the Conqueror and Suleyman the Magnificent. Legend played a part in his origin which claimed for his mother a fascinating Créole, cousin to the Empress Josephine of France. Captured while on her way home from her convent school in France to her father's plantation in Martinique, Mademoiselle du Buc de Rivry is said to have been sold in slavery to the Bey of Tunis who, impressed by her marvellous beauty, presented her in tribute to the Sultan of the day, Abdul Hamid I. Legend goes further and asserts that it was this resourceful French-woman who, at the time of the rebellion of the Janissaries, when both his brother and cousin were assassinated, saved her son's life by hiding him in an oven till his supporters had rallied to his defence. Whatever may be the truth of the story—and like all stories emanating from the harem it is based on hearsay rather than on record—the existing portraits and descriptions of Sultan Mahmud, the small bright eyes looking out of the clever foxy face, the short wiry figure and nervous

---

* Equivalent to the Coronation ceremony.

movements, so unlike the impassive countenance and measured gestures of the well-bred Turk, and, above all, his gigantic energy and enlightened views, give substance to the legend.

But one man's energy was not sufficient to weld together a crumbling empire. Flames of revolt fanned by Russian imperialism were already lighted in the Balkans; English liberalism nurtured an independent Greece; in Egypt one of his own pashas, the upstart adventurer Mehmet Ali, had thrown off the Sultan's yoke, and at home corruption and inefficiency undermined his government and obstructed his work of reform. It was Mahmud's misfortune, as well as his glory, to be in advance of his age, to attempt reform when no one in the country understood the meaning of the word and where no one was capable of assisting him in his task. Single-handed he battled on, a reformer who still used the methods of a medieval tyrant.

First to be suppressed were the Janissaries. That élite and pampered militia, originally recruited from Christian slave-children converted to the Moslem faith, had during the centuries developed into the most fanatical and reactionary of all the forces of Islam. In the great days of the Ottoman Empire the white felt bonnets of the Janissaries had been the first to appear before the walls of Constantinople, the last to retreat from the gates of Vienna. Proud of the fact that they were better fed and better paid than any other military corps, they took their titles from the kitchen. The colonel of the regiment was known as the 'Maker of Soup', the 'Soup Kettle' was their standard. But as the Sultans gradually became more effete, so the Janissaries became more powerful and more exacting in their demands. The clang of their kettle-drums dominated the city and successive sultans lived in fear of the overturned cauldron which signified revolt.

But Mahmud was not of a character to be cowed into submission. When the Janissaries rose in opposition to his reform he called on his people to defend themselves against their tyranny. The whole city took to arms, and ten thousand members of the corps perished in one day. Mahmud pursued his vengeance with a pitiless cruelty and for weeks the Bosphorus and the Sea of Marmara were infested with rotting bodies.

But, however savage and primitive might be the means with which Mahmud stamped out revolt, he created from the ruins of a medieval institution a modern army with naval and military colleges run on European lines.

For the first time in history regular ambassadors were accredited to the European courts, daily newspapers publishing world events appeared in Constantinople, and the Turk who till now had left all trafficking and commerce to the despised Greek and Armenian, was given a passport and encouraged to travel abroad. But in every measure of reform, particularly in those which alleviated the lot of his Christian subjects, Mahmud had to battle against Moslem pride and prejudice. An antiquated system of administration dating from the days of the Conquest, laws based on the teachings of the Koran, a conception of the world surviving from the time when the Turkish armies terrorised Europe and Christian ambassadors who incurred the anger of the Sultans were left to languish in the prison of the Seven Towers—all these combined to make the Turk not only indifferent, but opposed to progress. A Sultan who dared to create an order of merit to be awarded irrespectively both to his Christian and his Moslem subjects, and who gave grants of land to Christian Churches was bound to arouse the most dangerous of all opposition, that of the *mollas* and the *softas*, the doctors of the Sacred Law and the theological students. However westernised in his ideas, Mahmud still ruled as an eastern tyrant and an attempted rising led by the *mollas* was suppressed with the same sanguinary ferocity which had marked the suppression of the Janissaries. With iron hand he made his people understand that he was determined to carry out his reforms and that opposition to his will meant death.

If he failed to realise his ambitions, it was not from lack of resolution, but because his countrymen were not ready for reforms, and because he received no support from the foreign powers. The War of Greek Independence found those three habitual rivals, England, France and Russia, in alliance. Fired by their classical enthusiasms and blind to their true interests, English politicians allowed the Czar to attack the Sultan at a time when his defences were seriously impaired by the destruction of his fleet at Navarino. The loss of Greece, the humiliation of the Treaty of Adrianople, the culminating bitterness when England and France stood by and allowed his vassal Mehmet Ali to invade Syria, combined to break Sultan Mahmud's spirit and in 1839 he died, leaving his seventeen-year-old son the task of cleaning out the Augean Stables of Turkish misgovernment.

Whereas Mahmud had ruled by fear, Abdul Medjid aspired to rule with tolerance and mercy, and the *Hatti-Sherif* of Gulhané which inaugurated his reign promised equal privileges and fair taxation to all his subjects. Dictated by Reshid Pasha, one of the young men whom Sultan Mahmud had sent to complete his education abroad and who had returned from England full of liberal principles and ideals, this proclamation was hailed by Europe as the Magna Carta of modern Turkey. The Western Powers, inspired partly by fear of Russian aggrandisement and distrust of Mehmet Ali's ambitions in the East, gave to a weak and vacillating boy the support they had denied his father, but despite his good intentions, Abdul Medjid was far from possessing all the noble qualities which were attributed to him. The harem played a more important part in his life than the divan, and on many an occasion he allowed the reactionary influence of the eunuchs, who viewed with dread the westernisation of the Empire and the end of harem rule, to undermine the work of the young ministers who sincerely hoped to regenerate the Empire. Foreign ambassadors might regard him as the future saviour of his country, but the Kizlar Agasi, 'guardian of the gates of felicity', who saw him in those moments of intimacy when the omnipotent Sultan was no more than a capricious boy, knew him to be as frightened and as helpless as all those other princes of the House of Osman brought up in ignorance by slaves and eunuchs.

His father was already on his death-bed when Abdul Medjid saw for the first time the map of the Ottoman Empire. Since then he had been obsessed by the thought of those vast unknown dominions stretching from the Caucasus to the Persian Gulf, from the Danube to the Nile, an empire of thirty-five million people of whom twenty-three millions belonged to alien creeds. In his dreams he was haunted by the spectre of revolt, casting great tentacles across his empire—part of that legacy of fear which Mahmud had attempted to suppress, but which had returned to haunt his twenty-year-old son, shadowing the cradle of the baby, Abdul Hamid, whose mother's first reaction had been one of fear lest superstition and intrigue might rob him of his heritage.

Chapter II

THE YEAR OF Abdul Hamid's birth coincided with the return to Constantinople of Sir Stratford Canning, appointed for the fourth time as British Ambassador to the Sublime Porte. Both the urgency of the Eastern question and Lord Palmerston's growing conviction that it was in the interests of England to preserve the integrity of the Ottoman Empire had led to the reinstatement of an ambassador who by his fearlessness and independence of character had succeeded in winning the confidence of the taciturn and suspicious Turk.

Over thirty years had gone by since a supercilious young Englishman, acting as minister in the absence of his chief, had had his first interview with Sultan Mahmud in a kiosk of the old seraglio. Western innovations had not yet penetrated to the Ottoman court; a group of scattered pavilions still served the Sultan for a palace; the Janissaries camped round their kettles in the courtyards, and the officers of state wore the embroidered robes inspired by a dream of Suleyman the Magnificent. To all outward appearances Mahmud was still the godlike figure of Oriental legend, receiving western ambassadors in silence seated behind a golden grille in a small dimly-lit room with a half-drawn scimitar beside his throne.

From the day of that first interview, Stratford Canning's life had been dedicated to serving his country's interests in the East. As a young man he had fought the intrigues of Napoleon's agents, which threatened Britain's overland route to India, and now, in middle age, he had been sent to contend with the imperialistic pretensions of the Romanoffs. When Sir Stratford landed at the custom house of Tophane in the early spring of 1842 he had been absent from Turkey for over ten years and during those years Russia had profited by England's policy of non-intervention to consolidate her position both on the Black Sea and the Straits. Failing to find help from the Western Powers in his struggle with Mehmet Ali, Mahmud had had no other choice than to turn to his traditional enemy, the Czar. The treaty of Hunkiar Iskelesi, by which Turkey pledged herself to close the Dardanelles to all foreign warships whenever Russia was at war, the presence of Russian troops on the shores of the Bosphorus, and Mehmet Ali's ambitions to create a vast Egypto-Arab Empire finally convinced Lord Palmerston that it was no longer possible to remain neutral in Eastern affairs.

Sir Stafford's return to the Pera Embassy was a clear warning to the Cabinet of St. Petersburg that England was reverting to the traditional policy of William Pitt in regarding Constantinople as a gateway to India. And for the next fourteen years the over-lifesize personalities of Stratford Canning and of Czar Nicholas I were to dominate the near-Eastern scene.

Despite the warm welcome accorded him by the Sultan and his ministers, Sir Stratford was under no illusions as to the difficulties which lay ahead. For the moment the crisis which had nearly led to a European war had been averted. Faced by a common danger the rival powers had sunk their differences. Europe was in the throes of the 'Hungry Forties', voices strangled at the Vienna Congress were once more gathering strength, and the divine right of kings had to be protected, whether they were Hanoverian or Hohenzollern, Hapsburg or Romanoff, or even of the infidel house of Osman. Bombarded by an Anglo-Austrian squadron, the rebel Mehmet Ali had been forced to relinquish his claim to Palestine and Syria and to content himself with the hereditary Pashalik of Egypt, paying tribute to the Porte, while to show her good-will in the European concert, Russia had consented to the repeal of the Treaty of Hunkiar Iskelesi in favour of a convention of the Straits which closed the Bosphorus and the Dardanelles to all foreign warships except when Turkey herself was at war.

Outwardly all was serene, with the Great Powers vying with one another in courting the young Sultan. But though Abdul Medjid might proclaim his western tastes by receiving ambassadors in a simple fez and 'Stambouline', that hideous garment of European cut which had replaced the embroidered robes and sable pelisses of the past, the majority of the pashas who ruled his empire remained bitterly opposed to any suggestion of reform. In the outlying provinces local governors continued to do as they pleased, farming the taxes for their own profit and extorting money from the peasants. Three years had gone by since the proclamation of the *Hatti-Sherif* of Gulhané, promising equal rights to Mussulman and Christian, but beyond the walls of the Sublime Porte the *Hatti-Sherif* remained a dead letter. Not only the pashas, but the people themselves resented any attempt at westernisation. Conservative and fanatical, they continued to oppose any reform which threatened to infringe on the Sacred Law of Islam. The Ottoman Empire was above all a theocracy and there was no appealing against the dictates of the *Sheriat.** For all his high-sounding titles as the shadow of God on Earth, the Sultan himself could be deposed by a *fetva*† signed by the *Sheikh ul Islam*, the chief religious dignitary of the state.

Stratford Canning had returned to Constantinople with instructions to advise and, if possible, to assist the young Sultan in stabilising his government. But it needed more than Abdul Medjid's good will to stabilise an empire demoralised by defeat, hovering on the verge of bankruptcy. While salaries were in arrears and soldiers mutinied for their pay, the annual revenue of an entire province went to finance the wedding festivities of the Sultan's youngest sister. The roads of Anatolia remained no more than muddy tracks, often impassable during the spring and autumn rains, while Balian, the Sultan's Armenian architect, conjured up vast Italianate palaces on the shores of the Bosphorus.

No one had ever suggested to Abdul Medjid the possibility of cutting down on his personal expenditure. Brought up in the harem as the heir to the throne, his first words had been treated as a command. From his earliest childhood he had lived surrounded by parasites pandering to his slightest whim, and not even Stratford Canning dared to endanger his position by stressing the necessity for retrenchment and economy. There was no check put upon the wild orgy of spending in which Reshid Pasha's plans for the improvement of communications and the development of the natural

---

* The sacred law based on the Koran.
† An order.

resources of the Empire took second place to the demands of the harem.

Here behind closed doors was a world where Stratford Canning could never penetrate, where, in the arms of the favourite of the hour, Abdul Medjid would forget the promises he had made to Greek patriarch or Arab sheikh, to Maronite bishop or Armenian merchant. In this world of eunuchs and of women nothing had changed since the day when Mahomet the Conqueror broke down the walls of the Golden Palace of the Paleologi and a race of nomadic tribesmen became heirs to the heritage of Byzantium. The *gynacea* of the Greek empresses, breeding-ground of corruption and intrigue, livelihood of pimps and slave merchants, guarded by eunuchs and by deaf-mutes, was transformed into the Sultan's harem. An unnatural system bred unnatural vices and two centuries after Mahomet had unfurled the green standard of the Prophet on the altar of Aya Sofia, his descendants already numbered sots and perverts. The decadence of Byzantium and the soft air of the Levant helped to sap the vitality of a race of fighters, till gradually the Ottoman court became subjected to harem rule.

Not even Mahmud the Reformer had made any attempt to curtail the number of his eunuchs or his women. The Kizlar Agasi, or Chief Eunuch, who was usually by origin an un-educated negro slave, still ranked as one of the most important personages of the Empire and the very word of progress was anathema to a palace eunuch, whose whole existence depended on the survival of the harem system.

Abdul Medjid's fears of an ever-encroaching West, his terror of revolution which was beginning to outweigh his desire for reform, found an echo in a hundred fluting voices dwelling on tales of massacre and rape, of Christian rising against Moslem in the Balkans, of Maronite fighting Druse in the Lebanon. The weak and impressionable Sultan would emerge from the harem and the counsels of his eunuchs, ready to oppose the demands of the Western Powers, till the next audience with the British Ambassador, when the compelling personality of Stratford Canning and the consciousness of his empire's internal weakness would once more render him vacillating and conciliatory.

Even more dangerous was the part the eunuchs played in the education of the young princes who up to the time of their circumcision (which according to tradition occurred in their seventh or eighth year) lived with their mothers in the harem, knowing nothing of the outside world beyond what could be glimpsed from behind the closed curtains of an *araba*, those swaying painted carts drawn by bullocks, which conveyed the palace women on their rare expeditions abroad.

In the case of the little Abdul Hamid, his seclusion was still more complete. As the mother of a royal prince Pirimujgan remained as much an interloper in the harem as on the day on which she made her first appearance at Cheragan. The majority of her companions, who had been brought as children to the palace, resented the dancer from a pasha's harem who had won imperial favour, and seeing her neglected by their master dared to cast aspersions on her origin. 'A Jewess,' said some; 'An Armenian,' said others—and the pale little boy with the large hooked nose lent credibility to the rumours. All his mother's frustrated love was concentrated on the child who spent his days in the sick-room, listening to the unending complaints of an ill and unhappy woman. It is not surprising that he grew up with an abnormal horror of disease when his first memories were of the doctor's visits, of a dark curtain drawn across the bed, for no male physician visiting the harem was allowed to see more than his patient's hands or tongue thrust out between the curtains. Expected to give a diagnosis after the most cursory of examinations, it was hardly the doctor's fault that the rate of mortality in the harem was high, and the picture of his consumptive mother slowly dying from neglect was to remain with Abdul Hamid all through his life, influencing his relations with other women, embittering his attitude towards his young brothers and sisters whose mother had supplanted his own in the Sultan's favour.

In spite of the numerous abortions practised in the harem, Abdul Medjid's family kept growing year by year, but little Hamid rarely joined in the games of the other children, or if he did it was only in order to spy and report back to the sick-room. From his earliest youth he was adept at eaves-dropping, listening to the whispering of the eunuchs. The humiliation of some former favourite, the illness of one of his brothers, particularly if it happened to be that of the eldest, Murad, were eagerly seized on and reported as likely to give pleasure to his sick and lonely mother.

He was six years old when an event occurred which caused confusion in the harem. Abdul Medjid had fallen in love with a beautiful Egyptian and announced his intention of making her his wife. It was contrary to tradition for the Sultan to marry a subject and for centuries the Imperial harem had been peopled by slaves whom their masters rarely, if ever, made into their legal wives. In thirty-one reigns there had been only three exceptions to this rule, therefore this sudden decision of Abdul Medjid was interpreted as yet another sign of pernicious foreign influence, and viewed with dismay by the whole hierarchy of slaves from the Kizlar Agasi to the youngest of odalisques. In face of their opposition Abdul Medjid celebrated his wedding, building in honour of his bride yet another kiosk in the seraglio gardens. Standing on a jutting promontory between the Marmara and the Golden Horn, the Yeni, or New Kiosk as it is still called today, evokes the memory of a Sultan's fleeting passion, a whim expressed in stone. And it was here on a June day in 1848 that he received the congratulations of his courtiers amongst whom were His Majesty's two eldest sons, Murad and Abdul Hamid.

For the first time Abdul Hamid now ventured into the men's quarters, the *selamlik*, and all his underlying jealousy of his elder brother was aroused when he saw with what confidence Murad approached the throne, with what pride their father beckoned him to his side—only later seeming to remember that he also was his son with a right to share his glory.

Tentatively he made his way through the crowd of suppliants from the furthest corners of the Empire, through the parasites and courtiers with high-sounding titles fascinating to a child's ears; Keepers of the Imperial nightingales and parrots; Coffee-makers and Pipe-cleaners; Stirrup-holders and Sword-bearers; Barbers who had no other function than to trim the Sultan's beard, every hair of which was reverently preserved; singers of sacred verses, whose duty it had been to chant excerpts from the Koran while the Imperial turban was being washed, and who now that the turban was no longer worn, retained their sinecures in silence. Here were the last survivors of Byzantium, the white eunuchs, as thin and wizened as the black ones were monstrously fat; the jesters; the deaf mutes and the pages, plump little boys with painted cheeks dressed in the gayest of silks, children scarcely older than the little prince who now made his first appearance in the world of men.

The Sultan noted the hesitant walk, the instinctive shrinking away from human contact, noting it not in pity but in irritation. For though Abdul Medjid was gentle and kind-hearted by nature, he appears to have shown neither sympathy nor understanding for the small shrunken figure who reminded him all too forcibly of his own declining strength and of the innate decadence of his race. Nor was there anything lovable about Abdul Hamid to compensate for his unprepossessing appearance. At six, his dark, heavy-lidded eyes already looked around him with wariness and suspicion, his slightest gesture was surreptitious and the Sultan observed with disgust the furtive greed with which his son partook of the rich food and sweetmeats, stealing cakes from the laden tables and hiding them away. The secrecy with which his mother had concealed her pregnancy, the unhappiness that followed on his birth, combined with the jealousies and intrigues of the enclosed feminine world in which he lived, had made Abdul Hamid morbid and deceitful, longing to be loved, yet unable to trust or to be trusted. So much depended on winning his father's affection, but the remote omnipotent figure before whom all men trembled and no man dared to speak aloud, looked at him so critically and coldly that he realised he had failed his mother in her last hope.

The Sultan's attitude was noted and copied by his entourage. While Murad sunned himself in the adulation of his father's courtiers, his younger brother was ignored and no one noticed him creeping away alone from the crowded feast.

It happened by chance that Sir Stratford Canning was passing through the palace gardens on his way to the Sultan's reception when he came across a small lonely figure sitting by a fountain. A child in such a place could only be one of the royal princes, and bending low from his great height the

Ambassador greeted the little boy with an exquisite courtesy, as if he were already a reigning sovereign. His formal dignity, his impressive figure, the glittering uniforms of the members of his staff, were all balm to wounded pride and instinctively Abdul Hamid saw in him a protector and a friend. Sir Stratford must have sensed some of the humiliation and disappointment, for suddenly he forgot the prince and saw only a pathetic child, and spontaneously placed a hand on his shoulder in a warm fatherly gesture.

What to Stratford Canning was no more than a passing impulse was to be remembered by Abdul Hamid as the first kindness he ever received from a stranger. Many years later when he came to the throne, the British Ambassador of the day noted that it was largely due to the impression made by Lord Stratford de Redcliffe in the Sultan's youth that Abdul Hamid looked upon England as his natural ally. Unfortunately the events of the first years of his reign succeeded in dissipating these illusions.

Chapter III

HUMILIATED AND REBUFFED, Abdul Hamid paid no further visits to the *selamlik* till after his circumcision, which occurred in the summer of 1849. Despite the difference in their ages, the Sultan had decreed that his two elder sons should be circumcised at the same time, and to celebrate this event, he invited all the poor children of Constantinople and the surroundings born in the same years as the two little princes to become what was known as their companions in circumcision.

True to the traditions of their nomadic ancestors, the circumcision of the princes took place in a tent instead of in a palace, and for ten days the Sultan's court was transferred to the plain of Haydar Pasha on the Asiatic shore of the Bosphorus. Eye-witnesses recall the brilliance of the scene, with every pasha's garden from Scutari to Kadikeui, a forest of fluttering banners and golden tent poles, while at night the sky was lit by the illuminations of domes and minarets and the fireworks from ships at anchor in the Golden Horn. It was half a popular holiday, half a religious feast, with the gold-embroidered tents of the Padishah not a stone's throw away from the tents which sheltered the poorest children of his capital. All the familiar figures of the fairground, the sellers of sweetmeats and sherbets, the jugglers and the storytellers, not to omit the inevitable performers of *karagheuz**, mingled with the grave-faced *ulema*, and green-turbanned descendants of the Prophet.

Over a thousand children were operated on daily, tended by the Sultan's doctors, fed by the Sultan's cooks, who presided over the enormous fires on which cauldrons of pilaff were kept boiling day and night and sheep roasted whole on giant spits. Every evening after sundown the Sultan himself would visit the children's tents, presenting each child who had been operated on during the day with a new suit of clothes and a

* The Turkish Punch and Judy.

(18)

hundred-piastre gold piece. It was by gestures such as these that Abdul Medjid won the love of his subjects and the title of the 'Gentlest of Monarchs', so that even the most zealous of reformers lacked the courage to suggest that feasts on such a scale were costing the country money it could ill afford.

Abdul Hamid was barely seven when he was for the first time separated from his mother and put into direct contact with the people who were to be his future subjects. It was a proud moment when he found himself sitting beside the Sultan under the gold and purple canopy of the Imperial *caique*, rowed by fourteen oarsmen across the Bosphorus, but pride soon turned to panic when he saw the crowds assembled on the pier at Scutari. The eunuchs had already imbued him with their own terrors. Execrated by the people, who held them responsible for all the abuses and corruptions of the palace régime, these unhappy emasculated creatures retaliated by teaching the little princes in their charge to distrust their fellow men. With Abdul Hamid their lessons had fallen on fertile ground. Brought up on their stories, he saw in every out-stretched hand a weapon about to strike, detected in every shout of welcome a note of underlying menace; pathetically he tried to emulate his brother's self-confidence, only to shrink back in terror at the rows of staring eyes. But when it came to the actual ceremony, he neither whimpered nor flinched at the touch of the surgeon's knife. Innately religious, he suffered the ordeal with a composure which led people to predict that should he ever ascend the throne his reign would be glorious for Islam.

Little did Abdul Hamid realise at the time how suddenly and cruelly his childhood was to end, for no sooner had he returned from Haydar Pasha than he was summoned to his mother's death-bed. Too ill to accompany the Sultan's harem across the water, Pirimujgan had remained behind at Cheragan, and watching the illuminations from her window had caught a fatal chill. She was only twenty-six when she died and in history she survives as no more than a shadow cast over the childhood of her son, a shadow which gradually darkened as the child grew into a man, for the loneliness of the seven-year-old boy was not more acute than that of the future sultan, who throughout his life went in search of the mother he had lost.

Abdul Medjid's private physician, the Greek Zographos, described the inconsolable grief of the little boy, who after his mother's death crept back into the room and insisted on pulling back the sheets, so as to see her face for the last time. But custom decreed that Abdul Hamid must have a stepmother, and every childless woman in the palace aspired to a position which might one day make her into a Valide Sultana.

The Sultan's choice fell on the fourth of his *kadins*, the beautiful but barren Peresto, a woman loved and respected for her intelligence and charm. Her task was not an easy one, for in loyalty to his mother's memory Abdul Hamid rebuffed her first attempts at affection. But Peresto showed such tolerance and understanding, such a selfless devotion in her relations with her foster-son, that he gradually began to appreciate her qualities, and in her company the silent little boy learnt the arts of conversation and the exquisite politeness which in later years were to charm the visitors to Yildiz Kiosk.

All Peresto's efforts, however, were unable to soften Abdul Hamid in his attitude to his brothers and sisters. Burdened with the hatred he had inherited from his mother, he responded with coldness, even at times with cruelty, to their advances. There is a story told of how one summer's day when the children were sleeping in the heat of the afternoon, he crept up to each of his brothers and sisters in turn and stole his or her most treasured possession. It is not surprising if, after one or two such experiences, they preferred to avoid his company, nor were they the kind of incidents which when reported were likely to endear him to his father. The latent antagonism between the Sultan and his second son grew stronger every year. After their circumcision the young princes had passed from the harem to the *selamlik* and were now privileged to accompany their father at military reviews and at Friday prayers. But it was always Murad, never Abdul Hamid, who rode at the Sultan's side.

When Peresto pleaded in favour of her foster-son Abdul Medjid would reply that he had watched his son on several occasions and found him lacking in every grace, 'the only one of his children who gave him any trouble and promised badly

for the future.' The reports of his teachers and of his *lala**
were not encouraging; for whereas the *lala* reported that he
was shy and secretive by nature and apparently uninterested
in the young odalisques who were already being brought to
his notice, his teachers asserted that he displayed an altogether
abnormal curiosity in all that concerned the Empire.

Not only politics, but also history were taboo in the curriculum of the 'princes' school', where education was confined to
readings from the Koran, a superficial knowledge of music
and of French, and fabled stories of the glories of the Ottoman
Sultans. If a boy showed a scholarly disposition he was allowed
to perfect himself in Persian and Arabic, provided that his
reading was restricted to the ancient poets. But Abdul Hamid
was no scholar. He had a restless practical mind, displaying
from his earliest childhood an interest in current events and an
aptitude for figures which he was not allowed to cultivate.

The eunuch who acted as the treasurer of the harem would
often see the little prince creeping up to his account book,
turning over the pages, utterly fascinated and absorbed. But
to be interested in facts and figures were not qualities to be
encouraged in one who seemed destined to spend most of his
life in the shadow of the throne, and Peresto did her best to
draw her foster-son's interests into less subversive channels.
She was the first to encourage his talent for carpentry and fine
carving, which was to remain his favourite hobby. His nervous, restless nature found relaxation in weaving intricate
patterns in precious wood and in inlaying cedar and aloe with
silver and mother of pearl.

But for all Peresto's devotion to her foster-son and constant
interest in his welfare, his mother's ghost still stood between
them, preventing any real intimacy or affection, and when
Abdul Hamid came of an age to choose his own companions,
his first choice of a female friend was a woman old enough to
be his grandmother. In this he showed a certain discernment,
for Pertevniyal Sultana, mother to the Crown Prince Abdul
Aziz, was one of the most remarkable women of the day. She
had begun life as a bath-attendant in Stamboul, and her good
fortune dated from the time when Sultan Mahmud caught

* A eunuch who acted as a kind of tutor.

sight of her walking in the street with a bundle of fresh linen on her head, and, charmed by her luxuriant beauty and amused by her peasant wit, brought her back to the palace. He had loved her more than any of his other *kadins* and even when she grew fat and middle-aged she still maintained her hold. Unlike the pampered Circassians, who knew no other world beyond the palace, she remained to the end of her days a woman of the people, keeping in touch with the companions of her early youth and amusing the Sultan with salacious anecdotes and the gossip of the bazaars. Fanatically religious, with all the primitive superstitions of the Anatolian peasant, she was the first to warn her master of the opposition his reforms were encountering in the mosques and *medreses* of his capital and she remained firmly convinced that the disasters which overwhelmed the end of Mahmud's reign resulted from his sympathy with the Christian infidels.

Recognising in this clever but bigoted old woman a dangerous influence, whose intrigues might lead the reactionary party, the so-called Old Ottomans, into supporting her son the Crown Prince in opposition to Medjid, the Sultan's ministers advised him to get rid of an awkward encumbrance. But though his ancestors would have had no hesitation in committing an unwanted woman to the Bosphorus, the Sultan was of too kindly a nature to resort to such methods, and while the Crown Prince Aziz was encouraged to live the life of a country gentleman on his farms, his mother was graciously invited to remain an inmate of the Imperial harem, where her visitors could be carefully watched and her slightest movement was subject to the jealous eye of the Valide Sultana.

Separated from the son whom she adored, Pertevniyal immersed herself in the study of necromancy and astrology, seeking in mystic signs and the movements of the stars some escape from the barrenness of the present, peopling a dream world with waxen effigies of those whom by prayers and incantations she hoped to raise to power or doom to perdition.

It was in this strange old woman, whom the eunuchs feared as a witch, that the young Abdul Hamid found his first friend. Loneliness brought them together and a curious affinity developed between Mahmud's favourite and Mahmud's grandson. Hour after hour they would sit together, poring over some old Arabic book, searching for some magic formula, the old woman sucking at the amber mouthpiece of her *chubuk*, the little boy spelling out the words in his curiously deep, drawling voice, both of them absorbed and self-centred, filling the tobacco-laden air with creations of their own fantasy—visions of future power.

Chapter IV

WHILE THE GIPSIES and astrologers who frequented the harem were full of gloomy predictions of a war in which Moslem would be fighting at the side of *giaour*, the Sultan's ministers were sincerely attempting to carry out the reforms which Abdul Medjid had promised at the beginning of his reign. With Austria and Russia engaged in suppressing revolution in Hungary, Italy and Poland, the Ottoman Empire was at peace to put her house in order, and liberal opinion in Europe warmed in sympathy with the Sultan who, true to the tradition of Islam, gave hospitality to the Polish and Hungarian exiles from Russian and Austrian oppression. Another gesture which won Abdul Medjid the admiration of the West was the official abolition of negro slave markets throughout the Empire. The fact that no mention was made of the little Circassian girls who continued to be brought or kidnapped by the purveyors of the Imperial harem, was either overlooked or ignored by Turkey's well-wishers.

Vacillating and half-hearted even in his reforms, capable of a generous impulse rather than of sustained action, Abdul Medjid received the credit for carrying out measures such as the prohibition of tax-farming in the provinces, and the introduction of the first secular schools: measures which were largely due to the energy of his ministers Reshid and Ali Pasha, and to the unflagging support of the British Ambassador, Stratford Canning, who more than anyone else was responsible for putting 'the sick man of Europe onto his feet', and thereby countering the plans of the Russian Czar, already counting on the heritage of a moribund empire.

When in 1850, Austria and Russia attempted to coerce the Sultan into handing over Kossuth and the other Hungarian and Polish nationalists, to whom he had given refuge, Abdul Medjid's proud refusal was backed by the presence of the British fleet in Besika Bay.

(24)

There were those who asserted that Stratford Canning's high-handed action in summoning the fleet was dictated not so much on behalf of his country's interests as owing to a personal grudge against the Russian Czar, who in the past had refused to accept his nomination as Ambassador to St. Petersburg. But not even the appearance of British warships in Ottoman waters succeeded in dissipating the illusions the Emperor Nicholas had cherished, ever since a visit to London in the spring of 1844, when his success with the young Queen Victoria and her minister, Lord Aberdeen, had convinced him that England would never draw the sword in defence of the Ottoman Empire. Nor did the Czar believe that England and France, those two great rivals for the commerce of the Levant, would ever make common cause against him. And when 1851 saw the return of the Napoleonic eagles to the Tuileries and a Bonaparte once more assuming the Imperial crown, Russia remained convinced that England would prefer to share with her in the spoils of the Ottoman Empire rather than nurse it to recovery as the ally of a Bonaparte. No diplomatic considerations could induce Catherine's grandson to accept Louis Napoleon as a 'Brother' in the hierarchy of crowned heads, and the new French Emperor was never to forgive the Russian Czar for refusing to address him by that title.

It is difficult to ascertain to what extent these private grudges were responsible for the misunderstandings and prevarications which led to what must have been one of the most profitless wars in history.

Ostensibly the quarrel centred round the question of whether Greek or Latin monks should have the guardianship of the Holy Places in Palestine. On the one hand was France, avid for glory and prestige, laying claim to the privileges she had enjoyed since the days when Suleyman the Magnificent had granted to King Francis I the right to trade in all the ports of the Levant, complete religious liberty for all French nationals, and the guardianship of the Holy Places in Jerusalem.

Thus had originated the famous 'Capitulations'* by which privileges, which at the time of the Moslem conquest had been given only to the Venetian and Genoese communities in

---

* Extra-territorial rights granted to certain foreign powers.

Pera and Galata, were extended to a European power. And if, in the course of centuries, these concessions were granted in turn to the rivals and even to the enemies of France, and if, during and after the French Revolution, France herself had neglected the religious communities in Palestine, she nevertheless continued to regard herself as the rightful heir to the Latin Empire of the Crusader knights.

On the other hand there was Russia who, with nationalism in Eastern Europe trampled underfoot by the iron heel of the Holy Alliance, was once more free to take on the role of protector of the Christian minorities in Turkey, a part ill-fitted to the cold-blooded autocrat who had suppressed by flogging and the gallows the aspirations of his own minorities.

One's sympathy goes out to Abdul Medjid, forced into the invidious position of arbiter in a quarrel not of his own seeking. For what could it matter to him if 'the golden star of the anointing' marked with the arms of France was missing from the floor of the Holy Sepulchre, or whether Greek or Latin monks had the keys of the 'Sacred Manger'. All his interests for the moment were absorbed in his new palace at Dolmabagche with its white marble terrace on the Bosphorus, its throne room one hundred and fifty feet in length, with gilded corinthian columns reflected in the largest mirrors in existence.

Hours would be spent in discussing with his Armenian architect the furnishings for the harem or in despatching fantastic orders to European warehouses—orders for crystal chandeliers four tons in weight and solid silver candelabra, each with the mystic number of three hundred and thirty-three sockets. In their wooing of the Sultan, the Great Powers vied with one another in presents for his new palace: grandfather clocks from Queen Victoria, elaborate Bohemian glass from the young Francis Joseph, Buhl tables inlaid with porcelain miniatures of all the Bonapartes, rare white bear-skin rugs from the Russian Czar. But the gifts would be barely unpacked before his Imperial Majesty would be informed that the French or Russian Ambassador was requesting yet another audience. And if it was not the French or the Russian Ambassadors then it would be Stratford Canning, but lately returned from London with the added lustre of a British peerage. By the spring of 1853 Abdul Medjid had been forced to tear himself away from the delights of Dolmabagche, and to wake to the fact that what till now he had regarded merely as a quarrel among Christians had become a threat to his sovereign power.

When the wisteria hung in purple clouds above the Bosphorus and the tulips blazed in the pashas' gardens; when Abdul Medjid had no other wish than to enjoy in the company of his harem the pleasures of the spring, he was presented with the Russian ultimatum. As a threat, rather than as an offer of alliance, the Emperor Nicholas offered him his friendship on the one condition that Russia was given the protection of all the Greek minorities throughout the Ottoman Empire—a right which would not only lead to interference in all Turkey's European provinces, even in Constantinople itself, but would make Russia master not only of the Bosphorus and of the Dardanelles, but of the whole Greek archipelago.

Faced by what amounted to an abdication of his rule over twelve million of his subjects, one third of the entire population of his empire, the Sultan declared the Russian proposals to be incompatible with the integrity of the Ottoman Empire, and a few days later a combined British and French fleet steamed into Besika Bay, thereby convincing the Czar that the alliance he had refused to believe in had become an established fact.

Nevertheless negotiations, which were mainly conducted by Austria, continued throughout the summer, for it was not until the autumn that the Ottoman Empire, under pressure from her allies, officially declared war on Russia and allied warships entered the Dardanelles.

Turkey was now the ally of the Western Powers, but there were none of the hysterical excitement and Press polemics with which the Western nations prepared for war, none of the fervour and enthusiasm with which the Russian people hailed the appearance of the holy images which, by order of their Czar, were being paraded through every town and village. Five times in the course of a century the stolid Anatolian peasant had left his pastures to fight against the Russian enemy.

From the Euphrates to the Bosphorus, from Arabia to the Balkans, lines of uncomplaining soldiers, ill-clothed, ill-fed, had been marched across desert and mountain to die for their Caliph and to earn a place in the Prophet's Paradise. But till now there had been an element of fanaticism in each campaign. The green standard of Mahomet had only to be unfurled to make every soldier feel he was fighting *jehad*, a Holy War, and it was hard for the simple Moslem to understand how it had come about that *Giaour* and Turk should now be fighting side by side.

In Paris, the Emperor Napoleon talked about 'la gloire', while his soldiers crowded into troopships singing *'Partant pour La Syrie'*: in London, Lord Palmerston admitted in Parliament that England's real incentive to fight was in order to safeguard her route to India, but the Sultan had no need to make stirring speeches or to defend his actions. By instinct and by habit the Turk was primarily a fighter. The sufferings endured by the Allied troops during their first winter in the Crimea—the ineptitude of officialdom and the breakdown of supplies, the horror of the cholera-infested hospital at Scutari—scandals which newspaper correspondents made public to the world and which caused such indignation in England as to bring about the downfall of a Government, these things were accepted by the Sultan's soldiers as part of their daily life.

The Crimean War has come down to history as a record of heroism in disaster; pages of unrelieved gloom illumined by sudden flashes of light—young British officers leading their men to death in a glorious charge 'because, at headquarters, someone had blundered'; the French general, St. Arnaud, who when stricken with a mortal disease still insisted on riding into battle at the head of his troops; Florence Nightingale and her little band of selfless, dedicated women; and, on the Russian side, the epic defence of Sebastopol, the indomitable spirit of the dying Czar, who remaining to the end 'The Man of Iron', dictated from his deathbed the last grim words, 'The Emperor is dying.' But little is heard of the Turks who, half-starved and with their pay in arrears, defended the mountain passes in the Balkans and held out in Kars to the last man. Their heroism went unrecorded. It was their privilege to fight, their privilege to die in battle.

They were not stirred by war, but by the consequences of war. Cold and hunger left them unmoved, but the spectacle of unveiled women nursing soldiers in the hospital at Scutari aroused a bitter resentment. When Abdul Medjid visited the battlefields of the Crimea, his soldiers were profoundly shocked to see their Padishah riding in the company of foreign generals and giving the salute to infidel troops, while red-faced men in kilts exposed their bare and hairy knees before the 'Shadow of God on Earth'.

It was not only on the battlefield that the Turk had to endure the presence of the *Giaour*. Peace was to bring a greater invasion than there had ever been in war. In the wake of the soldiers who lay buried under the cypress trees of Scutari, came the speculators and the contractors, the financiers and the engineers. It was an invasion for which Turkey was not prepared and against which she had no defence. She was still a backward country. She needed time in which to stabilise her reforms and to educate her people to respect the rights of the minorities in their midst. Even the Sultan had only learnt the first lessons. At thirty-five Abdul Medjid was already too tired and ill to struggle on in the cause of progress. His actions had become little more than gestures to placate on the one hand his own people, on the other his Western allies.

What was even more dangerous was that no effort was being made to prepare his children for the future. No European influence was allowed to penetrate the doors of the princes' school. Their curriculum remained unaltered, and even the war took on a remote, impersonal aspect. Life in the palace had no contact with the crowded, vermin-ridden hospitals across the narrow strip of water at Scutari. While the Allied troopships passed up and down the Bosphorus, with the wash of the water lapping against the marble landing stages of Dolmabagche and of Cheragan, and the streets of Pera re-echoed to French and English voices, the young princes remained in ignorance of the existence of their new allies.

Chapter V

THE WAR WAS OVER and to celebrate the peace the British Ambassador was holding a fancy dress ball. But what made this ball different from all other balls was that for the first time in history the Sultan of Turkey and Caliph of Islam was honouring a foreign embassy with his presence.

Standing at the entrance, bare-headed in the snow, surrounded by his staff in full uniform, Lord Stratford was experiencing the crowning triumph of his whole diplomatic career. Forty-five years ago, when he knelt in front of Mahmud's throne, he never dreamt the day would come when Mahmud's son would be his guest. Even in the last week there had been times when he had wondered whether the reactionary palace clique would prevail over the counsels of his ministers and prevent Abdul Medjid from committing what the Old Turks considered to be a violation of his sacred privileges. But the flare of a beacon on the hills above Cheragan had announced the Sultan's departure from the palace, and already one could hear the cheering as the royal procession progressed down the Grande Rue de Pera, the full-throated cries of 'Long live the Padishah' mingling with the clapping of the European population. Then with a volley of cannon from the British artillery stationed at Galata Seray, the Imperial carriage escorted by a detachment of the Twelfth Lancers, followed by a glittering retinue of Turkish ministers and Allied generals, swung into view. The enthusiasm of the crowds rose to a crescendo as the Sultan passed through the gateway of the British Embassy under the decorated arch which traced in coloured lights the linked names of Victoria and Abdul Medjid.

Lord Stratford was not only a great ambassador, he was also a great showman, and, as the Sultan alighted from his carriage, an electric wire communicated the news to the British fleet at anchor in the Marmara, which responded with a salute of 101 guns. Mystified and delighted by this new manifestation of his ally's genius Abdul Medjid's usually melancholy face broke into a smile and, giving the Ambassador his hand (an honour till now denied to the highest of his subjects), he proceeded up the great marble staircase. A guard of honour composed of Grenadiers, Highlanders and Horse and Field Artillery presented arms, the band of the German Legion stationed in the gallery struck up the Turkish and English anthems and at the entrance to the ballroom the Sultan was greeted by his hostess wearing the somewhat unsuitable costume of a Dresden shepherdess. The sight of Lady Stratford exposing her faded charms in a flutter of lace and ribboned panniers was only one of the many incongruous features of what to Abdul Medjid must have been a fascinating, strange and utterly bewildering evening.

Seated on a throne at one end of the ballroom surrounded by his ministers and the ambassadors of the Allied Powers, he watched with astonished eyes the spectacle of Lord Stratford's guests revolving round the room, locked in close embrace with what appeared to be half-dressed women. And though *The Times* correspondent reported that 'His Majesty watched the dancing with evident pleasure,' and that 'the fancy dresses of the ladies served to enhance their charms,' it must have been hard for someone of Abdul Medjid's temperament and upbringing to remember that those pretty young women in their shameless costumes were not odalisques provided by Lord Stratford for his amusement, but the respectable wives and daughters of the European colony of Pera.

Nevertheless, from the Sultan to the youngest of subalterns, everyone enjoyed the ball. All the various sections and races of the city were represented, from the Greek Patriarch and members of the old Phanariote aristocracy to the Jewish Chief Rabbi and the Armenian Archbishop. Religious differences and quarrels were washed away on a tide of champagne; toasts to the Gallant Allies, the Victors of Sebastopol, toasts to the French Emperor and the English Queen, whose portrait looked down benignly from above the Sultan's throne, toasts to Abdul Medjid who, as a crowning mark of condescension, was seen to take refreshments with his host—a gesture trivial in itself, but without precedent, for in the past every detail of the Padishah's private life had been hidden from public view, and only the Chief Eunuch had been privileged to serve his meals.

On this night of January 31, 1856, everything seemed possible, and when the Sultan left the Embassy at midnight thousands of Christians and Moslems were still waiting outside in the snow to catch a glimpse of the frail figure in the blue, sable-lined cloak who held power of life and death over thirty-six million people. Instead of returning to the palace, Abdul Medjid slept at one of his brother-in-law's *yalis* outside the city. Lately he had been spending many nights away from his harem, and there were rumours circulating round the palace of a certain Armenian dressmaker in Pera whom the Sultan was said to visit in disguise. That model husband and impeccable character, Lord Stratford de Redcliffe, would have been surprised to hear that, according to the gossip of the harem, he was regarded as responsible for providing the Sultan with an Armenian mistress. But whether they were Armenians from Pera, or Circassians from the palace, it was all equally useless, for at the age of thirty-five Abdul Medjid was already physically impotent.

More important than the vagaries of the Sultan's sex-life was his growing addiction to drink, a vice particularly abhorrent to all good Moslems. At a time when Turkey was about to take her place in the Concert of Europe and another Imperial rescript was to confirm and amplify the guarantees for life and property laid down by the *Hatti-Sherif* of Gulhane, the Sultan was showing the first signs of cracking up both morally and physically.

On this night of triumph, Lord Stratford may have asked himself whether the Sultan would be strong enough to carry on alone, once he was no longer there to advise, persuade, and if necessary, coerce him to the reforms which were necessary to save his empire. These reforms demanded sacrifices, for the Ambassador was convinced that the only way of protecting the integrity of the Ottoman Empire in the future lay in a barrier of neutral and independent Balkan states acting as a bulwark against the encroachments of the Romanoff and Hapsburg Empires. Unfortunately the inevitable sacrifices which would have to be made to these autonomous and semi-autonomous Christian states made it fatally easy for the party of reaction to rouse public feeling against the Sultan's liberal ministers. Time after time Reshid Pasha had been in disfavour not only with the public, but with his master. Now, stricken with a mortal disease, he was gradually delegating his powers to the Foreign Minister, Ali Pasha. But would Ali be any more successful than his predecessor in converting the mass of the people to what was contrary to the fundamental principles of their religion? Would the Moslems ever consent to a constitution by which all subjects of the Sultan, irrespective of race or creed, were equal before the law?

Tonight, in the first flush of victory, Christian and Moslem had united in cheering their Padishah. Abdul Medjid had partaken of food in the presence of an unbeliever and invited Lady Stratford to pay a visit to his harem. But the fifteen-year-old Prince Murad had not accompanied his father to the Embassy. Though considered old enough to have a harem and establishment of his own, he was officially said to be too young to attend the ball, while on the other hand the thirteen-year-old Abdul Hamid was said to be too old to accompany his younger brothers to the Ambassadress's children's party the following day. These younger princes were not yet considered of an age to be contaminated by alien influences, but both Murad and Abdul Hamid were already victims of that pernicious system which condemned the heirs to the Ottoman throne to a life of idleness and seclusion. As for the Sultan's brother, the Crown Prince Abdul Aziz, the Ambassador had deemed it wiser not to send him an invitation which would only have placed him under suspicion. But there could be no guarantee of Turkey's recovery so long as her future rulers were kept from all contact with the outside world, and in this, as in all other matters dealing with the palace, the 'Great Elchi'* was powerless to intervene.

Nevertheless the faint breath of progress had succeeded in penetrating even into the princes' school. After being kept in ignorance of the hardships and reverses of the war, the Sultan's sons now shared in the fruits of victory to the extent of stand-

* 'The great Ambassador', the Turkish name for Lord Stratford.

ing by their father's throne while he received the congratulations and the presents of the high dignitaries of the Empire, and of riding through the streets cheered by enthusiastic crowds. Smiling faces were everywhere; a general air of gaiety pervaded the capital; Allied soldiers crowded the cafés; groups of sightseers loitered outside shops exhibiting European wares and, protected by the Powers, Greeks and Armenians bore themselves with a new confidence. The young princes, who till now had maintained in public the impassive dignity demanded of their rank, were instructed to salute Allied officers even when they appeared with unveiled women at their side.

These changes, which were accepted and welcomed by Murad, were resented by Abdul Hamid. Influenced by old Pertevniyal and the sheikhs and *mollas* charged with his religious education, he was shocked by the freedom with which foreigners behaved in his father's capital. He knew nothing of the Allied sacrifices, of the grim struggle in the Crimea; but other stories were repeated and magnified a hundredfold. The eunuchs were never tired of recounting how the Christians had refused to avail themselves of the privilege which for the first time granted them the right of serving in the Sultan's armies, but had preferred to go on paying the tax which exempted them from military service. Time after time he heard how the Armenian population of Van had constructed a magnificent barracks in preparation for the Russian troops, and how at Kars they had massacred the Moslem population before the Russians had entered the town. The palace seethed with stories of this kind, while other rumours which were never meant to reach his ears were heard and absorbed by a silent and precocious boy.

A certain relaxing of the rules of the harem had resulted in a scandalous incident. By permission of the Sultan the palace ladies were now not only allowed to drive through the town in open carriages, but actually to enter the bazaars instead of waiting outside to have their purchases brought out to them. This privilege was enjoyed to the full, and every day bevies of palace women, wearing the flimsiest of *yashmaks*, could be seen driving across Galata Bridge under the guard of mounted eunuchs.

It happened one day that two young and pretty women were crossing the bridge when they passed a French officer on horse-back. Struck by his good looks and emboldened by their new freedom, they kissed their hands in greeting, to which the Frenchman gallantly replied. But no sooner had he done so than he was struck across the face by a blow of their eunuch's whip. Unhesitatingly the officer unsheathed his sword and, without dismounting, ran the Negro through the body, in full view of the crowds gathered on the bridge. Pandemonium followed on what seemed about to become an international incident. One of the palace servants had been attacked by an infidel and anything to do with the palace was sacrosanct. But the days had gone when a eunuch could terrorise a foreigner into submission, and when General Canrobert, the French Commander-in-Chief, was summoned to the Porte he defended his officer's behaviour on the ground that, having been publicly insulted by a negro, he had no choice between killing him or handing in his resignation as being unworthy of his command.

Both the Sultan and his ministers had perforce to content themselves with this explanation of an incident which had enormous repercussions in the palace, where the eunuchs were thrown into a state of alarm lest the privileges they had abused for so long might now expose them to dangers from which there was no protection. The first signs of the subversive influence of the West had penetrated the harem and in his foster-mother's apartments Abdul Hamid heard the women whispering among themselves, relating half in horror, half in laughter, the incident of Galata Bridge. Now that whipping as a punishment had been formally abolished, the palace women no longer lived in such abject terror of the eunuchs and discipline was so far relaxed that European doctors, dentists and even pedicures were allowed to attend the harem. Money had never been more plentiful, for the fruits of victory consisted largely of foreign loans and, as usual, priority was given to the insatiable demands of the palace which, including eunuchs and servants, now numbered over three thousand mouths to feed.

Women, with no more idea of money than children, were

given *carte blanche* to shop in the bazaars. They were encouraged, in fact ordered, to bring their wardrobes into line with Western fashions. Voluptuous beauties who had never worn corsets in their lives, now squeezed their ample forms into contraptions of steel and whalebone; embroidered slippers were discarded for tight patent leather shoes as worn by the Empress Eugénie; sellers of Parisian lace, gloves and artificial flowers did an enormous trade, and even old Pertevniyal neglected her witch-craft for the more fascinating occupation of shopping. But to her young protégé this sudden orgy of spending seemed both profitless and extravagant. Fascinated from his earliest child-hood by the account books of the harem, Abdul Hamid had found among his masters a certain Kemal Bey, who was sufficiently courageous to give him some of the true facts re-garding the money which now flowed so lavishly into the Sultan's treasury. The three million pounds advanced by Eng-land was not a free gift from a grateful ally, but a loan guaran-teed by the Egyptian tribute, and the elaborate preparations which were being made for the arrival of the French Emperor (who, incidentally, never came) were because Turkey had need of further loans.

The *Hatti Humayun* (Imperial Rescript) of February 21, 1856, by which the Sultan confirmed the guarantees laid down by the *Hatti-Sherif* of Gulhane, was even more unpopular than its predecessor. The orthodox Moslem, whose religion was based on a literal interpretation of the Koran and the Sheriat law, bitterly resented the clause in which the Sultan referred to 'the happiness of his people, who without distinction of class or religion were all equally dear to him.' Thus the new charter, which offered them protection and security against former abuses, was rendered valueless by the fact that the same privileges were extended to all non-Moslem com-munities. This would not have happened had the people already profited by the benefits promised at Gulhane, but the average Turk who still lived at the mercy of corrupt officials was growing more and more convinced that the Padishah was favouring the Christian at his expense. It was a dangerous situation which the Sultan's ministers only realised too late, after they had committed themselves in the eyes of Europe to a policy which as Caliph of Islam, the Sultan was powerless to carry out.

Nevertheless the *Hatti Humayun*, which was largely the work of Lord Stratford de Redcliffe and of his French colleague, made an enormous impression on the statesmen gathered round the conference tables in Paris. The British and French Governments, who had pledged themselves to protect the integrity of the Ottoman Empire and prevent the Black Sea from becoming a Russian lake, were so impressed by the Sultan's pledges to alleviate the lot of his Christian subjects that they took no steps to see that the promises were put into action, and a special clause was inserted in the treaty which forbade any foreign power from interfering in Turkey's internal affairs.

Competent observers, like the future Austrian Chancellor, Baron von Beust, realised from the first that the treaty was unworkable, 'that the Sultan's zeal for reform was in direct ratio to his anxiety for self-preservation', and that, though in his hour of defeat the new Czar Alexander II might consent to the neutralisation of the Black Sea zone, it would be impossible in the future to prevent a great and growing power from rebuilding the arsenals and dockyards on her only warm sea coast, as impossible as it would be to prevent her from exercising a political influence on her brother Slavs living under Turkish rule.

On the one hand the treaty was too hard, on the other too lax. As the French Ambassador in Vienna said to von Beust, 'When you read the terms of the treaty, you will ask yourself who is the victor and who is the vanquished.' And from Constantinople the Emperor Nicholas' old enemy, Lord Stratford, warned Lord Clarendon:

> Nicholas' Russia is to all appearances on its knees, but the Russia of Nature is still in its growth, shorn of its most forward branches but capable of shooting into greater luxuriance at no distant period.

The old Ambassador still harboured fears for the future, foreseeing more accurately than the statesmen gathered in

Paris the dangers which beset a vast unwieldy empire surrounded by potential enemies.

> Greece, [he wrote] is but a scotched snake, Persia may well forget her neutrality. The slavic race from Serbia to Montenegro requires to be watched. The Sultan's Asiatic frontier is weakly defended. Circassia remains to be cleared and the Crimea to be disarmed.

For above all he was frightened of Russia, 'that power raised on a million of soldiers trained to implicit obedience and selected from sixty millions of ignorant and fanatical slaves.' This persistent fear is reflected not only in Lord Stratford's letters to Lord Clarendon, but in his own private diaries where he writes:

> Rome of old extended its sway by conquest, but wherever its eagles flew, the arts of civilisation followed, or the conquerors themselves were softened by the refinement of those they subdued. The Russian bird of prey has no such commission. It turns indeed towards the sun, but the shadow of its wings is blighting and moral desolation closes on its flight. The Russian soldier is not content with marching in a strait-waistcoat. His knapsack is stuffed with spare ones for the accommodation of his foreign victims, partisans or opponents, as it may chance to be.

Prophetic words of warning, ignored by the statesmen gathered in the Tuileries, where the Russian delegate, Count Orloff, was the success of the Parisian season. The mistakes committed in this year of victory were to bear fruit twenty years later in the year when Abdul Hamid came to the throne to find himself deserted by the very powers who had guaranteed the integrity of his empire.

Chapter VI

FIVE YEARS HAD GONE by since the night of Lord Stratford's ball, and the most eminent physicians of Asia and of Europe were gathered in the palace of Dolmabagche, trying to save the life of the thirty-nine-year-old Sultan. Consumption, of which he had had the germs since his early youth, was diagnosed as the cause of his illness, but the eminent specialists who had been called in from Vienna attributed the Sultan's rapid decline not so much to any specific disease, as to complete mental and physical exhaustion, brought on by his sexual excesses.

The years which had elapsed since the Crimean War had been years of disillusion. Abdul Medjid had seen his reforms derided, his resolutions come to nothing and the age-old hatred between Moslem and Christian venting itself in a fresh orgy of pillaging and murder. In 1858 the death of Reshid Pasha and the retirement of Lord Stratford de Redcliffe had deprived him both of his ablest minister and of his wisest friend, and since then he had lacked the strength to fight against the forces of reaction and the palace *camarilla*. After giving his solemn word to protect the Christian minorities in his empire, he had found himself powerless to curb the fanaticism which swept in a wave of flame across the Lebanon, leaving the charred ruins of Maronite villages and six thousand corpses in its wake. In Damascus the Christian quarters had been levelled to the ground: in Jeddah a French consul had been murdered when pilgrims on their way to Mecca attacked and massacred the European population, under the eyes of the Turkish garrison. There had followed the inevitable repercussions in Europe, with both France and England informing him that they could not be counted on to support a Government which allowed these massacres to occur, and in the end he had been forced to submit to the humiliation of foreign intervention.

The French troops who landed at Beirut to help in restoring order and who, according to diplomatic formula, 'had been sent by the Emperor Napoleon to assist the Sultan against the rebels,' showed the world that despite the Treaty of Paris Turkey was not yet ready to take her place in the Concert of Europe. And across the Black Sea, the Russia of Alexander II, which was gradually recovering from the wounds of the Crimean War, was quick to profit by this lesson.

It was a sad end to a reign so full of good intentions. Of all the thirty-eight articles of the *Hatti Humayun* of 1856, the only one which had become effective was the last, which stressed the necessity of 'profiting by the science, knowledge and capital of Europe.' The Ottoman Empire had become the happy hunting ground of speculators and company promoters. Undeterred by the fear of massacre, foreign adventurers of every kind were opening offices in Galata and Pera, insinuating themselves into the ante-chambers of the Sublime Porte, where they scattered *baksheesh* among underpaid officials and offered rapacious pashas a share of the spoils.

Railroads, banks and post offices; concessions for steamship companies and mineral rights; fantastic schemes for the irrigation of Mesopotamia; the piercing of the Isthmus of Suez; these were the spectres of progress which haunted the dying man in Dolmabagche. And neither Reshid nor Stratford Canning were there to dissipate his fears and give him confidence in the future. But on this lovely summer's morning of 1861, even the future had become indifferent to him, and neither the scent of the roses drifting in from the gardens, nor the weeping of the women in the adjoining room had any longer the power to rouse his consciousness. Gradually he was slipping into that grey, twilight world where the last human ties are severed and all that remains is the fading mutter of the *imams'* prayers.

Standing by the Sultan's bed, the two eldest princes paid their last homage to a father who now viewed them with the same indifference. But whereas Murad allowed his natural feelings to betray him to a few womanly tears, Abdul Hamid's pale, curiously unyouthful face remained cold and unmoved. Such love as he had to give had gone to the mother who had died twelve years ago. As a younger son he had nothing to

gain or lose by his father's death, beyond the vicarious satisfaction of seing the hitherto-favoured Murad reduced to the
same position as himself. From now on they were both virtually their uncle's prisoners, the unwanted heirs, who stood
between their cousins and the throne.

Abdul Medjid was dead, and by nightfall 'the Sultan of
Sultans, Commander of the Faithful, Guardian of the Holy
Places and Shadow of God on Earth' had been transported from
his marble palace on the Bosphorus to his father's mosque
in Stamboul, where, divested of the last earthly vanities,
he lay exposed on a straw mattress, his feet turned towards
Mecca.

Booming across the Golden Horn from the palace of the
Serasker, the salute of 101 guns announced the advent of a new
Sultan, and in every European chancellery the question was
being asked as to what manner of man was Abdul Aziz. So
little was known of the burly country gentleman who for the
past fifteen years had lived on his estates, breeding his prize
cattle, contenting himself with a few women and a small
establishment. He was said to be simple and unassuming in his
tastes, conservative rather than progressive, attached to the old
laws and the old customs, but now Dolmabagche awaited him
in all its decadent splendour, with nine hundred women in its
harem, three hundred cooks in its kitchens, an army of gardeners and of architects, who almost overnight could make
wildernesses flower and palaces rise at his command.

Even the strongest nature would have been affected by this
sudden change of fortune, and how could anyone as ignorant
and unprepared as Abdul Aziz avoid the pitfalls of absolute
power? Such qualities as he had came from his robust vitality
rather than from his intellect. He had Mahmud's autocratic
temperament allied to the superstitions and prejudices of his
peasant mother—a dangerous heritage for a Sultan called on to
rule over a vast empire in a period of revolution and transition.
His first spontaneous actions show him to have been both kindly
and humane. This was particularly apparent in his attitude
towards his brother's harem, for instead of condemning
hundreds of women still in the prime of life to perpetual
captivity in the Old Seraglio, he decreed that those who were

not the mothers of princes should, if they wished, be allowed to marry. His brother's numerous progeny (Abdul Medjid had fathered nearly thirty children, over half of whom had died as babies) were treated with generosity and his two eldest nephews were given large properties both in the capital and in the surrounding countryside.

Unfortunately it was not long before the inevitable jealousy of a Sultan towards a Crown Prince had embittered his relations with Murad. But during the first years of his uncle's reign Abdul Hamid enjoyed a greater liberty than he had known in his father's lifetime. In Dolmabagche every detail of his household had been controlled by the Sultan's eunuchs, but now he had not only a large *konak* in the fashionable district of Maslak, but also a summer villa at Therapia and a kiosk at Kiathane by the sweet waters of Europe. A monthly allowance equivalent to eight hundred and fifty pounds sterling was paid him from the Civil List and for a short while he appears to have been so inebriated by this new freedom that he indulged in an orgy of spending at variance with his true character.

The hitherto timid and unwanted boy had now two powerful protectors. The one was his old friend Pertevnyal who, as Valide Sultana, exerted her influence in his favour; the other was his foster-mother, Peresto, who had become the object of the new Sultan's stormy and passionate devotion. People are still living who remember the little woman with the heart-shaped face and enormous blue eyes, who won the heart of two successive Sultans. There is no greater tribute to Peresto's charm than that Abdul Aziz should have singled her out from all the beauties of his brother's harem. It is even asserted that he wanted to marry her, which is difficult to believe, for Peresto was not only known to be sterile, but, by oriental standards, was already middle-aged. Whatever may have been the truth, she appears to have shown little inclination to accept the Sultan's advances. As foster-mother to a royal prince she was free to leave the Imperial harem, and she now accompanied Abdul Hamid to his new home, which she would hardly have done if the rumours circulated by his enemies had been true.

Throughout his life Abdul Hamid was gentle and courteous in his relations with women, even on occasion trusting them in a way he never trusted any man, and the tale of his ingratitude towards his foster-mother is probably only one of the many legends in which the Crown Prince Murad is depicted as possessing all the virtues, whereas his younger brother is dismissed as cruel, reactionary and ignorant. One has only to study their portraits to see in Murad's loose-mouthed, weak-chinned face the incipient signs of mental degeneration, the fatal tendency to the same vices as his father. By contrast his brother's face is closed and secretive. The dark eyes under their heavy lids give nothing away. It is a clever, ugly face, dominated by the great hooked nose which shadows the contemptuous mouth. Yet, oddly enough, it is not devoid of charm, and, when Abdul Hamid set himself out to please, his rare illuminating smile and deep, drawling voice subjugated his listeners.

Already, as a boy, he impressed the few foreigners with whom he came into contact, and the Hungarian orientalist and traveller, Professor Vambery, has left a description of his first meeting with the young prince Hamid.

Vambéry, who was then at the beginning of that astonishing career which was to take him, disguised as a dervish, to the remotest parts of Asia, was earning his living in Constantinople by giving French lessons to the Imperial princesses, and it was at the palace of Sultan Medjid's eldest daughter, the Princess Fatma, married to a son of Reshid Pasha, that he first met the sixteen-year-old Abdul Hamid. The young prince used to visit his sister specially in order to attend her lessons, and Vambéry describes him 'sitting silent and immobile, only changing position when the eunuch in attendance brought him the usual cup of coffee, his black eyes fixed on the teacher's face, as if anxious to snatch every French word from his lips, and when his sister was called away on some domestic affair, addressing him in a timid, slow voice, rarely touching the subject of instruction, but asking questions about Reshid, his sister and her husband.'

From this it would appear as if Abdul Hamid had not outgrown the habit of spying on his brothers and sisters. But despite his suspicious nature, he seems at the same time to have been capable of friendship.

Thirty years were to pass before Vambéry saw Abdul Hamid again. In the intervening years the silent, unobtrusive boy had become the most feared of autocrats, but the old friendship survived, and though at first the Sultan barely recognised his visitor, no sooner had he reminded him of the Princess Fatma's lame teacher, than he stretched out both hands in welcome. And when Vambéry told him of some of the dangers and hardships of his adventurous life he asked him why he had not come to him sooner, as he would like to have shown him the faithfulness of his friendship. In that Court, where everyone was suspect, Vambéry remained, almost to the end, one of the few Europeans who was allowed to visit the Sultan without an interpreter.

Other less creditable friendships were formed in the first years of freedom, when Murad and Abdul Hamid made tentative excursions into the world beyond the palace. The Sultan Abdul Aziz was not yet beset by the fears and suspicions bred of absolute power, and acting on the advice of the wise and tolerant Ali Pasha, he allowed his nephews to frequent the company of Europeans. It was the time when French influence in Constantinople was at its height. Great Britain, represented by the wayward and eccentric Lord Bulwer, had forfeited much of the prestige she had enjoyed under Stratford Canning and, while the British Ambassador absented himself from his embassy to live in idyllic bliss with a Greek mistress on an island in the Marmara, the ablest diplomats of the Quai d'Orsay intrigued to re-establish French supremacy in the Levant.

Reshid's successors looked to France rather than to Britain for support. British officers who had stayed on in Turkey after the Crimean War and accepted posts in the Ottoman Army found themselves in competition with French technicians, sent out under Government auspices. French professors were put in charge of the new secular schools, French goods flooded the market, and in the drawing rooms of Pera the young princes found a slavish imitation of Parisian fashions, an uncritical admiration for everything that was French. Enthralled they listened to discussions on politics and foreign affairs, and learnt to sit at table with unveiled women and to appreciate French wines, a taste which was later to prove fatal to Murad. For the first and last time in their lives the two brothers appeared as boon companions, their natural shyness drawing them together. But no sooner had they familiarised themselves with European customs than they inevitably drifted apart. While Murad foolishly identified himself with the little group of journalists and philosophers whose open criticism of the Government was already attracting the notice of the police, his wiser and more cautious brother preferred the banking houses of Galata to the political cafés of Pera. Abdul Hamid's friendship with the Greek banker, Zarifi, and the Armenian broker, Assani, dates from these days. They were friends to whom he was always loyal, and many years later certain arrogant ambassadors were heard to complain of dinner parties at Yildiz where Levantine brokers of doubtful reputation were among their fellow guests.

Behind the beaded curtains of dark and frowsty counting-houses, Abdul Hamid was free to indulge in his passion for figures. Timidly at first, then gradually gathering courage, he began to play on the Bourse of Galata. Advised by Zarifi, he made his first investments, which appear to have been success-ful, for by the time he succeeded to the throne he had already amassed a fortune equivalent to seventy thousand pounds. But above all he learnt for the first time the power and value of money. Men talked freely and often indiscreetly in front of him. His very diffidence and apparent eagerness to hear the truth led them to forget that they were addressing one of a long line of autocrats. He heard that his father's extravagance had brought the Empire to the verge of ruin, and that in spite of the eight million pounds of foreign loans, the Treasury had had to resort to a fresh issue of paper money and to hand-to-mouth borrowing from private capitalists in Galata. But now private capital was exhausted, Treasury Bonds were acquiring a bad name and to save the Turkish lira the Government had no other choice than to beg for a further loan from the Western Powers.

The Allies of the Crimean War, who around the conference table in Paris had promised to regard any infringement of

Turkish independence as a *casus belli*, had failed to live up to their obligations. Wrangling among themselves, they had allowed the Danubian principalities to unite under one ruler and to proclaim their virtual independence of the Porte. Not a single French or British soldier had been mobilised when Serbia, in violation of the Treaty, had taken possession of two of the six fortresses still under Turkish control. The heroics of the Crimean War were of the past; interference had taken the place of defence, and every new loan gave the Western Powers a further right to interfere.

Rumours were rife in those narrow, tunnelled streets which fall from the blistered walls of Galata into the sunlight of the Golden Horn—rumours of the merging of the State Ottoman Bank with an Anglo-French foundation, under the tutelage of an advisory committee appointed by London and Paris; rumours of Fuad Pasha's attempt to produce a budget— a rumour which gave rise to scepticism, for how could any minister venture to introduce a budget when there were no reliable figures in existence on which to base it? And the young Abdul Hamid learnt that in his uncle's empire no government department kept regular accounts. There was no register of property owners and in spite of the reforms of 1839 and 1856, the condemned system of tax-farming was still being practised in the provinces. On every side he heard tell of chaos and disorganisation, of bribery and corruption, till he began to realise that for all his dislike of foreigners, a dislike carefully nurtured by old Pertevnyal and the sheikhs and *mollas* of his early entourage, it was only in the company of Europeans that he could learn how to govern an empire, and profit not only by their knowledge but also by their weaknesses.

Chapter VII

IN THE SPRING of 1867, the embassies of Pera re-echoed to the news of the Sultan's prospective journey to Europe. Till now no Ottoman ruler had ventured beyond the frontiers of his empire except in the role of a conqueror, and the first reaction of Abdul Aziz had been to refuse Louis Napoleon's invitation to attend the Paris Exhibition. But the ministers of the Porte looked upon the French Emperor's invitation as a heaven-sent opportunity to strengthen by personal contact Turkey's links with Europe and to obtain another loan. So with infinite tact and patience they succeeded in inducing their unwilling master to expose his sacred presence in a land of unbelievers.

But even after the Sultan's active opposition had turned to sullen indifference they had still to contend with the opposition of the Palace *camarilla*, led by the Valide Sultana, who had enlisted all the more reactionary elements in the country to put difficulties in the way. One by one these difficulties were solved and the irascible Sultan was persuaded that neither harem nor eunuchs would be in keeping with his role as a liberal and progressive monarch, while the vast army of retainers, the cooks whose duty it was to see that their master touched no food defiled by the unbeliever, the Coffee Makers, the Sword Bearers and the Keepers of the Imperial Wardrobe were gradually whittled down to reasonable proportions.

Among the first to receive invitations to accompany the Sultan to Paris were his two elder nephews, Murad and Abdul Hamid. It was not so much that their uncle desired their presence, for such friendly feelings as he had entertained on his accession had long since given way to the usual suspicion which characterised the relations of the Sultan and his heirs, but, given the ever present fear of a *coup d'état*, it was considered wiser not to leave the two princes behind. So, at the age of twenty-five, Abdul Hamid had the unlooked for and unhoped for opportunity of seeing Europe with his own eyes. Wiser than Murad, he displayed neither joy nor sorrow at the news. While the former jubilated at the prospect of a visit to Paris and boasted of his knowledge of the French language in front of the ignorant and irritated Sultan, he remained a silent, acquiescent shadow, too insignificant to be disliked. The boy who, according to Vambéry, had been so anxious to learn French that he appeared to snatch every word from his lips now feigned a complete ignorance of the language, acting so consummately that no one in Paris guessed that behind that bored, impassive mask he was observing and recording every impression, so that thirty years later he could still remember the name of every street through which he had passed and of every officer who had been presented to him.

Paris was enjoying the last halcyon days of the Second Empire and visitors from all over the world were flocking to the great Exhibition in the Champs de Mars, lining the streets and boulevards to cheer the unending procession of emperors and kings, princes and statesmen, who came and went from the Tuileries. Of all the galaxy of crowned heads no one aroused as much interest as His Imperial Majesty the Sultan of Turkey. The wildest rumours circulated before his arrival. He was said to drive in a golden carriage drawn by his vassal princes and to have his shoes filled with sand from the Marmara so that his feet might not be defiled by treading on Christian earth. Imagination soared to such heights of fantasy that by the time of his arrival the Sultan was credited with a retinue of lions and elephants led by negro slaves laden with golden chains. It must therefore have been somewhat of an anti-climax when, on the afternoon of June 30, 1867, a short, thickset man in a plain blue frockcoat and simple fez stepped out of the train onto the red-carpeted platform of the Gare de Lyon.

But though Sultan Aziz failed to live up to his reputation as a Caliph of the Arabian Nights, sightseers and reporters still waited all day outside the gates of the Elysée Palace to snatch some detail of his private life. Was it true, they questioned, that two roasted lambs and fifty hard-boiled eggs were consumed every morning at the Imperial breakfast table, and that girls from the Folies Bergères were brought at night into the palace? The bland-faced aides-de-camp and courteous but un-smiling secretaries refused to give the slightest information, horrified by a country where the common herd was permitted to pry into the sacred habits of 'God's Vice-Regent upon Earth.'

In apathy and gloom the Sultan attended the numerous entertainments in his honour, raising his hand to his forehead in oriental salutation, but displaying such a total lack of interest that it needed all Fuad Pasha's subtlety as an interpreter to convince the Emperor Napoleon that his master was 'so impressed by the power and glory of the French Empire that he had no greater wish than to be his friend and ally.' The only time when the Sultan was seen to smile was during a reception at the Tuileries, when the Empress Eugénie singled out his young son, Prince Yusufeddin, and offered him a box of chocolates. But the smile soon turned to a frown when the Empress engaged in animated conversation with Prince Murad, congratulating him on his excellent French, and after a few moments of wast-ing her charm on the polite but unresponsive Prince Hamid, turning once more to the elder brother.

In conversation with Fuad, Louis Napoleon commented upon the difference between the two brothers, the one so eager and full of life, the other so apathetic and indifferent. He little knew that this indifference was deliberately assumed to placate the suspicious Sultan, angered by Murad's success, and that at heart Abdul Hamid would have liked to rival his brother at a court abounding with beautiful women. He was as sensual and full-blooded as any other member of his family and it must have required considerable self-control to lower his eyes before the flamboyant charms of a Duchesse de Morny or a Madame de Castiglione. But stronger than any other emotion was his instinct of self-preservation, the inheritance of a childhood shadowed by fear, and he preferred the safety of obscurity to the fleeting triumphs which aroused his uncle's jealousy.

His very inconspicuousness gave him the greater leisure to observe his surroundings, and, as he toured the sights of Paris and dutifully admired the wonders of the Exhibition, he saw a France which, despite her prosperity and riches, lived in mortal fear of Germany, the new power on her eastern frontier. He saw an Emperor who, despite his flamboyant gestures, had been powerless to save the young Austrian Archduke who, supported by French arms and inspired by French ambitions, had been sent to his death in Mexico. In these very days Maximilian's short-lived empire, deserted by Europe and more particularly by France, was drawing to its tragic close, and no event was more calculated to shock a nature such as Abdul Hamid's, or more likely to prejudice him against the limitations of constitutional monarchy, where the force of public opinion could lead an Emperor to betray his word.

The young French officers on duty with the Ottoman princes confined themselves to initiating them into the charms of Parisian night life rather than in discussing politics, and there were intimate supper-parties at Maxim's with pretty girls from the Variétés, parties where Murad developed a taste for champagne-cup with brandy, which later was to have such a fatal effect on his health, and where Abdul Hamid was content to sit with his wine-glass scarcely touched, watching his brother grow more and more fuddled with drink, so that the following morning he would appear in front of the Sultan unable to control either his words or actions and in a mood most likely to arouse His Majesty's 'divine displeasure'.

His Majesty's 'divine displeasure' was easy to arouse these days, for Abdul Aziz was not enjoying his Paris visit. Fuad had failed to extort as much money as he had hoped from the barons of the *haute finance*, and the Sultan had taken an unreasoning dislike to his host from the day when, in an attempt to introduce a more personal element into the conversation, Louis Napoleon had dared to suggest that they were related through their Créole grandmothers: an attempted compliment, which Abdul Aziz regarded as the grossest of insults. It must have been with mutual relief that Emperor and Sultan said goodbye to one another at Boulogne, when the Ottoman Princes boarded the Imperial yacht, the *Reine Hortense*, which was to take them across the Channel to England, where, after weeks of argument, Lord Derby had succeeded in persuading the widowed Queen to come out of her retirement to receive the Sultan.

However unwilling Abdul Aziz had been to embark on his European tour, it was nothing compared with Queen Victoria's unwillingness to receive him. But too many political interests were at stake to allow either Queen or Sultan to follow their natural inclinations. The now-friendly understanding between France and Russia, the growth of French influence in the Levant, where de Lesseps' canal was nearing completion, and where Khedive Ismail was exploiting the importance of this canal to secure complete independence of the Porte, made it as imperative for Great Britain to strengthen her ties with Constantinople as for the Ottoman Empire to enlist British help in the event of a Franco-Russian alliance supporting the ambitions of the Egyptian Khedive. Although at first Lord Derby received neither co-operation nor encouragement from his Sovereign, he finally managed to convince her of the importance of the visit. So, consoling herself with the thought that 'the Sultan was not likely to come again', Victoria of England invited the Ottoman Sultan and Princes to lunch at Windsor Castle the day following their arrival in London. Prestige was gratified and pride was mollified, while the tedium of the interview was cut down to the minimum, the Queen hurrying back to her beloved Osborne and the Sultan and his suite returning to London.

The luncheon party at which the Queen entertained her guests with strictly English fare must have been a curious experience for the Turkish Princes. Even Abdul Aziz departed from his attitude of phlegmatic indifference, confronted by this dumpy, middle-aged woman in dowdy black and widow's bonnet, who ruled over vaster territories and more divergent races than those comprised in his own empire; while his young son, Prince Yusufeddin could hardly hide his horror and surprise at the motherly kisses bestowed on him both by the Queen and the Princess of Teck. But despite the fact that the very conception of a female sovereign was alien to the Moslem mind, Queen Victoria's innate dignity was such as to inspire both the Sultan and his nephews with respect and admiration. On no one did she make a greater impression than on Abdul Hamid, whose nervous nature found comfort and reassurance in the presence of this little Queen, so simple and unassuming, so supremely self-confident, representing in her very person the security and solid complacency of England.

The sun which had shone on the festivities in Paris was obscured by heavy clouds and rain from the moment they landed at Dover, but the charming welcome of the Prince of Wales who had come on board to meet them, the enthusiasm of the crowds who thronged the flower-wreathed platform, more than compensated for the greyness of the skies. However grudgingly Queen Victoria may have given of her hospitality, the hospitality once given left nothing to be desired, and both Her Majesty's Government and the City of London combined to impress the Sultan and his heirs with the wealth and power of Victorian England. As Punch commented in ironic vein:

> We've a Padishah to dazzle,
> We've a Pasha to amaze,
> We've to teach them England has all
> That makes prosper - all that pays.

The newest and fastest of trains had rushed the astonished Princes from Dover to London in a little over two hours. An escort of Household Cavalry accompanied them from Charing Cross to Buckingham Palace and from the balconies of Marlborough House a group of royal beauties cheered their arrival in the Mall. But more stirring than the official honours was the welcome of the people themselves. Though a new generation had grown up since the Crimean War, childhood memories of the gallant Turkish ally still lingered in the mind. Even the massacres of Lebanon and Arabia, though widely publicised by the Bible and Missionary Societies, had failed to destroy the legends of Alma and Sebastopol. Pan-Slav propaganda was as yet in its infancy and stories of Turkish atrocities and Christian martyrdom had not yet penetrated to the masses. The crowds in the London streets were there not only to see the exotic spectacle of green-turbanned sheikhs and Albanian chieftains agleam with gold embroidery and jewelled *yataghans*, but to cheer with a genuine enthusiasm the stout, bearded figure whom, with a singular lack of imagination, *The Times* described as 'looking like a typical Turk.'

In Paris the Emperor Napoleon had honoured his guests by transforming the Elysée Palace into a setting of the Arabian Nights; the Queen of England was subtler in her flattery, even if the flattery happened to be accidental. Accepting the Sultan as a European sovereign, she lodged him in her own house. There were no concessions to Oriental tastes or constitutions in the solid four-poster beds hung with flower chintzes, the empty fire-grates of an English July banked with rare plants brought from Kew. But so pleased was the Sultan by his reception and, for all his dislike of Europeans, so flattered by the attentions of his English hosts, that Fuad congratulated himself on the success of the visit. Not only was England making a good impression on the Sultan, but the Sultan was making a good impression on the English. At a banquet given at the Guildhall, where he delighted the London crowds by arriving on horseback glittering with orders, his fez surmounted by the traditional heron's feather clasped in diamonds, Abdul Aziz condescended to the length of making a speech through his interpreter. His words were cheered to the echo by the worthy City merchants who saw in the Ottoman Empire a vast and as yet barely exploited market for British merchandise. Even if the Sultan was a creditor he was a creditor on a large enough scale to inspire respect, and the recently floated Ottoman Loan Shares, by which all outstanding debts of the Porte had been consolidated in one loan guaranteed by a group of international bankers, were popular with English investors owing to the high rate of interest and low purchase price. The ordinary 'John Bull' was prepared to look upon the Turk as 'an honest fellow', and whether at a banquet at the Guildhall or a ball at the India Office the Sultan and his nephews were hailed as the lions of the day.

But Abdul Aziz was fundamentally too ignorant, too prejudiced and already too mentally deranged to derive any real benefit from his visit to England. If he admired what he saw, it was only in order to possess what he admired. Even his nephews were already too warped by their early upbringing to grasp the principles of a constitutional monarchy. While Murad spoke with enthusiasm of a democracy he did not begin to understand, Abdul Hamid, who was as ignorant but more cynical and intelligent than his brother, tried to probe the weaknesses of a government which at heart he admired.

Ten years later, Abdul Hamid, now Sultan, would often refer to this week in England, and the British Ambassador, Henry Layard, would be surprised to find how much he had managed to absorb in between the round of garden-parties and military reviews. He had seen how England's ever-growing industrial cities were making it increasingly difficult for her to feed her population, rendering her ever more dependent on her overseas possessions and how England, as well as Turkey, had trouble with her minorities. Layard found the young Turkish Sovereign familiar with every detail of the Fenian Rising, as if it gave him a certain pleasure to know that constitutional monarchs too lived in fear of assassination.

The climax to the visit was a naval review at Spithead, and the Queen's account in her diary enables us to recapture the atmosphere of that bright, windy day interrupted by squalls of rain, which not only made it difficult for the ships to get under way, but largely contributed to the discomfort of the royal guests. Though the navy was said to be his hobby, the Sultan was ill the moment he went to sea and it must have required a heroic effort to maintain a dignified bearing while clambering up a swaying accommodation-ladder on a rolling yacht, and to be greeted at the top of the ladder by the little Queen, as calm and erect as if she were in her own drawing-room at Windsor. Queen Victoria noted in her diary:

> It must have been a curious sight, the Sultan and I sitting outside the deck saloon, the others beyond. [And she added] The Sultan feels very uncomfortable at sea. He was constantly retiring below and can have seen very little, which was a pity, as it was a very fine sight.

She never knew how much was noted and remembered, if not by the Sultan, at least by one of his nephews. The review, which had been deliberately staged to impress the Ottoman princes with the power of the Royal Navy, had succeeded in its object. During a reign of over thirty years, successive British Ambassadors had only to threaten the appearance of the British fleet in Ottoman waters for Abdul Hamid to remember that rough, windy day at Spithead with the great iron-clads riding the waves, the guns firing at one another in mock battle—and remembering, accede to their demands.

After the Royal Yacht had passed through the lines, the Queen invested the Sultan with the Order of the Garter, though as she herself said, 'she would have preferred the Star of India as more suitable for a non-Christian, but he had set his heart on having the Garter.' The ceremony took place before lunch, where the Queen displayed so hearty an appetite as to impress her guests with her super-human quality. And no sooner had they swallowed the last morsel than the Sultan and the Princes once more went below, only appearing on deck to take leave of their hostess when she disembarked at Osborne pier.

The ordeal was over. That evening, from his bed at Buckingham Palace, enjoying a pilaff prepared by his own cook, Abdul Aziz dictated a letter to Queen Victoria, in which he professed himself, to be 'touche jusqu'aux larmes by the kindness of Her Majesty's reception.' But if one had asked the simpleminded monarch what had impressed him most in England, he would probably have answered, 'The fireworks display at the Crystal Palace', which had pleased him so much that he had given a thousand pounds out of his privy purse towards the reconstruction of the burnt-out wing.

The Queen had done her duty and it was the turn of the Royal Dukes to give balls and banquets in the Sultan's honour. Figures from the past, such as Lord Stratford de Redcliffe, came out of their retirement to pay homage to the Ottoman Princes. In a world of strangers Abdul Hamid found an old friend, and the veteran ambassador must have been flattered by the welcome he received from the young prince whom he remembered as a neglected little boy at his father's selamlik. But English food and the English climate (for it rained incessantly during their stay) proved too much for Abdul Hamid's delicate constitution and on the day of departure he could barely drag himself to the train. When the royal party reached Vienna he was too ill to attend the functions where the last two representatives of the principle of Divine Right, the descendant of the Holy Roman Emperors and the Caliph of Islam, met for the first time as friends. He was forced to stay behind when the rest of the party boarded the flower-decked flotilla of ships which were to take them down the Danube as far as the Turkish frontier.

Many years later, Abdul Hamid referred to the kindness with which he was treated at the Austrian court, 'the amiable and graceful' way in which the Emperor Francis Joseph made daily enquiries after his health, sending him presents of fruit and flowers from Schönbrunn, and the courtesy which in later years he showed towards European visitors to Yildiz was modelled on his memory of the Hapsburg Emperor.

Chapter VIII

ABDUL HAMID WAS twenty-five when he returned from Vienna stimulated by new impressions, and ideas and had he been able to take an active part in politics he might have benefited from the journey, but for nine years he was condemned to a life of idleness and obscurity by an uncle whose jealousy of his nephews was increasing with the years, and who was already nursing in secret the ambition to supplant them by his own son.

Since his journey to Europe, the Sultan had been obsessed by a megalomania which led him to believe that, in spite of the kings and queens who claimed to be his equals, he alone was the elect of God, the Sultan of Sultans. So long as Fuad and Ali remained in power, they were able to turn this megalomania to good account, in encouraging him to emulate and outvie his predecessors by introducing further reforms into his heterogeneous empire. But, in 1871, the deaths of these two enlightened statesmen brought about a complete reversion in Turkey's foreign and domestic policy. Freed of their tutelage, Abdul Aziz gave way to his most extravagant whims, and before long his courtiers were whispering among themselves what had hitherto been only hinted at in the private correspondence of the foreign ambassadors, namely that the Sultan was growing feeble-minded. Faced by the boredom bred of absolute power, he sought refuge in a world of fantasy. The dinner service of solid gold encrusted with precious stones, specially ordered from a Parisian goldsmith; the shimmering walls of Beylerbey panelled in mother of pearl in honour of Empress Eugenie's three-day visit; even the fleet of costly ironclads equipped in British shipyards and commissioned regardless of the fact that the sailors were not yet trained to man them, all bespoke the same pathetic attempt to foster an illusion of grandeur. His megalomania dictated his most trivial acts, leading him to exact an abject servility from his courtiers, whom he forced to grovel on their knees and to address him in language so inflated as to sound strange even to oriental ears. Then at other times he would grow bored at pretending to himself and revert to the most puerile and infantile amusements. His chamberlains would have to stand by with impassive faces while cocks and hens were let loose in the throne room to be chased by a delighted and perspiring monarch who, clutching at their feathered necks, decorated them with the highest orders of the Empire. No wonder people called him 'mad', reminding one another in whispers of the strain of insanity inherited from Ibrahim the Sot.

Meanwhile his heirs assisted as silent and helpless witnesses to the disintegration not only of the Sultan, but of the Empire. Corrupt and ineffectual ministers, whose talents lay in flattering their master rather than in administering the State, had ousted the reformers, and the new Russian Ambassador, General Ignatieff, profiting by their ineptitude, was to infiltrate his agents into key positions throughout the Balkans.

Thirteen years had gone by since the Treaty of Paris, and Russian ambitions were once more concentrated upon the Straits; the only difference being that the Czar had now exchanged the title of 'Defender of the Orthodox Faith' for that of 'Protector to his Fellow Slavs'. Under the new banner of Pan-Slavism the Sultan's European provinces were honeycombed with secret societies, directed by Russian consuls and financed by the Russian Embassy at Constantinople. Political circumstances favoured these intrigues. The Prussian cannon which shattered the Napoleonic eagles at Sedan shattered at the same time the whole balance of power in Europe and in the Levant. Barely a year after the opening of the Suez Canal, dedicated by de Lesseps to the glory of his country, France lay prostrate under the heel of Germany. A month after Sedan the Czar was already claiming from Bismarck the price of his neutrality—Germany's support in denouncing the 'Black Sea clauses' of the Treaty of Paris.

With France defeated and Austria still bleeding from the wounds inflicted at Sadowa, only England and Turkey were left to protest against the violation of the Treaty, but in England a Liberal Government was in power, led by Mr.

Gladstone, the champion of small nations, the inveterate enemy of Islam, and the Foreign Office confined itself to expressing profound regret at the 'arbitrary repudiation of a solemn engagement', insisting on a conference being held in London, instead of at St. Petersburg. This, though it may have helped towards saving Britain's face, in no way prevented Russia from getting her own way.

Deserted by her former allies, the Ottoman Empire lay at the mercy of Russian intrigues, and the new Ambassador took full advantage of the situation. Years of diplomatic training in the Far East had prepared General Ignatieff for the task of dealing with oriental politicians—and no one was more versed in the art of flattery and lies, or more single-minded in his passionate belief in the future of Pan-Slavism.

When insurrection broke out in Bosnia, an insurrection deliberately incited by Russian agents, and the Governor wrote asking for reinforcements, General Ignatieff was able to persuade the Porte that, according to the reports of the consuls on the spot, the troubles had been grossly exaggerated and that it was far wiser to let them quietly subside and not give them undue importance. With its Christian peasant population and its Moslem landlords, Bosnia offered a particularly fertile ground for Pan-Slav intrigues and, thanks to the efficiency of the Russian agents and the inefficiency of the Sublime Porte, it was not long before a small-scale peasant insurrection had developed into a widespread rebellion, with the Sultan in the shameful position of accepting Austrian and Russian mediation in negotiating with the rebels.

In 1875 the Sultan's insane extravagance brought matters to such a pass that he was forced to inform his European creditors that he was unable to pay the interest due to the shareholders in the Ottoman Debt. This decision aroused a storm of protest from every country except Russia, whose envoy officially congratulated His Imperial Majesty on what he described 'as a wise and precautionary measure.' Russia had every reason to be pleased, for Turkey's partial repudiation of her debts aroused so much indignation in Europe, particularly in England, as to alienate any pro-Turkish sentiment which had survived from the Crimean War. Tempted by the high rate of

interest, thousands of small shareholders had invested their
life savings in Turkish Bonds, and the hardships to which these
unfortunate people were now exposed vented itself in anger,
not only against the Sultan and his ministers, but against the
Turkish nation as a whole.

Russian diplomacy now triumphed in every field, penetrating even the jealously guarded doors of the Imperial
harem, where General Ignatieff's fascinating wife was a
favoured visitor of the Valide Sultana. Abdul Hamid's old
friend Pertevniyal had become a political power dominating
her feeble-minded son and dispensing largesse on such a scale
as to make severe inroads into the Public Treasury. Her passion
for finery had increased with the years and she would think
nothing of buying as many as fifty dresses in one day and,
on returning to the palace, of discarding them as unsuitable for
her years and distributing them among her slaves. This habit of
what she called 'spreading happiness around her' once reached a
point when Ali Pasha dared to suggest that her expenditure
should be controlled, an insult she never forgot nor forgave,
and after Ali's death, she used all her influence to prevent his
party returning to power. Her hatred of the so-called Young
Turks made her into the Russian Ambassador's most powerful
ally, and she richly deserved the jewels and sables presented
by his Imperial master.

However unrelenting in her hatreds, Pertevniyal had a certain
peasant loyalty, and this loyalty was particularly evident in
her attitude to the Sultan's nephews. While she looked upon
the popular Murad with suspicion and dislike, fanning the
Sultan's natural jealousy of his heir, Abdul Hamid continued
to enjoy her friendship and protection. In her eyes, her splendid
virile son had nothing to fear from this shy, diffident young
man who gave the impression of being the most devoted of
his uncle's servants, always ready to report a disrespectful
whisper overheard in a corridor or some slighting remark
against the Sultan uttered in the presence of his brother Murad.
And the Valide Sultana, who for all her pride was still as
garrulous as any other bath attendant of Stamboul, continued to confide in the attentive young prince who appeared
to be so grateful for her friendship. In between the puffing and

sucking at the amber mouthpiece of her *chubuk*, the interminable cups of coffee and the nibbling of sweetmeats, Abdul Hamid learned of some of the intrigues which gather round a throne.

He was leading such a retired life at the time that he had little opportunity of hearing about the political situation, beyond what he read in the heavily censored newspapers. When he attended his uncle's *selamlik*, he was prevented from mixing either with the ministers or with the foreign diplomats and latterly the bankers of Galata had grown cautious of discussing politics in front of the Sultan's nephew. In these circumstances he welcomed the confidences of the Valide Sultana. From the old lady's garbled accounts, he learnt of the new orientation of Turkey's foreign policy and of the sudden popularity of the Russian Ambassador. He heard her praise the tact and wisdom with which the new vizir Mahmud Nedim had persuaded his master to make friends with the Egyptian Khedive, who was now building a palace on the Bosphorus and scattering *baksheesh* with so lavish a hand as to win all hearts.

One morning in Galata, Abdul Hamid had chanced to overhear a Greek banker commenting in an unguarded moment on how Abdul Aziz was selling his sovereign rights in Egypt in return for certain sums guaranteed by the Khedive's Armenian bankers. But Pertevniyal knew nothing of these transactions, nor would she have understood them had she known. In her primitive fashion, she was ready to acclaim the unscrupulous Mahmud Nedim as a heaven-sent genius because he had found new sources of income for the Sultan's privy purse.

Hour after hour she would rattle on in her hoarse old voice, interposing confidences with reminiscences, and Abdul Hamid would listen with his gentle smile, his half-closed eyes, expressing no opinion, venturing no confidence in return, yet so sympathetic in his manner as to give her the illusion he was agreeing with her every word.

It is difficult to gauge his reactions to the events which were gradually leading the Empire to ruin. On the one hand there was his ingrained belief in the inviolability of the Caliphate:

on the other the fear that his uncle's megalomania might end by robbing him of his inheritance. The Sultan was known to have consulted with certain *ulema** regarding the possibility of changing the succession and, though this was directed against his brother Murad rather than himself, it can hardly have left him unmoved for since his earliest childhood he had had nothing to look forward to other than the hope of one day becoming Sultan.

If confidences had called for confidences he might have told Pertevniyal of a prophecy of a sheikh from Sidon whom he had met through his Syrian chamberlain. Hearing that the sheikh was famed for his prophetic gifts, he had invited him out to his kiosk at Kiathane and there one summer's afternoon, as they were sitting on the terrace overlooking the Golden Horn and the cypress groves of Eyub, the sheikh had uttered his prophecy: 'Within two years you will be invested with the sword of Osman in the mosque of Eyub and acclaimed as Padishah and Caliph of Islam.' Spoken as in a trance, the words were never repeated. His eager questions met with no more than a blank stare, an embarrassed silence, and the sheikh returned to Sidon without throwing any further light on the prophecy. But those few words had been sufficient to convince Abdul Hamid he had not long to wait and they helped him to endure the monotony of a life where he had nothing to occupy his restless energy beyond the running of his farm at Kiathane and an occasional gamble on the bourse at Galata. Boredom had for a time tempted him to give way to the weakness both he and Murad had inherited from their father. But an addiction to *raki* had resulted in a serious illness and his Greek physician, Mavroyeni, had warned him that unless he could cure himself of the habit his health would be permanently undermined. Since then he had given up all forms of alcohol other than an occasional glass of bordeaux to stimulate his circulation.

It was the same thing with women. Though by nature a voluptuary, he soon realised his constitution was not suited to a life of debauchery. While Murad spent the greater part of his income on his women, Abdul Hamid's harem, presided

* Doctor of Sacred Law.

over by Peresto, were few in number and modest in their expenditure. Throughout his life he appears to have been in search of something beyond the sensual yet curiously impersonal relations of the harem. The women who attracted him were charming and intelligent rather than beautiful, women whom he valued for their companionship as much as for their physical attributes. And, in search of this companionship, he ventured into the Christian quarters of Pera where he formed his first serious attachment with a little Belgian glove-seller.

No portrait survives of Flora Cordier, 'the fair-haired girl with the laughing eyes', whose shop in the Grande Rue was a favourite rendezvous for the young gallants of the European quarter. Her ambitions, which stopped at nothing less than marriage, dated from the day when her customers included an Ottoman prince—and from all accounts Abdul Hamid appears to have gone through some form of marriage ceremony with her. But even at her proudest moment, Flora Cordier would never have guessed that no less a person than a British Prime Minister would record her conquest. Two years later, when Abdul Hamid ascended the Ottoman throne, Mr. Disraeli wrote to Lord Salisbury:

> The new Sultan has only one wife, a *modiste* from Pera, a Belgian. He was in the habit of frequenting her shop, buying gloves, etc., and much admired her. One day he said 'Do you think you could marry me' and she replied '*Pourquoi non*', and it was done. It is she who has set him against Seraglio life and all that. In short a Roxelana. Will he be a Suleyman the Great?

For all the British Prime Minister's poetic licence, Mademoiselle Cordier was not destined to become a sultana, still less a Roxelana—though for a few years she gave Abdul Hamid the warmth and affection which till now had been lacking in his life. She had also other attributes in her favour, for her glove shop on the Grande Rue was a focal point for all the gossip of the capital, and no gossip was too trivial to amuse the Prince Hamid. To her surprise, she found that this mature and adult man knew nothing about the everyday problems of life in the European quarter; of the corruption of the Mixed Courts;* the heavy bribes necessary to secure the simplest permits, and the venal customs officials who kept goods sequestered for months in the warehouses of Tophane. She must have been even more surprised by his political ignorance; of how he ignored the activities of the Reform Party and the growing demand for a constitutional government in which Christians and Moslems were united. From the unguarded chatter of his Belgian mistress Abdul Hamid heard for the first time of the grievances of the despised Christians; of how their hopes were centred in a certain Midhat Pasha, who as governor of the Danube Vilayet and President of the Council, had introduced sweeping reforms in favour of the Christian population, and though the aspirations of Midhat and his party meant little to a Belgian glove seller, Flora Cordier merely voiced the general feeling of bitterness and resentment which had gradually infected every class and which only the Palace continued to ignore.

---

* An international tribunal by which, according to the terms of the Capitulations, certain Powers had the right of jurisdiction over their nationals.

Chapter IX

Like a ship without a rudder, Abdul Aziz drifted towards the storm, and in the spring of 1876, the British Ambassador, Sir Henry Elliots noted that:

> From the pashas down to the porters in the street and the boatmen on the Bosphorus no one thinks any longer of concealing his opinions. The word 'constitution' is in every mouth and, should the Sultan refuse to grant one, an attempt to depose him appears almost inevitable.

It had been a hard winter, and thousands had died from starvation and exposure in the snow-bound steppes of Anatolia. Constantinople was crowded with refugees, and the mosques and *medreses* were full to overflowing. Beggars were as numerous as the pariah dogs and the traditional hospitality of Islam was being taxed to the utmost. Rich and poor alike inveighed against the Government, and while discontent augmented in the capital, the news from the provinces became ever more alarming. Volunteers from Serbia and Montenegro were flocking to the support of the Bosnian insurgents: in Bulgaria Pan-Slav intrigues had roused religious hatred in villages where, of recent years, Moslem and Christian had been living as peaceful neighbours: in Salonika an outburst of Moslem fanaticism had caused the murder of the French and German Consuls, and, by the spring of 1876, the Eastern question was once more claiming the attention of every European chancellery. The three partners of the *Drei Kaiser Bund*, the Emperors of Austria, Germany and Russia were openly accusing the Sultan of having failed to carry out the long-promised reforms, warning him that unless these promises were redeemed, the Powers would have to intervene 'to protect his Christian subjects'.

There was one element which the European Powers did not

take into sufficient account, and this was the growing discontent of the Turkish people themselves, to whom the threat of foreign intervention was the last drop in an already overbrimming cup of misery and humiliation. Though officially banished and proscribed, the Young Turk party was secretly growing in strength and Christian and Moslem now looked to Midhat Pasha as their leader. Even the theological students, who usually represented the most conservative element in the capital, were siding with the reformers. And on May 10, two thousand of these students stopped the Sultan's son, Prince Yusufeddin, on his way to the War Office, demanding the dismissal of the pro-Russian Grand Vizir and the reinstatement of Midhat Pasha.

Frightened by the threat of revolution, the Sultan recalled Midhat from exile. But Midhat had not been in the capital a week before he realised that no measure of reform would ever be carried through so long as Abdul Aziz remained on the throne. Unable to face a crisis, the Sultan shut himself up in his harem, where he spent the greater part of his days and nights in the arms of a seventeen-year-old Circassian who had obtained such an ascendancy over his failing mind that he was reputed to have spent nearly a million Turkish pounds in gratifying her whims. There was no alternative other than to depose him and Midhat turned in despair to the Heir-Apparent who was now living as a virtual prisoner in his *konak* outside the town.

There are no details as to how Midhat established contact with the Heir-Apparent, or whether Abdul Hamid was included in these meetings, but his behaviour in the light of future events leads one to believe that he had some previous knowledge of them and that he was confided in, if not by Midhat, by his brother-in-law, a certain Mahmud Djelaleddin Pasha who played a considerable part in the rising. In ordinary circumstances Abdul Hamid would have been the last person to identify himself with a conspiracy against the Throne, but fear for his future was for the moment stronger than the fear of revolution, forcing him to make friends with men whom he distrusted and to support a brother whom he hated and despised.

The Prince, whom Midhat and his party represented to the world as 'Murad the Reformer', a paragon of all the virtues, was very different from the high-spirited young man who, on his visit to Europe, had embraced so wholeheartedly and with such complete lack of understanding all the slogans of democracy. His restricted life had told on his health: what had been a weakness had developed into a vice, and over-indulgence in champagne laced with brandy had turned him into a physical and mental wreck living in continual fear of the assassin's knife, and so fuddled by drink that at times he could barely find the notes on the piano which remained his only consolation. Owing to the seclusion in which he lived, few people knew of Prince Murad's failings and, even if Midhat suspected him of being weak and self-indulgent, it was probably an added attraction in the eyes of an ambitious man who envisaged the future Sultan as little more than a puppet in his hands.

Ambition appears to have been Midhat's dominating characteristic, but it was an ambition directed to his country's good, rather than to his own personal ends. To the Turkey of the nineteenth century he appeared as a phenomenon, stamping out corruption in every province under his jurisdiction, cleaning out the cluttered corridors of the Sublime Porte with a brilliant and ruthless efficiency. But above all he was a patriot ready to sacrifice wealth, his position and even his life to obtain a free constitution for his country. At the crucial hour, when even the members of the Government in power had agreed as to 'the indisputable necessity of deposing the Sultan Abdul Aziz', Midhat and the Minister of War were the only ones who volunteered to risk their lives in the hazardous enterprise of a *coup d'état*.

It is strange how at a time when public resentment of the Sultan was so openly expressed that the British Ambassador reported: 'It can only be a question of days before Abdul Aziz is deposed,' no rumours of a rising appear to have reached either the Palace, or the Russian Embassy whose spies were quartered all over the city. On the night of May 29, the date fixed for the *coup d'état*, Abdul Aziz is said to have gone to bed in a particularly good humour after staging a cock-fight in his throne room, while General Ignatieff was dining at the

Austrian Embassy to discuss the final draft of the Berlin memorandum. This memorandum, to which Great Britain had refused to be a partner, declaring the terms to be too peremptory and to favour the Bosnian rebels at the expense of the legitimate power of the Porte, was to be presented to the Sultan the following day and General Ignatieff seems to have had no suspicions that, while he was sipping the excellent Tokay provided by his host, troops acting under the orders of the Minister of War were moving in on the palace from land and sea.

It was a wild stormy night with a bitter wind from the Black Sea lashing the Bosphorus into clouds of spray, drenching in rain the little group of men waiting for a *caique* on the Asiatic shore. These men were not conspirators by nature, but respectable middle-aged politicians unused to bivouacing on rainy nights or to furtive midnight boat trips. In front of them loomed the dark bulk of Dolmabagche Palace with here and there a light still showing in the windows, throwing a wet and gleaming reflection onto marble, lights which shone like so many danger signals. Nor were matters improved when, having crossed the Bosphorus with difficulty, they found that the horses and carriages which should have been waiting on the European shore had gone to the wrong place and nearly an hour was wasted before they were found. Then Midhat set out for Stamboul to prepare the people for the news of the *coup d'état*, while his companions proceeded direct to the Palace Barracks.

The clocks of Dolmabagche struck one o'clock, the last hour of the Sultan's reign, and in this last hour one's heart goes out to Abdul Aziz lying trapped in his white marble palace while his soldiers were throwing a cordon round the gates and the new battleships, in which he had taken so much pride, were steaming up the Marmara to cut off his retreat by sea. All unsuspecting he lay in his gilded bed, with the little slave girl nestling at his side, when shots rang out in the dark and the silent gardens became alive with voices and the crunching of gravel under army boots. The loyal Albanian Guards were resisting, but it was only a question of moments before they were overwhelmed and the attackers had forced their way into the palace.

It cannot have been a pleasant task for a bluff, straightforward soldier like the Minister of War to force his way into the Throne Room, where he was confronted by a mass of hysterical eunuchs headed by a gigantic Nubian in a white nightgown, no less a person than the Kizlar Agasi, and, in the midst of this confusion, to find the Sultan standing half-dressed at the top of the stairs, an unsheathed sword in his hand, the little Circassian clinging to his arm and sobbing with terror, yet in spite of her terror still remembering to pull the veil over her face.

Abdul Aziz's first impulse was to resist, and he only consented to sheath his sword when the Minister produced the *fetva* signed by the Sheikh ul Islam who, as the highest spiritual dignitary of the Empire, possessed the right to depose the Sultan according to the canons of the Sacred Law. On hearing the decree of the Shériat, the Sultan submitted to his *kismet*, the Will of Allah no man can strive against. But now there emerged from the harem the vast, incongruous figure of the Valide Sultana who, with tousled hair and uncovered face, flung herself on the Minister of War, clawing him with her hennaed nails, kicking him in the stomach with her jewelled pattens. In this one instant half a century of harem training had fallen away. Pertevniyal Sultan had reverted to Besma the Bath Attendant of Stamboul, fighting like any other peasant woman to save her son, but Abdul Aziz had grown strangely quiet, too dazed and stunned to speak, never remonstrating when the soldiers grappled with his mother on the floor, nor offering any resistance when they led him away to the carriage waiting outside.

Meanwhile, over in Stamboul, Midhat was going through some anxious hours. He had arrived at the War Ministry unattended and drenched to the skin, so that he had difficulty in persuading the night watchman of his identity and still greater difficulty in persuading the commanding officer to order out the troops from the neighbouring barracks. Had there been one rumour of failure these troops might well have turned against him, for it was not until nearly dawn that a gun fired from Dolmabagche landing-stage announced the successful conclusion of the *coup d'état*. Then Midhat was able to go out into the square to announce the news which was received with shouts of joy. So universal was the resentment against the late Sultan that there was not one murmur of dissent, and the soldiers pressed forward to volunteer for a guard of honour to escort him to Prince Murad's *konak* on the outskirts of the city.

Were the conspirators to blame that, when Midhat arrived at the Prince's residence, Murad was still asleep and apparently unaware of what was happening in the capital? After assuring themselves of the Crown Prince's loyalty and of his willingness to accept a constitution, they appear to have proceeded with their plans, ignoring the chief protagonist, so that when a devoted eunuch rushed into the Prince's rooms to wake him with the news of the *coup d'état*, Murad's first reaction was of fear instead of joy. Living in continued dread of assassination, he suspected the news of being a hoax to betray him to his uncle. Even Midhat's presence failed to reassure him and, crouching on his bed with a look of frightened cunning in his eyes, he kept murmuring 'Let my uncle rest in peace.'

Faced by this abject spectacle of fear, Midhat saw everything he had risked his life for in danger of being lost. Falling on his knees before the Prince, he exhorted him to courage. It was too late, he told him, to go back on his promises, for his loyal subjects were already waiting to acclaim him in his capital, and his ministers were gathered at the War Office. But Murad's only answer lay in tears, pathetic, helpless tears, as if he already felt the heavy burden of the throne. It was then that Midhat recalled the Prince Hamid and how, ever since the days of Abdul Medjid, the two brothers had hated and distrusted one another and, in a harsher voice, he added 'If your Royal Highness declines to accept the throne, the next in succession is your brother, the Prince Hamid.' The hated name seemed to infuse new life into the weeping Prince. Jumping up from his bed in a state of uncontrollable excitement, he cried 'Never shall that happen,' then, regaining control of himself, he said 'I will come to my people—let Allah's will be done.'

While Midhat was persuading the unwilling Murad to accept the throne, his colleagues were already gathering at the War Office. The first of the ministers had barely arrived when the Prince Hamid was announced. There was general surprise as to how the Prince, who was supposed to have no previous knowledge of the *coup d'état*, had managed to get there so quickly, but his presence was explained when he was seen to be accompanied by his brother-in-law, Mahmud Djelaleddin, one of the richest and most powerful of the pashas, whose influence with the high-ranking officers of the Army had forced the conspirators to take him into their confidence. With imperturbable politeness the young Prince greeted the embarrassed ministers, to most of whom he was practically a stranger. The cold, pale face cut by the scimitar-shaped nose was as impassive as ever; the dark eyes half-hidden by their heavy lids gave nothing away, only a slight stiffening in his bearing, a prouder turn to the head, betrayed the fact that he was now Crown Prince, with only one life between him and the throne. Admittedly his relations with his brother were such that his position as Crown Prince was hardly to be envied. But Murad had promised to rule as a modern constitutional monarch, and constitutional monarchs did not imprison or murder their heirs. In the grey, wet dawn he had waited for the signal of the firing of the gun from Dolmabagche and without stopping for further confirmation had hurried to the War Office, to be the first of his brother's loyal subjects to congratulate him on his accession.

In the past months, Abdul Hamid had been taking a growing interest in his brother's health, and had learnt that Murad's doctors believed him to be suffering from an inherited nervous disease, aggravated by an excessive use of stimulants, and that any sudden shock or excitement might easily prove fatal to his already unbalanced mind. This morning the appearance of the new Sultan confirmed the gloomiest of these prognostications. For Murad gave a pitiable impression when he entered the council chamber of the War Office accompanied, or rather supported, by Midhat Pasha. The Prince, whose accession was to herald the dawn of a new era, came forward to greet his ministers with vacillating steps and red-rimmed eyes, trembling so violently that he could barely grasp his sword, pronouncing the solemn oath of accession in little more than a whisper.

'*Padishahim Chok Yasha*', shouted the soldiers in the square. Out in the Marmara, a salute of naval guns proclaimed the advent of a new sovereign. But in the War Office, the ministers looked at one another in consternation and dismay. Then involuntarily their eyes turned in the direction of the Crown Prince Hamid.

Chapter X

TURKEY HAD A new sovereign acclaimed throughout the Empire, for the legend of 'Murad the Reformer' had circulated the bazaars from Salonika to Baghdad. The news was received with the same enthusiasm in Europe and General Ignatieff was the only foreign ambassador in Constantinople to maintain an attitude of cold reserve, deliberately strengthening the guards round the Embassy in order to foster an atmosphere of uncertainty and fear among the European population of Pera. But even General Ignatieff was gradually forced to realise that the *coup d'état* was being equally welcomed by Christian and by Moslem. The state of emergency proclaimed as a measure of precaution lasted no more than a few hours and by the afternoon of May 31 the cafés had re-opened and were packed with gay holiday crowds, while both churches and mosques were illuminated in honour of the new reign. In the market-places and fair-grounds the performers of *kharageuz* had already introduced a new set of characters, whose misfortunes delighted their audiences, characters ranging from the pro-Russian ex-Grand Vizir now nick-named 'Mahmudoff' to a thinly veiled impersonation of the Russian Ambassador himself.

But the jubilation in the streets found no echo in the palace, where doctors and ministers were making every effort to rouse the young Sultan from his melancholy. With the docility of a child, Murad signed the *irades* and *firmans* issued in his name, but when it came to receiving the congratulations of the ambassadors he was seized by such a violent fit of excitement that the doctors judged it wiser to defer their visits. So serious was the situation that Midhat did not dare to leave his master's side and the official ceremony of the *Biat*, or proclamation, had to be indefinitely postponed. It was hoped that rest and quiet would gradually restore Sultan Murad's shattered nerves, but the events of the next few weeks combined to prove fatal to these hopes.

When the news circulated round the town that the ex-Sultan had committed suicide, there was not a person from the British Ambassador downwards who did not suspect him of having been murdered. But the testimony of nineteen of the most reputed doctors of the city, including those of the foreign embassies, and the evidence of the eunuchs and the women belonging to the ex-Sultan's harem all point to suicide. According to the evidence, Abdul Aziz was in such a state of despair that, the day after his deposition, he had made three attempts to throw himself out of the window and, as a measure of precaution, his women had removed all sharp instruments out of his reach. If this was true, then his mother, the old Valide, was guilty of little less than murder, when on the morning of June 4 she complied with a request for a pair of scissors with which to trim his beard. The request in itself was sufficiently strange to arouse her suspicions, for the trimming of a Sultan's beard was part of an elaborate ritual in which every hair was reverently preserved, and the office of Imperial Barber ranked high in the intricate hierarchy of the Ottoman court. Yet Pertevniyal not only handed the scissors to her already half-demented son, but allowed him to shut himself up in his room, taking no other precautions than to post some of his women at a window which overlooked his room. It was the Circassian favourite who gave the first alarm, when, watching the back of the Sultan's chair, she saw his head fall forward and a stream of blood gush to the floor. By the time the door was forced open it was too late. Abdul Aziz lay dead with the veins of his arms slit open, the fatal scissors lying on the floor.

Such was the story pieced together from the wailing and sobbing of hysterical women by an old English doctor who for the past forty years had been attached to the Imperial harem. According to Dr. Milligen's account, the most distracted of all was the old Valide who, when asked if she was in any need of medical attendance, answered, 'I am not in need of a doctor, but of an executioner, for I have murdered my son.' Dramatic words, worthy of a mother of the Gracchi, tempting one to believe in the doctor's story, and to see old Pertevniyal for once in the light of a heroine before she passes out of history to join that melancholy host of unwanted women immured within the tiled courtyards of the Old Seraglio. But Dr. Milligen, who nearly half a century earlier had attended Lord Byron at Missolonghi, was an old man, his mind and memory clouded by years of harem intrigues, and his evidence, even when added to that of eighteen other doctors including his English colleague Dr. Dickson, still seems to have left some room for doubt.

These doubts persist to the present day for, though an official report stated that after a careful examination of the corpse the doctors had given a unanimous verdict that the wounds were self-inflicted, the fact remains that no doctor, still less an infidel, would have been allowed to make a thorough examination of the dead Sultan's body. It would have been considered as sacrosanct, only to be touched by the holy men who prepared it for burial. But whether suicide or murder, Sultan Aziz's death had a disastrous effect on his successor. In his unbalanced state of mind the unfortunate Murad saw himself as his uncle's murderer and his condition became so alarming that his mother, the new Valide, prevailed on Midhat Pasha to send to Vienna for the leading specialist on nervous diseases.

Meanwhile the Sultan remained invisible to his people, and the crowds waiting on Fridays outside Dolmabagche Mosque were rewarded by no more than the sight of a closed carriage. Jubilation began to give way to uneasiness and the ex-Sultan's 'suicide' had unpleasant repercussions among the older and more conservative element in the capital. A few days later, when his Circassian favourite died in childbirth, a vast crowd followed her coffin to the burial grounds of Scutari. But her death was only one of a series of tragedies. Her brother, a young Tcherkess officer noted as a brilliant pistol shot and devoted to the ex-Sultan, had been ordered to Baghdad, and, resenting the order, set out to revenge himself on the Minister of War. Maddened with Indian hemp and armed with four pistols, two in his boots and two in his belt, he burst in on a Cabinet meeting, killing with two successive shots first the War Minister and then the Foreign Minister. The attendants who tried to disarm him were shot down one by one and it was not until he had killed seven people and wounded eight others that he was finally captured.

Hanged in front of a large crowd, he maintained his dauntless bearing to the end, insisting that he had no accomplices and no other motive other than to revenge himself on the Minister of War. But this isolated act of a young fanatic signed the death warrant of the new reign, depriving Sultan Murad of the last vestige of sanity, so that by the time the celebrated alienist, Dr. Leidersdorff, arrived from Vienna, both his own physician and the head of the Constantinople lunatic asylum had declared the Sultan to be incurable. Dr. Leidersdorff, however, was of another opinion. Diagnosing the disease as chronic alcoholism, aggravated by a series of shocks, he held out a hope of recovery provided the patient could have complete rest during a period of three months and not be subjected to any form of excitement. This diagnosis placed the ministers in even more of a quandary than before, for it left the Ottoman Empire virtually without a sovereign at one of the most critical periods of its history.

Throughout the Empire, the Sultan's subjects were waiting for the promised constitution. The *Irade* issued by Midhat on the first day of the new reign had not only promised wide-sweeping reforms, but had gone so far as to hint that certain portions of the Sheriat might have to be suppressed, so as to ensure the complete equality of all the Sultan's subjects. Hailed as the forerunner of a liberal and progressive reign, this *Irade* had made such a good impression in Europe that Prince Bismarck and Count Andrassy had combined in persuading Prince Gortchakoff, that for the moment the Berlin Memorandum had better be shelved and the young Sultan given time to put his house in order. But since then a month had gone by —a month of ominous silence during which the international situation had been steadily deteriorating and the Balkans had burst into flame.

Dictated by ambition, Serbia and Montenegro had joined forces with the Bosnian insurgents in an unprovoked and aggressive war against the Porte: in Bulgaria the intrigues of the Russian agents had prepared the way for a rebellion on the same pattern as the Bosnian insurrection, and in the month

of May armed Christians fell on their peaceful Moslem neighbours, raping their women, burning their villages and murdering over a hundred Turkish soldiers and policemen before the
Moslem population, reinforced by bands of hastily levied
irregulars, could retaliate in kind. And when they retaliated,
it was on such a scale that the world recoiled in horror before
the news of the Bulgarian Massacres. Faced by a situation which
was daily becoming more untenable, the harassed ministers met
in council and, in the first days of July, decided to offer the
Crown Prince Hamid the regency during his brother's illness.

For the past months, Abdul Hamid had been living at his
villa at Therapia, the popular resort on the Bosphorus where
the embassies had their summer residences. Few places are more
enchanting than Therapia in the summer, with its wooden
yalis, silvered by wind and sun, set against a background of
green lawns and giant magnolia trees, its little harbour crowded
with many-coloured sails. But there was nothing peaceful
about Therapia in the summer of 1876. It was a hotbed of
rumour and intrigue, with all the shops and cafés run by spies,
long-fingered Levantines, Greeks, Jews, Syrians and Armenians
in the pay of the Great Powers. And among the many estab-
lishments opened for the season, was Flora Cordier's glove
shop from the Grande Rue, now selling bathing articles and
perfumes to an international clientèle. Mademoiselle Cordier
had also her part to play, as she leaned her blonde head over
the counter charming her customers with her pretty insinuating
ways, extracting the latest diplomatic gossip to be reported
later in the evening, when a closed carriage brought her to the
Crown Prince's villa on the hill.

Abdul Hamid had left his harem behind in the capital, which
first gave rise to the rumour of his marriage to Mademoiselle
Cordier. This summer was probably the one time in his life
when he was genuinely in love, happy in the company of a little
Belgian woman so different in upbringing and character from
the monotonous beauties of his harem. He was young, passionate, and the rose gardens of Therapia offered the perfect setting
for a love affair. Also for the first and last time in his life he was
free, so long as his brother reigned from behind a padded door
and the ministers were divided in their councils.

At Therapia he lived a far simpler life than many of the rich pashas. His suite consisted of no more than an aide-de-camp, a secretary, and his friend and physician, Mavroyeni, who every few days was sent back to the capital to inquire after the Sultan's health. From his reports it appeared as if the famous Viennese specialist was having no more success than his despised colleagues, for in the last few weeks Murad had made two attempts to throw himself into the Bosphorus and the windows of his apartments had had to be fitted with bars.

Even Mavroyeni, who knew him so well, could not gauge Abdul Hamid's reaction to the news or guess what lay behind those half-shut eyes, those carefully worded phrases of commiseration and regret. Years of humiliation and frustrated ambition were about to be atoned for, but the Crown Prince refrained from betraying himself either by word or gesture. He stayed quietly on at Therapia, spending his nights with Flora Cordier, his days with an English neighbour, a Mr. Thomson, the head of a big business firm in Constantinople.

Mr. Thomson was flattered when the Crown Prince invited him to go riding or walking with him in the hills, and during these excursions plied him with questions on British politics and the working of the Constitution. Abdul Hamid appeared to be shocked and horrified by what was happening in Bulgaria and concerned by the inevitable repercussions in Europe. It was unusual to find an Ottoman prince so sensitive to public opinion abroad and so anxious to be well informed that he had gone to the lengths of having some of the Parliamentary Blue Books translated for him. Mr. Thomson was struck by the Prince's evident sincerity and genuine desire to understand the European mentality and outlook. There was something very disarming about the way in which he openly confessed his ignorance, even going so far as to say, in a moment of intimacy, 'What can you expect of us, the children of slaves brought up by eunuchs?' But when the Englishman began to expound his own solid Liberal principles, and to criticise the Moslem attitude towards the despised Christian, then the Prince's manner immediately became cold and distant, and the subject would be politely dropped.

Yet Abdul Hamid learnt enough from his conversations with

Mr. Thomson to impress Midhat Pasha when he came to offer him the regency. From all accounts it appears to have been their first meeting, except for a brief instant on the morning of Murad's accession, and Midhat was surprised to find the Prince so well informed of the political situation, yet so modest and so surprisingly unwilling to accept the regency.

Abdul Hamid was well aware of the dissension in the Cabinet, of how the veteran Prime Minister, Mehmet Rushdi, shrank from taking any decisive steps till he was assured that the Sultan's position was hopeless, while on the other hand, the new Minister of War, Redif Pasha, who as commander of the corps d'armée of Constantinople had played a leading part in his uncle's deposition, and his brother-in-law Damat* Mahmud, a proud ambitious man, who saw himself in the role of a kingmaker, were both pressing for Murad's abdication. Midhat Pasha belonged to neither of these parties, for he was interested not so much in the Sultan as in the constitution and the role he himself would play in the making of this constitution. To accept the regency was to play into Midhat's hands, to be no more than a puppet carrying out his orders and, if one ever dared to defy these orders, to find oneself deposed and Murad's sanity miraculously restored. But while declaring himself to be unworthy of the honour paid him by His Majesty's Government, and expressing hopes of his brother's quick recovery, Abdul Hamid set out to charm and impress his visitor, pretending to opinions more advanced than the most advanced of his ministers, and in favour of a more democratic constitution than the one already prepared by Midhat.

It is strange that a hard-headed, uncompromising politician like Midhat should have believed in the promises of a young man whom he now met for the first time. But the situation was becoming desperate. Pressure from above, and in particular from Russia, was forcing the Cabinet to a decision: Dr. Leidersdorff's latest reports held out little hope of Sultan Murad's recovery, and the great feast of Ramadan was drawing near, a time when it was imperative for a Sultan to appear in public.

* *Damat*, title given to a Sultan's brother-in-law.

However bitterly he was later to regret his action, it was Midhat more than anyone else who was responsible for persuading his colleagues, and, in particular, the Grand Vizir and the Sheikh ul Islam, into taking the decisive step which placed Abdul Hamid upon the Throne. On August 30, 1876, a *fetva* was read aloud in full Divan, declaring that according to the law of the Sheriat, a Sultan suffering from mental aberrations was considered unfit to rule. Thereby the Sultan Murad was officially deposed in favour of his brother Abdul Hamid who now succeeded to the throne as the thirty-fourth Sultan of the House of Osman.

Chapter XI

EARLY on the morning of August 31, Abdul Hamid set out from his foster-mother's house at Nishantash to be proclaimed as Sultan in the Topkapou Palace in Stamboul—the hour when Constantinople was at its most beautiful, with the minarets cutting like silver lances through the pale haze of dawn, and the sun rising behind the hills of Asia, chasing the last shadows from the islands in the Marmara, transforming the cupolas of Stamboul into bowls of golden light. To the heights of Nishantash came the sounds of a waking city, the cry of the *muezzin* calling the faithful to prayer, the wailing note of the water-carriers and the raucous shouts of the Kurdish porters, people to whom it was just the beginning of another day, while for Abdul Hamid it was the most momentous and perhaps the loneliest day of his life. By spending the night at Peresto's house* he had recognised his foster-mother as Valide Sultana, but today of all days his thoughts must have gone back to the neglected sick-room of his early childhood, to the mother whose frustrated dreams were justified at last.

His highest ambitions were about to be realised, but it was a sad joyless face which looked on his people for the first time. His people—the very phrase still sounded strange, for what did he know of them—these men of a hundred races and religions who already at this early hour were crowding the streets, from Taxim Square to the Sultan Ahmed Mosque. Could he hope to satisfy their aspirations, so that his name would be equally honoured in the tents of Arabia and the homesteads of the Balkans? All that he knew of his empire was his capital, beautiful and alien in itself, turning its back on Europe, shutting its eyes to Asia, his corrupt Byzantine capital which century by century had slowly sapped the vitality of its conquerors.

* While living in her foster-son's harem, Peresto had kept her own house, to which she occasionally retired.

In their turn the people stared at the pale young man with the large hooked nose and melancholy eyes who, for all his delicate appearance, sat astride his horse as a true descendant of Osman and of Ertughrul. There had been no time for the Press to extol his virtues or dispel the legend of 'Murad the Reformer,' which had taken hold of the public imagination. Was it his nervous fancy, or were there men in the crowd who looked upon him as a usurper?

These doubts and hesitations were dispelled in the triumphant moment when he arrived at the palace of his ancestors, and, escorted by the Grand Vizir and the Sheikh ul Islam, passed through the courtyards and the gardens he had known when he had been a lonely child, to the sanctuary of sanctuaries, where the Prophet's mantle and other sacred relics were preserved. Here took place the religious ceremony of the *Biat*, or proclamation, in which the Sheikh ul Islam pronounced him to be 'Abdul Hamid Khan, son of Abdul Medjid Khan, Sultan of Sultans, Commander of the Faithful, Lord of Two Continents and of Two Seas, Guardian of the Holy Cities.'

The short ceremony was soon over and he came out into the sunlight in the courtyard of Orta Kapou*, where he mounted the Golden Throne which his ancestor, Selim I, had brought back from his Persian conquests while the *ulema*, grouped round in a semi-circle, intoned the thrice-repeated chant of the proclamation. Then the musicians struck up the Imperial anthem, the soldiers presented arms and from all the courtyards of the palace re-echoed the cry of 'Long Live the Padishah'. At the same moment, the Sultan's standard was unfurled on every public building in the city, and a salvo of guns re-echoed across the Golden Horn.

Abdul Hamid was Sultan. At his feet knelt the first suppliants, foremost among them the leaders of the five non-Moslem communities of the capital, who, in return for their congratulatory addresses, were assured that their sovereign had only one desire—the progress of his country and peace for all his subjects. Ministers and notables pressed forward to kiss the hem of his cloak, hour after hour he listened to presentations and petitions with only a brief pause for rest and

---

* Orta Kapou the third, or inner gate of the Seraglio.

refreshment, and it was already late afternoon when a tired young man with a strained white face embarked from Seraglio Point to return to Dolmabagche.

Shimmering in the evening sunlight, Dolmabagche waited on its new master, its gardens ablaze with summer flowers, its fountains flashing plumes of light. The bars had been taken down from the windows of the royal apartments, the padding removed from the gilded doors, and Sultan Murad was no more than a memory to the host of sycophants waiting with bowed heads on his brother's first command. Quietly, almost furtively, they had removed him the previous night to that same ill-fated palace of Cheragan where his uncle had ended his days in humiliation and despair. With Murad went his harem, beautiful young women in the prime of life, children already adolescent, babes in arms, all committed to that same twilight world peopled by the ghosts of madness. But the splendour of Dolmabagche held no charms for its new master, haunted by the memory of Abdul Aziz lying trapped like a rat in his own palace.

The flamboyant beauty of its marble façade so proudly exposed to the Bosphorus only served to emphasise the vulnerability of its position, a target for any long-range gun from a warship in the Marmara, or cannon posted at Scutari. Abdul Hamid's timid nature, which craved security and peace, felt restless and ill-at-ease in these vast halls peopled by silent servants, while his modest harem seemed lost in quarters built to house the nine hundred women kept by Abdul Medjid in the last years of his life. Everything in the palace bespoke the extravagances and debaucheries of his predecessors, from the three hundred lambs which were daily consumed in the Royal kitchens to the cabinets of erotic drugs and instruments, pathetic heritage of a father who died surfeited of his own excesses. But however appalled by the extravagance and waste, Abdul Hamid was at heart too much of a traditionalist to question of the closely woven hierarchy of a court where the lowest scullion held a grade as officer of the Imperial Household and where men justified a lifetime of service earning such sinecures and titles as 'Cleaners of the Imperial *narghiles*', 'Keepers of the precious porcelain reserved for the Sultan's

use' and 'Bearers of the trays and spoons' no other hand
could touch. During the week which elapsed between the
ceremony of the Proclamation and that of the Investiture, the
new Sultan gradually learnt to adapt himself to the lonely
grandeur of a throne.

Meanwhile, from every corner of the Empire, wherever
there was available means of transport, his loyal subjects con-
verged upon the capital to assist at the ceremony of 'the girding
of the sword.' And by the morning of September 7, the streets
and quays of Constantinople were teeming with fezzes and
turbans, keffiahs and billycock hats, all craned to see the procession of Imperial *caiques* proceeding from Dolmabagche to
the Mosque of Eyub on the Golden Horn. Everyone wore
their finest clothes, from the Kurdish porters at the Custom
House and the melon vendors on the quays, to the captain
pasha waiting to receive his master at the Admiralty Pier. All
along the waterfront, the route was lined with soldiers and
marines, Turks, Albanians, Arabs and Circassians, their decorations gleaming in the sunlight, their native music mingling
in a wild cacophony of sound.

The Sultan proceeded up the Golden Horn, seated under
a crimson canopy in a white and gold *caique* rowed by
fourteen pairs of oars, while the flags of the foreign Stationnaire ships dipped in salute and a hundred thousand voices
cheered from the shore. The prophecy of the sheikh from
Sidon was about to be realised, and Abdul Hamid had
not shown himself ungrateful, for the old man had been
summoned from his *tekke* in the Lebanon to accompany
the Sultan to the ceremony at Eyub. Built by Mahomet the
Conqueror to enshrine the bones of the Prophet's Standard-
bearer, the Mosque of Eyub is the most venerated of all the
four hundred mosques of Stamboul, and it was here that the
Ottoman Sultans were invested with the legendary sword of the
founder of their House. Now it was the turn of Abdul Hamid
to stand before the silver shrine. The heavy sword, made
for men of heroic build, pressed against his slender body, the
huge, bearded sheikh who presided at the ceremony had to
bend down to give him the traditional kiss on the left shoulder,
but there was a quiet dignity about him, an air of calm

assurance which led men to forget the insignificance of his stature. The simple ceremony was witnessed only by a few dervishes and priests but now the whole world seemed to converge on Eyub, ministers and aides-de-camp, pashas and sheikhs, blocking the village streets with their horses and their retinue, all part of the great procession which was to accompany the Sultan back to his capital.

Through the gate of Adrianople, which once led the Sultans to the conquest of Europe, past the ruined walls of Byzantium, came the royal cortège, wending its way through the narrow streets of Stamboul, under the overhanging eaves of latticed windows, the carved stone arches of the old Phanar quarter— zaptiehs, spahis and bostandjis in their magnificent gold-embroidered uniforms and scarlet cloaks: the Sheikh ul Islam on horseback, wearing his white cashmere robes bordered in gold, preceded by the green banner of the Prophet. And half hidden by a double file of infantry, the plumed *kalpaks* of the Albanian guards, the Sultan appearing not so much a man as a symbol of divine authority, not so much the Sultan of Turkey as the Caliph of Islam, successor to that sacred trust which his ancestor Selim had won by right of conquest of the holy cities.

Astride his white horse bridled in gold, wearing a simple fez, unadorned by diamond or aigrette, one small hand holding the reins, the other clasping his sword hilt, Abdul Hamid received today the acclamations due to God's Vice-regent upon Earth. But when the procession reached the Sublime Porte, and he was faced by the various members of the foreign diplomatic corps seated on an estrade of honour, then he was reminded of all the problems which awaited him when the ceremonial robes had been laid aside and he had returned to the emptiness of Dolmabagche, a lonely, frightened young man struggling to preserve an empire from disruption.

He had so much to learn, so little time to learn it in and so little trust in his advisers. From the very first, he appears to have feared and disliked the men who had put him on the throne. And for all the diffidence of his manner, his eagerness to listen and absorb, there was something about his attitude which was beginning to worry his ministers for, when they left the palace on the night of the investiture, the old Grand Vizir, Mehmet Rushdi, turned to his colleagues saying 'We have been in a great hurry to get rid of Murad. May we never live to repent what we have done.'

Two days later, Midhat Pasha submitted for the Sultan's approbation the first draft of a speech outlining the policy of the new reign. It was almost identical to the one already published on the occasion of Murad's accession, and as such, was hardly calculated to please Abdul Hamid, reminding him both of his indebtedness to Midhat and of the promises he had made at Therapia. But outwardly he appeared to receive it with every mark of approbation. And it was only when he returned it, so blue-pencilled and edited as to be changed out of all recognition, that Midhat began to realise his constitution was in danger.

Curiously enough, Abdul Hamid made no secret of his distrust of his ministers. Already as Crown Prince he had confided to his friend, Mr. Thomson, that should he ever come to the throne, he was determined not to put himself in the hands of any ministers, and to get rid as soon as possible of those who were already in office. Other ministers, he said, would have to be found, who would think of the public good rather than of their own aggrandisement. His first task would be to restore the state finances and see that Turkey's creditors were not defrauded, and this could only be accomplished by the most rigorous economy of which he himself would set the first example.

If he confided so much in Mr. Thomson, it was because he knew these conversations would be faithfully repeated to Mr. Thomson's intimate friend, the British Ambassador, on whom Abdul Hamid was particularly anxious to make a good impression. In his seemingly ingenuous fashion, he confessed to being young and inexperienced. He hoped in all things to be guided as much as possible by the advice of Her Britannic Majesty's government. It was a difficult position for Sir Henry Elliott, who was both a friend and adviser of Midhat Pasha, for though he was inclined to agree with Disraeli 'that the young Sultan promised well', he nevertheless felt called upon to warn him through his friend Mr. Thomson, that for the moment it would be unwise, not to say impossible, to get rid of men like Mehmet Rushdi and Midhat, both of whom were looked up to by a large section of the public.

Had Sir Henry Elliot possessed any knowledge of Abdul Hamid's character, he would have realised that nothing was more calculated to arouse his resentment than to be told of the popularity of his ministers. Mehmet Rushdi was an old man waiting to be relieved of the cares of office, but Midhat at the age of fifty-four was still in the prime of life, energetic, aggressive, too little of a courtier to manage the susceptibilities of a young man brought up in the tradition of a long line of autocrats.

It is open to question as to whether Abdul Hamid's dislike of Midhat, the vindictiveness with which he pursued him to the grave, was based on purely personal grounds, or because Midhat was in possession of a certain document he had forced the Sultan to sign on the day of his investiture. In this document, Abdul Hamid is said to have given his solemn word to abdicate the throne in the eventuality of his brother ever regaining his normal faculties, and there are many stories told of his frenzied efforts to regain possession of a paper which placed him at the mercy of a commission of doctors who, acting on his ministers' orders, paid regular visits to the royal patient at Cheragan. But for the moment he did not dare to dispute these orders, and it was only gradually that there transpired the iron determination to keep the reins of government in his own hands.

In the oppressive luxury of Dolmabagche, where every detail was calculated to rouse the senses and distract the mind, he set to work with feverish energy, insisting, to his ministers' dismay, on interesting himself in all that was happening in the remotest corners of his empire, reading the reports of every provincial governor, and equally ready to discuss a tribal feud in Kurdestan or a railway concession in Anatolia. At the first call to prayer he was already at work and his labours continued far into the night. Nothing was too trivial to escape his notice, no one was too humble to be refused an audience during those first months in which Abdul Hamid set out to grapple single-handed with the problems of his empire.

Chapter XII

In the Sultan's private apartments hung a map showing the Ottoman Empire in the days when its frontiers stretched north to the sea of Azov and west to the gates of Vienna. It was a map Abdul Hamid was never tired of studying and European professors were summoned to the palace to instruct him in those aspects of history which had not been taught in the princes' school—the story of his country's gradual decadence, the details of every lost campaign and humiliating treaty since the days when the conquering sword of Islam had turned into a weapon of defence and the Romanoffs had succeeded the Hapsburgs as the hereditary enemy.

Kutchuk, Kainardji, Bucharest and Adrianople, names which pricked like so many thorns, lacerating the Sultan's pride, reminding him of the loss of his richest provinces, of Russia's gradual infiltration in the Balkans. Supported by Russia, Greeks and Slavs had risen in revolt; the Danubian principalities had united under a Hohenzollern prince; Serbia and Montenegro had proclaimed their virtual independence of the Porte, and the Great Powers who, at the conference tables of Paris, had promised to uphold the integrity of the Ottoman Empire, had turned a blind eye to the violation of Turkish territory, to the breaking of solemn promises.

In fear and apprehension the young Sultan studied on the map all that was left of Turkey in Europe, a wild, mountainous region between the Adriatic and the Aegean, inhabited by primitive, turbulent people—Greeks, Albanians, Serbs and Bulgars, hating one another as bitterly as they hated any Turk. His ancestors had not troubled to classify them race by race. To the early sultans they were all Greeks or *Roums*, free to pursue their private feuds and practise their own religion so long as the blood tribute to the Porte was regularly paid, the levy of slave children, which replenished year after year the ranks of the Janissaries and of the Civil Service: but now the

(88)

names of Bosnia and of Herzegovina, of Macedonia and of Bulgaria were on every tongue. Slavs bled for their fellow Slavs and simple peasants were taught to handle modern rifles made in Russia.

As a child, Abdul Hamid ignored the existence of Bulgaria, except for the Bulgarian *yoghurtchus*, the yoghourt-sellers, and the old peasant women who provided the harems with attar of roses and sorbet from the celebrated rose valleys of Varna. But now every ambassador he received in audience respectfully drew his attention to recent events in Bulgaria. In front of Europe he stood accused of crimes committed before he had come to the throne, crimes which no European would admit had been committed in self-defence. Abdul Hamid may have been sincere in condemning the Bulgarian Massacres, for already as Crown Prince he had informed his friend, Mr. Thomson, that 'the hard words used in Parliament were not stronger than was warranted, if applied to those who were responsible for the atrocities.' But what he deplored even more than the savage reprisals inflicted by his Bashibazooks★ were the inevitable repercussions in Europe.

In search of friends abroad, he had made the first overtures to England, the only power who did not appear to covet any part of his dominions, yet whose interests lay parallel to his own. The figure of the 'Great Elchi' was still fresh in his memory and in his first audience with Sir Henry Elliot he referred to his father's admiration for England and for her great Ambassador, Sir Stratford Canning. He was only seven, he told the Ambassador, when one day he was summoned to his father and found Sultan Medjid in intimate conversation with an elderly Christian gentleman, whom he had once met in the palace gardens. On seeing him, his father had called him to come nearer and to kiss the hand of the Christian, which was so contrary to all accepted habits and tradition that he had burst into tears; whereupon his father grew angry, saying, 'Do you know who this gentleman is? It is the British Ambassador, the best friend of our house and country, and the English are our most faithful allies.'

★ *Bashibazooks*, Irregulars.

With these flattering words, Abdul Hamid offered Sir Henry Elliot the role of the Great Elchi. But though both the British Ambassador and the British Prime Minister would have been only too glad to avail themselves of this opportunity of safeguarding their country's interest in the Levant and Far East against the threat of Russian Imperialism, that incalculable force known as 'British public opinion' made it momentarily impossible for even a statesman like Disraeli to defend England's traditional policy.

Gladstone's pamphlet branding the whole Turkish race as the 'great antihuman specimen of humanity,' and calling on the civilized world to throw them, bag and baggage, out of Europe, appeared on the very day of Abdul Hamid's investiture. In the name of outraged Christianity, a great political campaign was launched against the Tory government. Bishops and philanthropic peers, journalists and missionaries enrolled under Mr. Gladstone's banner, and swelling this chorus of righteous indignation were Turkey's defrauded shareholders mourning over the graves of butchered Christians the loss of their eight per cent. Mass meetings were held all over England and when Disraeli stood up in the House of Commons to counsel moderation, pleading that 'though the slaughter of twelve thousand individuals was certainly a horrible event, it was not sufficient reason to make the British Empire denounce its treaties and change its policy,' he was shouted down not only by his political opponents, but by some of his own party.

Many years later Abdul Hamid referred to the Bulgarian Massacres as, 'the most unfortunate event which could have occurred both to him and to his country.' He had come to the throne genuinely believing in England's friendship, offering to be guided by the advice of her Government, and he found the Government helpless in the hands of that strange phenomenon, 'public opinion.' Russia was the first to profit by the situation, pushing forward her claims for a military occupation of Bulgaria, openly intervening on Serbia's side when, contrary to expectations, Serbia's war of wanton aggression against the Porte had culminated in a series of Turkish victories. As General Ignatieff cynically admitted, 'The Bulgarian Massacres brought Russia what she had never had before, the support of

British public opinion.' Faced by a divided Cabinet, Disraeli consented to a conference of the Great Powers to be held at Constantinople; a conference at which Turkey was to be persuaded, or rather coerced, into accepting proposals drawn up by the Concert of Europe for the pacification of her insurgent provinces and the termination of a war of which she was to be denied the victories.

Nothing could have been more calculated to wound the pride and susceptibilities of the new Sultan, who with regard to the Bulgarian Massacres had offered to do all and more than it was in his power to do. Sir Henry Elliot testifies:

> By the end of the summer, complete tranquillity had been restored in Bulgaria. The Moslems had recovered from the panic under which they had committed their excesses, a renewal of which was made impossible by the presence of a large body of regular troops; the devastated villages were being rapidly rebuilt, partly by the Government and partly by public subscriptions, and the dispersed inhabitants, including many hundreds who had been counted among the slain, were quietly returning to their houses.

But when it came to the punishment of those who were directly responsible for the outrages, the Sultan's promises became more evasive. Mosques had been desecrated and Turkish women violated by the insurgents, and the law of the Koran decreed that the violators should be put to the fire and the sword. Officials could be dismissed, or rather transferred to distant parts of the Empire, to placate the ambassadors of the Great Powers who understood so little of the problems which beset a monarch who was both Sultan of Turkey and Caliph of Islam. But as Caliph, Abdul Hamid was powerless to shed the blood of men who had acted in defence of their religion. From the very beginning of his reign he stressed the spiritual importance of the Caliphate and his resentment at what he considered to be the unfairness and prejudices of European statesmen only served to strengthen this attitude.

How much of it was genuine is open to question, for there are those who maintain that Abdul Hamid was not really religious at heart. This doubt is expressed by no less a person than Professor Vambéry, one of the few Europeans who really knew him well. According to Vambéry, Abdul Hamid

> leant towards mysticism and was often subjected to excesses of fanaticism. But on the other hand, his incontestably sharp mind brought him into collision with theories founded on supernatural matters, and in spite of his first decision to keep up his holy character as a successor of Mahomet, he would enter into the discussion of delicate religious matters by which he betrayed a good deal of scepticism.

Judging from all he saw and heard, and in spite of the religious fervour which Abdul Hamid exhibited in the society of sheikhs and *mollas*, Vambéry came to the conclusion that

> the Sultan was not at all an unshakable believer, but accommodated himself in public life to the duties of a pious moslem.

This was already apparent in the first weeks of his reign, which fell in the month of Ramadan. Day after day, Abdul Hamid would be seen crossing the wooden drawbridge over the Golden Horn, or arriving by *caique* at Seraglio Point, on his way to one or other of the Imperial mosques. Apart from these official acts of piety, the people of Stamboul would often see their Sultan praying in one of the family mausoleums, and the one he visited more frequently than any other was that of his grandfather Sultan Mahmud.

Did Abdul Hamid come here to pray for strength from that lion-hearted Sultan who had handed down to him so many of his qualities—shrewdness, intelligence, statecraft—all but one quality, that of courage? The problems confronting them were the same, following in the same pattern: revolution in Bulgaria instead of Greece, the far-flung web of Russian intrigue, with Ignatieff in the place of Capo d'Istria, and the same lack of comprehension on the part of the Western Powers. But Mahmud had had the strength to challenge his destiny, to open his door to progress with all its attendant evils, whereas Abdul Hamid was too timid to risk or gamble one tithe of his inheritance, or sacrifice in the cause of progress the most obsolete of his prerogatives. He was Pirimujgan's son as well as Mahmud's grandson, the son of a frightened little slave girl, not of a proud Creole.

Abdul Hamid was not the only visitor to Sultan Mahmud's *turbe** during these days of Ramadan. As he rode out of the courtyard he would often pass a closed carriage preceded by a gigantic Nubian on horseback. The carriage would stop at the entrance, and a stout figure wrapped in black would emerge and pass with slow shambling steps into the *turbe*. But a Sultan rides with his head in the air, looking neither to left nor right, and it was not for Abdul Hamid to notice the Imperial arms on the carriage or disturb an old woman's grief. Pertevniyal Sultana had retreated into the shadows of the past, part of the memories of a little boy who, sitting at her feet, had spelled out the Arabic words of some magic formula, and dreamt his first dreams of power.

Pertevniyal was forgotten, but the interest in the supernatural and the occult she had fostered in an ambitious child persisted with the years. Ministers would be kept waiting for an audience while dervishes and astrologers were admitted at all hours into his presence, and on those nights of Ramadan, when the minarets and cupolas of Stamboul glitter in the light of a thousand torches and the silver crescent above Aya Sofia shines brighter than the moon; when the *Bairam* lamb turns on the spit in every Moslem household and the poorest eats his fill, the Sultan would often invite the old sheikh from Sidon to break the day's fast in his company—an honour he never accorded even to his Grand Vizir.

For the first time in many years, fasting was rigorously observed in the palace, with the Sultan himself setting the example. So strictly did he attend to his religious duties that no Christian was received in audience during the days of Ramadan. This applied not only to the ambassadors, but to the Sultan's closest friends, such as the Englishman, Mr. Thomson, the Greek banker Zarifi, and his physician, Mavroyeni.

It is not known whether this rule applied to Flora Cordier of whom little had been heard from the day when the summer idyll at Therapia was interrupted by the news of Murad's

* *Turbe*, Mausoleum.

deposition. Her shops, both on the Grande rue de Pera and at Therapia had been suddenly closed and there were rumours of her having been shipped off to Europe, while others asserted that she had been taken into the Imperial harem, thus leading the British Prime Minister to indulge in a flight of romantic fancy on the possibility 'of a little Belgian milliner developing into a second Roxelana'. From all these rumours and counter-rumours there gradually emerged the somewhat surprising fact that Mademoiselle Cordier had become a convert to Islam. Whether she was fired by ambition and tempted by marriage, or whether she merely coveted the idle, luxurious life of a harem favourite, the decision to adopt the *yashmak* and *feradje* proved fatal to her interests. Her charm for Abdul Hamid had been the charm of novelty, her ability to entertain and if necessary instruct him in the customs of a world of which he was completely ignorant. In spite of his habitual melancholy and shy reserve, there was nothing he enjoyed so much as really salacious gossip, the kind of anecdote no self-respecting Moslem would dare to repeat in front of his sovereign. This accounts for his friendship with the Greek banker, Zarifi, who in conversation with Henry Layard he once described as 'being fond of his Sultan, but fonder of Mr. Zarifi, and so amusing, it did not matter his being a rogue.' And it explains his being attracted to a woman like Flora Cordier, with her shrewd earthy common sense and spontaneous wit. Removed from the cheap polyglot world of Pera, she forfeited the very qualities which constituted her charm. In the restricted world of the Moslem woman, Flora had nothing left but her physical appeal and she was neither as young, nor as beautiful as the odalisques whom the Kizlar Agasi and the Valide procured for the Sultan's pleasure.

Little transpires of her life as the Sultan's favourite, bar the fact that she never entered the Imperial harem and that Abdul Hamid made no attempt to bring her into contact with his foster-mother who feared and distrusted her influence. Peresto was both intensely religious and politically astute and remembering the days of Abdul Medjid and the resentment aroused by his Armenian mistresses, she did all in her power to break

off the Sultan's relationship with a Pera shopgirl. Circumstances played into her hand, for isolated in a *konak* on the
outskirts of the city, removed from all contact with her
former friends, poor Flora soon lost her gaiety and sparkle and
it was not long before the Sultan had tired of a woman he is
said to have loved to the extent of offering her marriage as the
price of her conversion.

In a sense Flora Cordier may be said to have been a sacrifice
to Abdul Hamid's principles as Caliph of Islam. From now on
his amorous life was confined to the prescribed limits of the
harem. And it is in the harem that we find him at his most
human, a kind and considerate master, gentle and affectionate
both with his women and his children. But in that brief year
Flora Cordier had succeeded in giving him, if not the substance,
at least the illusion of love, the warmth and reassurance of a
normal, bourgeois relationship untrammelled by fear and inhi-
bitions, a relationship such as he could never hope to find in a
palace inhabited by slaves. As one of the more intelligent of
his kadinés said of him many years later, 'He was the kindest
and most understanding of masters, but he never loved anyone, least of all himself.'

Chapter XIII

'WE HAVE AGREED to invite the Powers to a conference, the place to be Constantinople and each Power to be represented by two plenipotentiaries. I assume the ambassadors at Constantinople and six greater men, what you call swells. Who is to go for England? I have a good mind to go myself.'

So wrote Disraeli, now Lord Beaconsfield, to his friend and confidante, Lady Bradford, on November 4, 1876, and the history of the ill-fated Constantinople Conference might have been very different had the English Prime Minister carried out his first intentions, for his subtle oriental mind and far-sighted vision would have been more than a match for what he called 'General Ignatieff's machiavellian combinations'. But in his place went the Secretary for India, Lord Salisbury, solid, unimaginative and profoundly sceptical, whose whole attitude to the conference is summed up in the way in which he broke the news to his wife: 'It is the kind of proposal one is bound in honour not to decline, but an awful nuisance, not at all my line, involving sea-sickness, much French and failure' —a curious avowal from a man who was later to become one of England's most successful Foreign Secretaries. Even Disraeli appears to have had some last-minute doubts on the wisdom of the appointment, when he saw his colleague set out accompanied not only by several secretaries, but several members of his family: 'Lady Salisbury, his eldest son and daughter, the latter of whom I fear will not be as serviceable as the secretaries.'

Lord Salisbury and his family were only a few of the unwanted guests to whom the Sultan was forced to offer hospitality in this winter of 1876. Since early autumn the Sublime Porte had been bludgeoned and coerced into consenting to an armistice with Serbia and Montenegro while, in the so-called interests of peace, the Czar had proposed the military occupation of Bulgaria and autonomy for the insurgent provinces of Bosnia and Herzegovina. Though fully aware of Russia's double game, circumstances led the British Government to fall in with her plans, and the Foreign Secretary, Lord Derby, wrote to the Queen:

> It is hard to believe that Russian volunteers for Serbia who have of late poured in at the rate, in one case, of three hundred in a day, come without the tacit or implied consent of the Emperor. But the present state of popular feeling makes all action in the anti-Russian sense practically impossible.

Forced to believe in the hollow fallacy of Russia's good intentions, England had taken the initiative of convoking a conference of the Great Powers to discuss the necessary measures for the pacification of the Balkans and, in his own capital, the Turk was to be made to submit to the decisions of the Concert of Europe. But however humiliated and angry, the young Sultan preserved the diplomatic tact which, throughout his life, was to be his greatest asset. No sooner had Lord Salisbury arrived in Constantinople than he was received in audience, and Sir Henry Elliot, who was present, states that 'nothing could have exceeded the cordiality of the Sultan's welcome.' Instead of receiving the English delegates in the formality of the throne room, where the Sultan stands apart on a sacred carpet no other foot can tread, Abdul Hamid received his guests in the intimacy of his own private apartments, with only his Master of Ceremonies to act as interpreter.

It must have been a curious scene, with Lord Salisbury, unversed in the arts of Eastern compliments, sitting massive and foursquare, perilously·balancing a fragile cup of coffee while, as a crowning mark of affability,.the Sultan leant forward to light him his cigarette with his own hand. At this first interview, Lord Salisbury does not appear to have suspected the iron will behind the inscrutable eyes and sad mouth shadowed by the moustache and sparse beard which, according to tradition, every Sultan has to grow from the day of his accession. In his slow drawling voice, with every word faithfully translated by the interpreter, Abdul Hamid told Lord Salisbury

(97)

how anxious he was to recover the friendship and sympathy of England, and how ready to be guided by the advice of Her Majesty's Government who, in the matter of concessions and reforms, would find him prepared to go as far as a regard for his independence and the interests of his empire would make it possible.

To this Lord Salisbury cautiously replied that for the moment he could not tell His Majesty the extent of the measures which would be necessary, but that he hoped to be able to speak more plainly after he had had further communication with his colleagues. It was therefore arranged that as soon as he had the necessary information, he would forward it to the Sultan, who would expect both him and Sir Henry Elliot to dine with him the same day, in order to discuss the situation. But day after day passed, no sign was made, and the messengers who were sent from the palace asking when Lord Salisbury was coming to dine, returned without an answer, excuse or explanation.

It is difficult to understand what prompted Lord Salisbury's behaviour, beyond the fact that he allowed himself to be governed by his own prejudices and dislikes. He had arrived in Constantinople distrusting everyone and everything, and though conscious of his ignorance of Turkey and of Turkish affairs, refusing to profit by the knowledge and experience of his Ambassador, whom he suspected of being pro-Turk and the friend of Midhat Pasha, to whom he had taken an instantaneous dislike. More unfortunate still was his attitude to General Ignatieff, for though at first he had dismissed both the Turkish minister and Russian Ambassador as being 'one as false as the other', it was not long before he had fallen a victim to the latter's charm, even to the extent of believing in Russian promises.

Sir Henry Elliot relates that, from the day of his arrival, Lord Salisbury never once of his own accord entered upon the subject on which they were associated, hinted at the course he proposed to follow, or informed him of the arrangements he was making with General Ignatieff, till he learnt of them at the meeting, when they were communicated to his foreign colleagues. Before long the rift between Lord Salisbury and his

Ambassador was common knowledge in the coffee-houses of Pera, where the British colony made no secret of their indignation at seeing Lady Salisbury driving round the town in Madame Ignatieff's carriage.

Once more Ignatieff had triumphed by working on Lord Salisbury's sympathies as a high-churchman and flattering him in the illusion of being the real arbiter of the conference. Contrary to expectation, he showed himself conciliatory, willing to abide by the English proposals, reducing Russia's demands to what he declared to be 'the minimum any Christian representative should consider himself in honour bound to impose upon the Turk', and, what was most dangerous of all, leading Lord Salisbury to believe that the Sultan and his advisers distrusted him, that there was no use in offering the Turks advice, and that the only means of dealing with them was by addressing them in peremptory language and threatening them with violent measures. At the same time, General Ignatieff's secret agents in the palace, many of whom occupied high positions in the Sultan's entourage, represented Lord Salisbury as an overbearing, violent and dangerous man, a bitter enemy of Turkey and the Turks. Having thus sown the seeds of mutual distrust, the Russian Ambassador persuaded the British delegate to a course of action most calculated to arouse Turkish obduracy and pride.

Nine preliminary meetings—a conference in all but name— were held at the Russian Embassy, to which not a single Turkish delegate was invited, and where the Great Powers decided on the terms to be imposed. Even when whittled down to General Ignatieff's minimum, they offered the Christian minorities in Bulgaria and Bosnia such a large measure of autonomy as to be completely unacceptable to the Turks. Yet more humiliating even than the proposals themselves was the way in which they were presented—without any question of discussion or negotiation, to be accepted or refused at the risk of war.

Such was the situation which confronted Abdul Hamid only three months after he had come to the throne, three months in which he had learnt enough about his country to know that it had little hope of financial survival without the help of

Europe. But in those three months he had also learnt to know his people, to realise that they valued their national pride and dignity far more than property or life. In their shabby uniforms and leaking boots, his soldiers in the Balkans were winning victory after victory over the presumptuous Serbs and their elegant Russian officers. To submit to European, or rather to Russian dictation meant robbing them not only of the fruits of victory, but of lessening himself in their eyes, and in the eyes of all the millions of Moslems who acknowledged him as 'Caliph'. To refuse, on the other hand, meant war, war without a single ally, for the Russian armies were already massing on the Pruth and, faced by these two alternatives, Abdul Hamid was ready to listen to the solution offered by Midhat Pasha.

'This was the moment,' said Midhat, 'to proclaim a constitution, to make the magnanimous gesture, which would put the European delegates to shame. By giving equality and freedom not only to the Christians of the disaffected European provinces, but to all the people of his empire, he would destroy the Russian case and disrupt the conference, for even the Czar would hardly dare to press his claims when general public opinion was on Turkey's side.' It was not an easy decision for Abdul Hamid to make, when for three months he had been doing all in his power to sabotage Midhat's plans. From his earliest youth the very word 'Constitution' had been anathema to him. And in Europe he had been shocked to see how the most powerful sovereigns had to submit to the dictation of their people. Of all his ministers, Midhat was the one whom he feared and distrusted the most, making him aware that he ruled not by the grace of God, but by the will of man, and that the shadow of his sick brother in Cheragan still loomed over the throne. But for the moment, Midhat and his constitution represented the only means of safeguarding his prestige and three days before the official opening of the conference, Midhat, the 'Father of the Constitution' was appointed as Grand Vizir.

The stage was set for the solemn drama which Abdul Hamid never intended to be more than a tragic comedy. On the morning of December 23, 1876, the representatives of the

Powers gathered in the Great Hall of the Admiralty building to decide the fate of Turkey. It was a cold wet day, and the grey light filtering through the windows made the diplomats' faces appear colder and more sceptical than usual. Already they were thinking not of the conference, but of what was going to happen when the conference had failed. Despite the so-called unanimity of their decisions, each envoy was secretly intriguing in the interests of his own country—and a heavy, hostile atmosphere pervaded the room, an atmosphere as depressing as the winter's day outside.

The preliminary formalities had barely been concluded when the echo of a hundred and one guns boomed from across the Golden Horn. Had the Turks revolted? Was this their answer to the bullying and coercion of Europe? Involuntarily, all eyes turned in the direction of the Turkish delegates. Pale with suppressed emotion, the Minister for Foreign Affairs, Safvet Pasha, rose to announce, 'Gentlemen, the cannon you hear from the tower of the War Office notifies the proclamation by His Majesty the Sultan of a new constitution, guaranteeing equal rights and liberties to all the subjects of his empire. And in the presence of this great event, I think our labours become superfluous.'

A chilly silence greeted this announcement, a silence broken after a few moments by the hard, clipped accents of the Russian Ambassador who, ignoring Safvet with a studied rudeness, moved that the conference should proceed to the business of the day. But who except the delegates themselves were interested in the maps and graphs, the blue books and statistics, so carefully compiled by their secretaries and clerks, when outside in the streets ecstatic crowds of Moslems and of Christians were cheering themselves hoarse for the Sultan and the constitution? Carrying banners inscribed with the red letters of liberty, bands of *softas* were parading the town, distributing leaflets with the text of the constitution. And in wonder and amazement, some of them not realising what it was all about, the citizens of Constantinople read that from now onwards they were to have a voice in the government of their country, schools for their children, religious freedom and an uncensored Press, while from a flower-decked platform erected in front of the Sublime Porte, Midhat Pasha gave public thanks to the Sultan for the liberties he had granted his people.

Over at the Admiralty the day's session was concluded and, wrapped in their furs and ulsters, the European delegates drove home through illuminated, flag-decked streets, knowing at heart their discussions to be futile now that Turkey had taken a hand in the shaping of her destiny. Ignatieff had stated his claims and made it clear that if they were not accepted, the Russian armies were ready to cross the Pruth. The Austrian delegate had been more conciliatory. As representative of the Dual Monarchy, he pursued a dual policy, faithful to the *Drei Kaiser Bund*, with a predatory eye on Bosnia, but at the same time doing all in his power to prevent Russia from penetrating south of the Balkans. The Turks throughout had been obstinate and proud and when the French envoy ventured to refer to the Bulgarian Massacres they had not hesitated to remind him of St. Bartholomew and the September Massacres. Only Lord Salisbury continued to maintain his attitude of Olympian calm, conscientiously doing his best to settle problems of which he was completely ignorant, homesick for England and the oaks of Hatfield, envisaging with horror the prospect of spending Christmas in the uncongenial atmosphere of the British Embassy. The day before the opening of the conference, Sir Henry Elliot had again attempted to convince him that 'Midhat and his party were genuine in their efforts of reform, and that the moment was exceptionally favourable for an English Cabinet Minister to acquire influence over the Turkish Government.' But later Lord Salisbury had dined at the Russian Embassy and over the vodka and caviar Ignatieff had insinuated that their work would be considerably facilitated if Sir Henry Elliot was recalled, for the British Ambassador's friendship with Midhat Pasha gave the Turks reason to believe that the Concert of Europe was not united.

So completely had Lord Salisbury fallen under Russian influence that he went to the lengths of writing a letter to Lord Derby suggesting Sir Henry's recall—a letter which, when shown to Lord Beaconsfield, aroused his justifiable indignation.

Salisbury seems most prejudiced, and not to be aware that his principal object in being sent to Constantinople is to keep the Russians out of Turkey, not to create an ideal existence for Turkish Christians. He is more Russian than General Ignatieff, *plus arabe que l'Arabie.*

In later years Lord Salisbury was the first to admit that he had fallen a victim to the plots and counter-plots and machiavellian brains against which the Prime Minister had warned him, that it had been a mistake to ignore his Ambassador's advice, and still more of a mistake to ignore the Sultan. When he became Foreign Secretary, he impressed on England's ambassadors to Turkey the supreme importance of obtaining a personal influence over Abdul Hamid, who exercised an arbitrary control over the administration of the whole Empire. But at the time he had failed to recognise that the young Sultan possessed the most machiavellian of all the machiavellian brains at the conference.

Abdul Hamid had staked on his highest card and Europe had ignored his bid. All his anger was now directed against Midhat who had manoeuvred him into a position from which there was no retreat. On this night of rejoicing, when every mosque and public building was illuminated, Dolmabagche remained in darkness, and when Midhat came to call at the palace, he was told that His Majesty was indisposed. But behind the closed shutters the lights burned all night in the Sultan's study. Abdul Hamid was revising the draft of the constitution, or rather of one particular clause of the constitution bearing the unlucky number of 113, and referring to the measures to be taken during a state of emergency. By adding a short rider to this clause, he reserved for himself the right of banishment. It was no more than a few lines so short it could easily be ignored, but the secretary who handed him the Imperial seal saw that he was smiling as he affixed his seal to the document, before despatching it with his compliments to His Highness the Grand Vizir.

Chapter XIV

POLITELY BUT FIRMLY the Turks had said 'No' to Europe, and after a month of futile argument the envoys-extraordinary were packing their trunks. What was pushing the Turks to their present resistance? Was it the weakness of Russia, or the belief that, in spite of Lord Salisbury's insistence on the unanimity of the Concert of Europe, England could not afford to remain a disinterested observer in the event of a Russian attack on the Ottoman Empire? The exasperated diplomats were at a loss to find the answer, for as Lord Salisbury wrote:

> If they had said the scheme diminishes the Sultan's power, or his revenue, or makes the Christian too nearly equal with a Mussulman, or deprives the Turk of a vested right in provincial good places, all these things would have been intelligible, but all they talk about is compromising their dignity.

None of these diplomats had taken into sufficient account the part played by Abdul Hamid behind the scenes. The Sultan had two objects in view; to rid himself of the tutelage of Europe and, secondly to rid himself of his Grand Vizir.

It was snowing on the day the envoys left Constantinople, but in spite of the intense cold Abdul Hamid was seen on the terrace of his palace looking through a telescope at the last of the ships rounding Seraglio Point.

There had been none of the traditional presents or diamond-studded Orders of the Medjidie to speed the departing guests. When Lord Salisbury had asked to be received in audience, His Majesty had excused himself, saying that he was suffering from a bad attack of toothache. General Ignatieff had not even had the manners to ask. In a speech so violent as to shock not only the Turks but some of his own colleagues he had denounced the Sultan and his ministers for obstructing the peace of Europe and, declaring Russia's patience to be at an end, had walked out of the conference, which broke up without the delegates even waiting to hear the Turkish protests at the Russian speech.

The European diplomats had left in anger, but Abdul Hamid was not afraid, for he knew that in spite of all the talk about 'unanimity of ideas', each power was suspiciously watching the other. Russia's two partners in the *Drei Kaiser Bund* had shown no inclination to follow General Ignatieff's example in his bullying of the Turks, and the conciliatory tone of Lord Beaconsfield's public speeches and the report of a London meeting, presided over by the Duke of Sutherland, to raise funds for the Turkish soldiers fighting in the Balkans at which one generous peer had contributed no less than one thousand guineas, all helped to convince the Sultan that neither England nor the Central Powers would allow Russia to advance unmolested in the Balkans. In a way he was grateful to General Ignatieff for having put an end to the expensive farce of the conference, for now he was free to deal with his own internal problems and to settle the score with Midhat. The enthusiasm with which his subjects had acclaimed the prospect of a freely-elected Parliament forced him to carry out his promises. But the Constitution would be no more than a dead letter, once it was deprived of the man who gave it its life force. Before the last of the diplomats had left the city Abdul Hamid was already planning the downfall of his Grand Vizir.

Midhat's relations with Abdul Hamid are important in showing us into the dark and hitherto unexplored recesses of the Sultan's mind. In his dealing with his Grand Vizir we see operating for the first time the fear-complex, which was to be responsible for so many of the future tragedies of his reign. Midhat's harsh and dogmatic manner did little to alleviate the suspicions Abdul Hamid had harboured against him from the day of their first meeting: the tone of his letters when addressing his Sovereign held none of the flattery and obsequiousness which an absolute monarch has the right to expect from his subjects, and one can hardly blame Abdul Hamid for resenting being told 'that the object of promulgating the Constitution was to abolish absolutism, to indicate Your Majesty's rights and duties, to define and establish those of your ministers, in a word to secure to the nation complete and entire liberty.' For underlying these words was the unpleasant reminder that Midhat had not hesitated to dethrone two Sultans for the good of his country, and that, if the necessity arose, he was equally ready to dethrone a third.

Abdul Hamid bided his time, waiting for the various chancelleries to digest the reports of the conference, and for Midhat to negotiate an honourable peace with Serbia—a move calculated to show Europe that the Ottoman Empire was capable of managing its own affairs. Then suddenly he struck. Midhat had dared to impinge on his royal prerogatives by insisting on the dismissal of the Minister of Finance. Certain public funds were missing and the Grand Vizir had had the audacity to suggest that the money had been secretly transferred to the Sultan's Civil List. For all his preaching of economy, his simple almost abstemious habits, so contrary to those of his forebears, Abdul Hamid was passionately attached to money. He loved money for its own sake and was never so happy as when juggling with figures or discussing his investments with his Greek banker Zarifi. The compliant Finance Minister, who had doubled the Sultan's Civil List by the simple expedient of paying it out in gold, was often included in these discussions. But now Midhat had exposed the whole sordid story of irregularities in the Treasury accounts and the disappearance of State Bonds and the Sultan had no alternative but to dismiss his favourite minister, an affront he refused to forgive.

On the morning of February 5, 1877, Midhat Pasha was summoned to the Sultan to discuss the long-promised reforms with which he had been assured His Majesty was now ready to comply. All unsuspecting he drove to the palace and it was only when passing his house on his way that he noticed a cordon of soldiers round the gates and received the first intimation that he was walking into a trap. On arrival at Dolmabagche, he was ushered into a small ante-room and told to await the Sultan's orders. His suspicions deepened when looking out of the window he saw the Imperial yacht *Izzeddin* moored by the landing stage. It was unusual for the Sultan's yacht to be out at this time of the year, and seeing the smoke pouring from the funnels, the boat all set to sail, even the bravest of men must have felt the cold premonition of disaster.

There were none of the obsequious courtiers usually so ready to welcome a Grand Vizir, none of the bevy of cringing eunuchs to whisper in his ear some favour requested by one of the Sultanas. Alone he waited in the airless, stuffy room, while in the distance, from the direction of the harem, came the faint notes of a piano playing a tune from Offenbach. After an hour of waiting the door opened to admit His Majesty's First Secretary, Said Pasha, who, with obvious embarrassment, kissed his hands and presented him with the Sultan's *irade*, requesting him to deliver up the seals of office and to accompany him to the yacht which was waiting to take him into exile.

Abdul Hamid had struck. The few lines added to the one hundred and thirteenth clause of the Constitution—a rider so insignificant that it had passed unquestioned, now came into effect. The Sultan reserved for himself the right of banishment, and his Grand Vizir was to be his first victim. But behind the bronze doors of the harem the Sultan was nervously awaiting the reactions of his people. Supposing they refused to accept the dismissal of the popular Grand Vizir. In that case he would have no alternative but to recall him to the capital and await a more favourable opportunity. The captain of the *Izzeddin* had been ordered to anchor for twenty-four hours in the Marmara. If no message had been received at the end of that time, then he was to proceed to Europe to any port of call Midhat might choose to name. The Sultan had laid his plans with care but at heart he was afraid. In dismissing Midhat he raised for the first time in his reign the spectre of revolt. From now on he would always have to reckon with an opposition, secretly undermining his power, for Midhat was not a man to suffer his disgrace in silence. He had influential friends in Europe and the European Press would be mobilised on his behalf. In spite of the high-handed attitude he had adopted towards the Constantinople Conference, Abdul Hamid was susceptible to public opinion abroad and he knew that the only way of placating the Powers was to convoke Parliament and prove to the world that he was ready to rule as a constitutional monarch.

Seated at the piano, playing the tunes of Offenbach and

Meyerbeer, which helped to soothe his nerves, his foster-mother realised that Abdul Hamid was going through one of the most crucial moments of his reign. By now she had learnt to interpret his slightest gesture, the nervous way in which his hands, small as a woman's, played with the beads of his *tesbieh*, the way in which he sat silent, hunched up in a chair, then suddenly lifted his head to listen with a wary, frightened look as if listening for the first echoes of a revolution.

With those blue, tolerant eyes which had seen and accepted so much, Peresto watched her foster-son, if not with love— for such love as she had to give he had killed a long time ago— at least with pity and affection. Gratitude also played a part, the gratitude of a sterile woman towards the Sultan who had exalted her above all other women in the Empire. She was grateful that he came to her in his loneliness and misery. Pirimujgan's ghost had been laid at last; behind the wall of the Old Seraglio the old witch, Pertevniyal, had lost the power to intrigue against her: even the little Belgian glove seller, who last summer had given her so many anxious moments, was no longer in the ascendant, for, in the strictest confidence, the Kizlar Agasi had informed her that in the past month His Majesty's visits to the *konak* in Maslak had been growing less frequent and there was nothing more to fear from that quarter. Remembering the wild orgies of the preceding reigns, the jungle warfare in which she had fought for survival, the female jealousies and hatreds deliberately encouraged by the weak and vitiated Medjid, Peresto had good reason to congratulate herself not only on the position she had achieved but on the courtesy and gentleness with which her foster-son treated the women of his harem. Nevertheless, she often found herself watching him, as she was watching him now, fearing the unpredictable burst of rage, the savage manner with which once his suspicions were aroused he would turn to strike down a former friend.

The raising of a hand stopped her playing. Abdul Hamid had drawn back the brocaded curtains and in the fading winter daylight was watching the *Izzeddin* steaming out into the Marmara. Speaking to himself rather than to Peresto he murmured, 'It was foolish of Midhat to try to cross his Sultan,' and there

was something in the tone of his voice which made his foster-
mother suddenly turn cold.

For twenty-four hours he stayed on in the harem while the
eunuchs brought him the latest reports of the bazaars. Taken
by surprise the people had been too bewildered to protest.
Certain calumnies circulated by the palace had been believed,
for Midhat was a man of many enemies, all of whom had
helped to swell the chorus of defamation. But in spite of his
triumph the Sultan remained nervous and ill-at-ease and neither
his foster-mother nor his *kadins* were able to distract him.
Restlessly he wandered from one *daire** to another, where
dressed in their prettiest and most transparent *entaris†*, *kadins*
and odalisques vied with each other in his entertainment,
but neither the lilt of a Georgian love song nor the dancing of
a negro slave girl could distract his attention, and only a cursory glance or a disinterested caress rewarded their efforts.
Dolmabagche, with its echoing halls, its galleries of mirrors
reflecting his own image, had grown hateful to him. It was too
near to the foreign Stationnaire ships at anchor in the Marmara,
too near to Cheragan and the brother whose existence he would
willingly have forgotten. Neither the searching of Midhat's
house nor the sequestering of his effects had revealed the
missing document in which Abdul Hamid had pledged himself to abdicate in the event of Murad recovering his sanity,
and to reassure himself on the state of his brother's health the
Sultan chose the night after Midhat's departure to visit Cheragan for the first time since his accession.

The glittering, fairy-tale palace of his childhood had become
a place of shadows, haunted by ghosts and memories. Tarnished
gilding and broken tiles bespoke the neglect which reigns in all
Eastern palaces from which the Sultan, the central figure round
whom the world revolves, has withdrawn his warming
presence. Eunuchs, gossiping idly in the ante-chambers,
prostrated themselves at his approach. The doctors wore the
apathetic look of those who know they will never be called
upon to effect a cure and, with an eye to preferment, hastened
to reassure him that the ex-Sultan's condition had considerably

* *Daire*—Apartment of the Kaoure.

† *Entari*—A loose robe.

deteriorated in the last month. But Abdul Hamid trusted no doctor's report; he had come to see for himself and, asserting his royal prerogative, he entered the harem where Murad had retired for the night.

In all this melancholy palace no place was more melancholy than the harem, from where all gaiety and happiness had fled. Even the children spoke in subdued voices so as not to disturb the royal invalid. Laughter was no more than a ripple on the surface, instantly hushed into silence and, however bitterly Abdul Hamid may have hated his brother, he must have felt some pity at the sight of all these young and beautiful women condemned to a life of imprisonment in a madman's company. It was pathetic to see their faces light up in his presence, the pleading looks from despairing eyes to whom he represented the only means of escape. Their very unhappiness gave them a reality and warmth lacking in the stereotyped beauties of his own harem and excited him more than all the provocative glances, the songs and dances to which he had been entertained in the past twenty-four hours. Even the painful effort with which Murad's mother, a proud majestic woman from the Balkans, was attempting to conceal her hatred, gave him a certain feeling of exultation, remembering with what cruelty she had persecuted his unfortunate mother. Graciously he now kissed her hand, complying with her requests, the trivial little requests which prisoners make. Murad had already retired for the night. His mother complained he was sleeping too much. Perhaps it was the effect of the sedatives with which the doctors were attempting to control his attacks. Not even the ex-Valide dared to suggest that in her opinion these drugs were draining her son of his last remains of vitality and strength. It would be unwise to awake him if he was already asleep for any sudden shock might have dangerous repercussions, though perhaps shock was hardly the way to interpret the sudden visit of a beloved brother. But Abdul Hamid was already at the bedroom door. A eunuch was commanded to open. The ex-Sultan was awake and the two brothers found themselves face to face for the first time since Murad's abdication. Even the eunuchs with their ears to the keyhole were unable to hear what passed between them. Perhaps they remained in silence, the one content to watch and gloat over the shrunken figure with vacant eyes who would no longer haunt a throne, the other, paralysed with terror, or maybe sane enough to know that words were only a waste of time. From now on Murad was his brother's prisoner and no prying minister or commission of doctors would disturb his shadowed room. Out in the Marmara, the one man who might have saved him was on his way to Europe, but adrift in a nebulous world the ex-Sultan may not even have remembered Midhat's name.

Chapter XV

As an exile, Midhat was to prove more formidable than Abdul Hamid had anticipated. European reaction to his downfall was unfavourable both in Press and Parliament. In the French Chamber of Deputies, Monsieur Thiers went so far as to say that 'Turkey's most inveterate enemy could not have devised a more diabolical piece of advice to give the Sultan.' Before long, Abdul Hamid had come to the conclusion that it would have been better to have rewarded Midhat with a high-sounding title and sent him to moulder in some Eastern province, for the Ottoman Empire possessed many delectable spots—where, forgotten by the outside world, presumptuous pashas could repent their indiscretions.

Incensed by what he regarded as a lack of comprehension on the part of the Western Powers, with no political guidance other than the reports of his Ambassadors, Abdul Hamid faced a Europe where tension over the Eastern question was rapidly mounting to a crisis. While Russia mobilised her armies, General Ignatieff toured the Western capitals feeling the pulse of the various governments in the event of a Russo-Turkish war. Exploiting his friendship with Lord Salisbury, he stayed as a guest at Hatfield at a time when some of Lord Salisbury's colleagues in the British Cabinet, in particular the Prime Minister, were already preparing blueprints for the defence of Constantinople, should Russia over-reach herself in her ambitions.

How could Abdul Hamid begin to understand the tortuous workings of the British Cabinet, divided in its inner councils? How *could* he grasp the complicated ramifications of Bismarck's policy, encouraging all other countries but his own to founder in the pitfalls of the Eastern question, or probe into the secret meetings between the Austrian and Russian Emperors at Reichstadt, when Alexander secured from Franz Joseph the promise of neutrality? He had nothing but his own intuition to guide him, allied to the unshakeable belief that in the end England would come in on Turkey's side. To impress England he now identified himself with the Constitution, opening the doors of his palace on March 19, 1877, for the solemn inauguration of the first Ottoman Parliament.

It was a historic event, but the gesture was made too late to impress Europe. In the opulent setting of Dolmabagche, deputies, wearing every variety of garment from burnous to sheepskin, gathered from the four corners of the Empire to assist for the first time in the governing of their country. The gigantic crystal chandeliers, throwing cascades of light on to mirrored walls and luminous marble floors, reflected the earnest faces of men from Sivas and Erzerum, from Adrianople and Baghdad, who had come to discuss and, if possible, to remedy what each believed to be his own particular problem, only to find that the corruption they had thought to be confined to their own province extended throughout the Empire, that misgovernment in Salonika was the same as that in Beirut.

It was a gathering of every race and religion presided over by the Sultan in the role of the 'Father of his People'. For whatever may have been his private sentiments, Abdul Hamid now proved himself to be a superb actor. Who could fail to admire his tolerance and wisdom in appointing an Armenian as vice-president of the Assembly, and in choosing two Israelites as aides-de-camp? The Speech from the Throne, read by his secretary, Said Pasha, bespoke the same spirit of enlightenment and progress. From now on all his subjects were to be considered children of the same country and placed under the protection of one law. All he asked in return was their cooperation to derive full benefit from a constitution based on justice and public security. Nor was this tolerance confined to politics alone. It extended even to members of the Imperial family and for the first time in many centuries, the Sultan's brothers were admitted to the Councils of State. It was all the more surprising as Abdul Hamid had never shown any affection for his younger brothers. But the presence of the Princes Reshad and Vahdeddin standing beside the throne helped to silence voices still inclined to ask awkward questions regarding the health of the royal invalid in Cheragan.

Dressed in black, one gloved hand on his sword, Abdul Hamid listened to his secretary reading the speech, and watched through veiled lids the reactions of his people. How he must secretly have hated all those eager, questioning faces who presumed to govern in his place. They had not yet learnt to criticise their Sultan, so far they restricted themselves to his *valis* and his *kaimakams*, but given the blessings of democracy, the day would come when every provincial lawyer would dare to question the decisions of 'God's Vice-Regent upon Earth'. It was not a pleasant prospect for a Sultan jealous of the smallest of his prerogatives, and it only served to intensify his hatred against Midhat who had been the first to evoke the genii of a Constitution.

After the opening ceremony in Dolmabagche Palace, Parliament moved to the offices of the Ministry of Justice on the Golden Horn. In later years, when it had been indefinitely prorogued and Abdul Hamid had succeeded in reducing the Constitution to an empty formula published every year in the official almanack, it came to be regarded almost as an act of treason for anyone, whether he be a foreigner or a Turk, to glance up at the grimy windows of the building which had seen the brief flowering of Turkish freedom. For contrary to what the Sultan had hoped, the experiment in democracy proved a success. The Turk is a democrat by nature and, in spite of inexperience and lack of knowledge of parliamentary procedure, the majority of the deputies were both intelligent and sincere in attempting to reform abuses. Outside observers were impressed by the enthusiasm and goodwill which prevailed among them, the loyalty with which the Sultan's Christian subjects showed themselves ready to defend the Empire from all foreign aggression. For a while it seemed as if the first breath of spring had succeeded in penetrating the stuffy offices of the Sublime Porte, with Abdul Hamid as the idol of his people.

During these weeks in which he forced himself to play the role of a democratic monarch he would escape from his palace in the evening, and accompanied only by an aide-de-camp, ride up into the hills by the rough dusty track which leads from the village of Beshiktash to a small kiosk on a wooded slope. Built by his father for a favourite odalisque, it was known as Yildiz—or Star Kiosk—and few places can have been more enchanting than this white, marble pavilion with a terrace commanding a view both of the city and the whole Asiatic coastline. But it was not so much its beauty which attracted Abdul Hamid, as the remoteness of its position. Here he could feel safe from prying eyes and escape the attentions both of dangerous revolutionaries and of his all too effusive subjects. At the foot of the hills curved the wide sweep of the Bosphorus; to the right lay the Golden Horn with its forest of sails merging into the cypresses of Seraglio Point. From the slopes of Yildiz one could watch through a telescope the approach of every ship coming from the Marmara or the Black Sea, and watching, feel secure. For what Abdul Hamid craved above all else was security. He did not want to impress the world by the magnificence of his palaces. The Italianate mansions on the water front were alien both to him and to his people. At Yildiz he could revert to the scattered pavilions of his earlier forebears, and build an encampment, rather than a palace, set in a large park surrounded by high walls, with subterranean passages and secret exits, where he would be free to come and go unknown to his chamberlains and aides-de-camp.

Evening after evening he returned to Yildiz, till the secret project became a concrete plan. Hundreds of workmen were drafted to the lonely hillside, builders who worked apart and in separate shifts, architects and engineers who were consulted as to detail but never entrusted with the completed plan, and in later days, when the ramifications of Yildiz spread over a wide area, it was said that only the Sultan knew the exact layout of his fortress home.

The planning and building of Yildiz seemed to fill him with a new courage which reflected itself in his foreign policy. For in this month of March, 1877, when the Western Powers were making a last bid for peace, Abdul Hamid remained obstinately opposed to any form of compromise.

In England, General Ignatieff's powers of persuasion had obtained little beyond the signing of a somewhat ambiguous document known as the London Protocol, in which the Great

Powers 'recognised with satisfaction the peace concluded between Turkey and Serbia, but declared their intention of
watching carefully the way in which the promised reforms of
the Ottoman Government were carried into effect, and if the
lot of the Christian population was not improved, then
they reserved to themselves the right to consider in common
as to the means best fitted to secure general peace in the
East.'

Some of the signatory powers themselves appear to have
been sceptical as to the outcome of this diplomatic *ballon
d'essai*. As Lord Beaconsfield commented, 'The protocol is
signed and everyone writes to me about our triumph and the
humiliation of Russia, but I can't yet quite make head or tail
of it.' And though England was at pains to persuade the Sultan
to consider the protocol in the light of a friendly overture,
which it would be unwise for the Sultan to reject, Abdul
Hamid refused to recognise the right of Europe to interfere
in the internal problems of his empire.

The rejection by Turkey of the London Protocol brought
matters to a head, for though Ignatieff's charmed tongue had
not succeeded in bringing England, France, Germany and
Austria in on Russia's side, to share in the spoils of the 'sick
man of Europe', Russia now had an excuse for what she claimed
to be a crusade in defence of Eastern Christendom. The Russian
armies were already on the Pruth when England sent to the
Porte a new ambassador to advise the Sultan 'to make every
possible sacrifice to prevent war'.

Henry Layard, equally known as a diplomat and as an archaeologist, had all the necessary qualifications to succeed in his
mission. His pro-Turkish sympathies dated back from the days
when he had served as a young man under the Great Elchi and
made his famous discoveries at Nineveh. But when he landed
at Constantinople on April 20, 1877, the Ottoman Empire
was already on the brink of war, and the Sultan no longer
had the power of decision. Without allies and without resources, with nothing to sustain them but their faith in the
power of Islam, the Turks, stolid and fatalistic, waited on
the Russian onslaught. In the Sublime Porte, Layard found
apathy on the one hand and confusion on the other, procras-

tination allied to inefficiency. Edhem Pasha, the new Grand
Vizir, was 'more desperate than warlike'; the Foreign Minister,
Safvet, was in a state of nervous collapse; and the Sultan was
already living at Yildiz and no one could issue the simplest
order without it being sent to Yildiz for confirmation.

Four days after his arrival the new Ambassador was received in audience. As he drove in a state carriage through the
gates of Yildiz, accompanied by the Foreign Secretary and
escorted by postilions and outriders, he must have speculated
as to what manner of man was the new Sultan, of whom he
had heard such contradictory reports, and who, while shutting
himself away from his people, had been the first to give them
a voice in the governing of their country. High walls flanked
by the barracks of the Albanian Guards protected his domain,
which in less than a month had been transformed from a wilder-
ness into a formal park, with lakes and fountains and flowered
parterres where the tulips so loved by Turkish gardeners
flamed in flamboyant pride. Exotic birds flitted from tree to
tree, strange animals stared out from the bushes. Layard had
still to learn that this ruler so shy and distrustful of his fellow
men loved all animals and birds.

The carriages stopped in front of an unpretentious three-
storeyed house, which was the main building of Yildiz. Here
the Ambassador and members of his staff were met by His
Majesty's First Secretary, Said Pasha, and conducted up a
flight of marble steps, leading directly to the reception rooms
on the first floor where, after partaking of the traditional
coffee and sherbets, they were handed over to the Chief
Chamberlain. For though Yildiz bore little resemblance to a
palace, Abdul Hamid still maintained all the pomp and trappings of an Oriental court. Pages and eunuchs, equerries and
chamberlains in uniforms blazing with orders and stiff with
gold embroidery bowed them from room to room till they
found themselves in the sacred presence. A slight, lithe young
man in a plain frockcoat and fez rose to greet them and
Layard's first impression of Sultan Abdul Hamid was one of
profound melancholy, accentuated by the 'pallor of his skin, his
jet black hair and beard'. On greeting him the face was lit by
'a very pleasant and winning smile', but when he spoke his

tone was that of a man almost in despair and his extreme nervousness was painfully apparent.

The Foreign Minister acted as interpreter, as with tears in his eyes the Sultan insisted on his desire for peace. 'For how could he otherwise hope to carry on with those reforms which were necessary to the prosperity and happiness of all classes of his subjects, and in which it was his firm desire to persevere.' Sadly and without bitterness he spoke of the estrangement between their two countries, an estrangement due to causes for which he could not be held responsible. By the end of the interview he had convinced Layard both of his simplicity and sincerity. And one finds the Ambassador writing to the Foreign Office 'the Sultan gave me the impression of a very amiable, well-intentioned, honest, thoughtful and human man, truly desirous of doing his utmost for the welfare of all classes of his people.' Nor was Layard alone in his opinion, for almost every man and woman who came into contact with Abdul Hamid at the beginning of his reign was struck by his charm and evident sincerity.

Was this air of sincerity assumed or did Abdul Hamid genuinely want help and advice? Swayed by conflicting moods, he may have been equally sincere when, with tears in his eyes, he insisted on his desire for peace or when, under the influence of his brother-in-law, the proud and belligerent Mahmud Pasha, he defied the Russian Czar. But the decision for war or peace no longer rested with the Sultan. When Henry Layard drove away from Yildiz on the evening of April 24, 1877, the Russian armies had already crossed the Pruth and for the fourth time in a century Turkey found herself at war.

Chapter XVI

SPRING HAD COME to the Bosphorus, bringing in its wake the threat of foreign invasion; and the crowds outside the Russian Embassy in Pera saw the Imperial Eagle being covered in tarpaulin and the first recruits from Asia landing from Scutari. This time there were no Allied troopships anchored in the Marmara, no red-faced men in kilts swaggering down the streets. War had become again a struggle of Islam against the West, with the green banner of the Prophet unfurled in the Imperial mosques, the dervishes marching with the troops.

Infected by the general enthusiasm, Abdul Hamid saw himself in the role of a great military leader, following in the victorious traditions of his ancestors. At one time he even contemplated joining his army on the Danube, but was dissuaded by his brother-in-law, Mahmud Pasha, who, as Grand Master of Artillery, excercised a fatal influence on the military councils of Yildiz. Time after time in these crucial months, when the Russians by the sheer weight of manpower were forcing their way through to the Danube, orders were issued and countermanded, incompetent generals put in command and able officers dismissed merely because they had failed to pay court to the Sultan's brother-in-law.

General Valentine Baker, a former English cavalry officer serving in the Ottoman Army, gives a heart-rending account of a war in which the uncomplaining heroism of the soldiers, who still gave thanks to their Padishah for the biscuits and water which were sometimes their only rations, was offset by the criminal negligence of the generals in command and the intrigues and jealousies of the great pashas in the capital.

In spite of his unflagging efforts to do his duty, Abdul Hamid possessed none of the qualities of a military leader. With his changing moods excessive optimism alternated with black despair, religious exaltation gave way to scepticism, courage degenerated into cowardice. The new British Ambassador, who within a few weeks of his arrival had succeeded in getting on such terms of friendship, even of intimacy, with Abdul Hamid, that hardly a day passed without a message from Yildiz asking for advice or information, gives a sympathetic and understanding picture of the young Sultan grappling with problems beyond the limit of his experience, insisting on keeping all the reins of government in his own hands and exhausting himself by his attention to petty detail. When Abdul Hamid complained that the 'burden on his shoulders was greater than was carried by any *hamal**,' Layard would respectfully point out that His Majesty was wearing himself out with work that could be left to any office clerk, whereupon the Sultan would reply with infinite sadness that there was no one in the whole palace he could trust.

His suspicions and fear of a conspiracy to put his brother back upon the throne were exploited by the ambitious Mahmud, whom Layard regarded as the Sultan's most dangerous counsellor, 'a Turk of the bad school, typical of the governing classes which had brought about the ruin of the Empire, sensual, bigoted, proud and obstinate.'

Abdul Hamid appears to have had some justification for his fear of a conspiracy. In a letter to the British Foreign Office, Layard writes of how a secret messenger from Sultan Murad's mother had succeeded in gaining access to the British Embassy, bringing a letter in which the ex-Valide solicited England's sympathy and support for her son whom she declared to be completely recovered from his illness and now capable of governing the Empire. She even suggested smuggling the Ambassador by night into the Palace of Cheragan so that he could see Murad and judge for himself; a proposal so fraught with danger that Layard thought it better to ignore it, particularly as he heard from other and more trustworthy sources that the unfortunate Murad was completely imbecile.

In this atmosphere of plotting and intrigue it was fatally easy for unscrupulous characters like Mahmud Damad to keep the naturally nervous Sultan in a continual state of agitation till it gradually affected his whole mentality, and suspicions be-

* *Hamal*—A porter of the docks.

came obsessions while fears degenerated into terror. It was during these months of tension that Abdul Hamid began to compile the famous *djournals* which later were to form such an essential and such a disastrous part of his régime.

The first direct reference to these *djournals* comes from Layard, who writes:

> The Sultan rarely forgets anything that is told to him and is in the habit of noting in a *djournal*, which he carefully keeps, and which he usually has at hand, any observation or statement which he considers worthy of remembering, and which he frequently refers to in our interviews.

But the Ambassador only mentioned the *djournals* kept by the Sultan, ignoring the existence of those mysterious files which in the years to come were to accumulate in the vaults of Yildiz; files ranging from the private despatches of the Turkish ambassadors which, contrary to established custom, were sent direct to the Sultan instead of to the Sublime Porte, to the badly written and often illiterate reports of the spies employed in the coffee-houses of Stamboul and in the households of His Majesty's trusted ministers. There was not a man of substance in the capital, from the Sultan's Greek banker, Zarifi, to the Grand Vizir, who did not have his dossier in the files of Yildiz. Even at the most critical moment of the war, when the Russians had succeeded in crossing the Danube and the capital was directly threatened, Abdul Hamid still found time to study every evening what must have been irritating, disturbing and at the best boring accounts of the gossip of the bazaars. At times he would fall asleep from utter exhaustion before the day's reports were finished and some lovely young woman who had been detailed to read them aloud and was only waiting for a word or gesture to change the subject to the more pleasant theme of love, would close the files with a weary yawn and resign herself to yet another lonely night.

There were other times, particularly in moments of nervous stress, when Abdul Hamid was the tenderest and most passionate of lovers, constantly requiring a woman's presence, clinging to her as a child clings to its mother and for days on end refusing to leave the harem. Generals and ministers would be summoned at night to Yildiz and conducted by a black eunuch to a remote pavilion in the middle of the park. Here, in a small room, furnished in oriental fashion, surrounded by cages containing his favourite canaries, they would find the Sultan lying on a divan, while from behind an embroidered curtain came the stifled sound of women's voices. It must have been an unnerving ordeal for even the most stalwart of generals to find himself in the presence of the Padishah and to know that every word he said was being overheard by the women behind the curtain. In his slow, drawling voice, the Sultan would put question after question without ever commenting on the answer, and it needed both courage and discretion to escape from one of those interviews without having given something away either about one's colleagues or oneself.

Were there times when Abdul Hamid regretted Midhat's ruthless efficiency, his knowledge of Europe and European statesmen, or did the sense of loss only serve to intensify the bitterness? The Grand Vizir, Edhem Pasha, was loyal and honest, but he lacked the courage to tell him the truth and there were moments when this lonely autocrat wanted to hear the truth, moments when he reacted against the flattery of Mahmud and his sycophants. For this reason he protected Said Pasha, a young man who first came to the palace as Mahmud's nominee, but who had rapidly disassociated himself from his patron and by his own talents had risen to the position of First Secretary. During a reign of over thirty years, Kutchuk, or Small Said (so called on account of his diminutive stature), remained in the shadow of the throne. Even when he fell, a temporary victim to the machinations of his enemies and to the suspicions of his master, he always came back stronger and more influential than before.

Henry Layard describes his first meeting with Kutchuk Said at a dinner given by the Sultan in one of the smaller kiosks of Yildiz. As a special mark of favour, Mrs. Layard was included in the invitation and dinner was served in European fashion. While waiting for their host, the Layards were amused and rather touched to see through the open doors of the conservatory the Sultan and his secretary walking round the dinner table to see that everything was arranged correctly, so that there would be nothing to criticise. Layard's first impression of the secretary was somewhat unfavourable; he noted the truculent expression, the eyes that never looked one in the face, the sharp, wolf-like teeth: but later in the evening, when the Sultan was showing Mrs. Layard round his illumin-ated conservatory, discoursing on flowers and birds in such a way as to win her English heart, Said took Layard aside to discuss the precarious state of his master's health. The young man spoke with such genuine concern that the Ambassador warmed towards him. And later he had many occasions to be grateful to Kutchuk Said for his loyalty and political integrity.

When acting as interpreter, Said never attempted to soften the Ambassador's words, even when Layard told the Sultan that 'England, owing to the bad effect of the Bulgarian atrocities, was pledged to neutrality;' words to which Abdul Hamid listened without any show of anger or of irritation. The Sultan rarely allowed his bitterness to transpire, though many of his ministers spoke openly against what they considered to be the defection of a former ally. Only on one occasion did he show how much he resented the attitude of Europe. In dis-cussing the question of the atrocities committed by the Russians in the Caucasus, he asked whether the raping of Moslem women and the murder of their children would stir up as much resent-ment in England as the alleged Turkish atrocities in Bulgaria; or was it, he asked, a matter of Christian against Moslem?

Layard had never seen the Sultan angry before. 'We are accused in Europe', he said, 'of being savages and fanatics, but we are not the savages who brought on an unjust and horrible war which will lead to the sacrifice of innumerable human beings, nor are we the fanatics who have incited Greeks, Armenians and Bulgarians to exterminate those who differ from them in religion.'

For the first time the future leader of Pan-Islam hinted at the large spiritual forces at his command. 'Unlike the Czar, I have abstained till now from stirring up a crusade and profiting from religious fanaticism, but the day may come when I can no longer curb the rights and indignation of my people at seeing their co-religionists butchered in Bulgaria and Armenia. And once their fanaticism is aroused, then the whole Western world, and in particular the British Empire, will have reason to fear.'

The Sultan spoke, knowing that the Ambassador was watching apprehensively the coming and going of emissaries from Afghanistan and Russian Turkestan, all of whom were treated by the Sultan as favoured allies. Ostensibly their intrigues were directed against Russia, but England had too many interests at stake to ignore any form of religious agitation on her Indian frontier. By acquiring the Khedive's shares in the Suez Canal and by crowning the Queen as Empress of India, Lord Beaconsfield had extended Britain's sphere of influence from Cairo to Kabul. Both he and Layard were fully aware of the dangers attendant on neutrality, with the Russian thrust in the Balkans and Armenia threatening not only Constantinople, but the whole of the Euphrates Valley and the Persian Gulf.

Even more conscious of the danger was Queen Victoria, indignant at the indifference with which the majority of her Cabinet treated the warnings expressed in her Ambassador's reports. In July 1877, one finds her writing to Lord Beaconsfield, begging him to call his followers in the House of Commons as well as in the House of Lords, and to tell them that the interests of Britain were at stake, 'that it was not for the Christians (and they are quite as cruel as the Turks) but for conquest, that this cruel wicked war was waged'. Lord Beaconsfield, who would have been only too ready to carry out the orders of his beloved Queen, had respectfully to inform her that there were not three members of her government who were prepared to go to war with Russia.

Abdul Hamid was probably never aware of the battles fought by the Queen of England on behalf of 'those poor allies whom we so cruelly abandon to a shameful and detestable invader.' They were brave words and in keeping with a memory treasured through the years of a little figure standing firm and confident on the deck of a rolling ship at Spithead. Despite his secret bitterness at England's policy, the Sultan never lost his admiration for Queen Victoria, an admiration tinged with envy of a woman who shared his Empire over the Moslem world.

Meanwhile the Russians were advancing in Bulgaria; the Balkan passes had been stormed and their light troops were raiding the Thracian plain. Pathetic hordes of refugees fleeing from their ravaged homes brought terror to Constantinople and both in Parliament and in the Sublime Porte there was talk of the necessity for coming to terms with Russia. By the end of July, Layard was warning the Foreign Office 'to be prepared for a peace between Russia and Turkey, made under pressure and dictation of Germany, without reference to the interests of England, which might be greatly compromised and imperilled.' As a safeguard, he urged the Government to abandon neutrality, to occupy the Gallipoli peninsula and to obtain the Sultan's consent to bring the British fleet into Turkish waters.

But before Layard's despatch had reached the Foreign Office an event occurred which changed the whole course of the war. At Plevna, a great road centre on the right flank of the Russian advance into Bulgaria, the Turkish General, Osman Pasha, inflicted a resounding defeat on the enemy. Instead of carrying the town by storm, the Russians were compelled to besiege it and for five months the small Turkish garrison held one hundred thousand Russians and Rumanians at bay.

Across the telegraph wires of Europe flashed the news, to the Ball-Platz and the Quai d'Orsay, to Downing Street and the Wilhelmstrasse, casting a new light on the Eastern question: 'The sick man of Europe has still the power of recovery.'

Chapter XVII

FOR FIVE MONTHS Abdul Hamid fostered the illusion of being the leader of a victorious nation, exhorting his generals to further sacrifices over the private telegraph wires which connected Yildiz to the army headquarters on the Bulgarian front. The eyes of Europe were concentrated on Plevna, where the Russians had thrown in division after division, only to be repulsed time and again. But as autumn turned to winter and disease and starvation took their toll, it became evident that the heroic Turkish garrison could not hold out for long. On December 10, the last communications broke down and after a day of ominous silence the Turkish people learned that Plevna had fallen and that the road to Constantinople lay open to the enemy.

So great was the chaos that the Sultan had to rely on the British Ambassador for details of the news from the front. Layard paints a pathetic picture of Abdul Hamid, hollow-eyed from lack of sleep, begging him to ask the Queen of England to intervene with the Czar on behalf of the wounded Turkish prisoners, then towards the end of the interview breaking down and admitting that what he needed from England was not only her intervention on behalf of the prisoners, but her help in negotiating an armistice.

His country's resources were at an end and, as a final blow, Serbia had joined arms with Russia. The Sultan's voice rose to a shrill scream when speaking of the treachery of a country which the previous year had only been saved from destruction by the intervention of the Great Powers and his own misguided generosity. Looking at that haggard face, grey under the rouge (for a Sultan may not show himself to his people as a sick and harassed mortal), Layard remembered Said Pasha warning him that His Majesty's mind might in the end give way under the strain. The slightest sound, such as the crack of a dry twig in the garden or the sudden banging of a door, was sufficient to bring a hand to a pocket of the sable-lined coat which always held a small gold and ivory automatic. Even as he talked his eyes kept wandering round the room as if in search of a hidden foe. What was Abdul Hamid afraid of most? Was it the enemy advancing on his capital or the representatives of his own people?

On Layard's advice, he had agreed to re-open Parliament and the interview at which he asked for England's mediation took place in Dolmabagche immediately after the inauguration ceremony. It was a ceremony he had thought never to attend again and he had only consented to do so in the hope of persuading the ambassadors of the neutral Powers to associate themselves in a combined appeal for peace. These hopes had been dissipated by the machinations of Prince Bismarck who favoured the partition of Turkey for his own ends, as a means of providing a perpetual source of friction between Germany's two powerful neighbours, Austria and Russia.

The effort of attending Parliament had drained Abdul Hamid of his last reserves of strength. It had been a very different gathering to the crowd of cheering deputies who·had hailed the declaration of war. Criticism had now reached the throne, led by the followers of Midhat; those whom the Sultan described as 'scamps and revolutionaries, without religion or morality, who made use of the chamber for bad purposes, employing the names of Midhat and of Murad to undermine his authority.' They had refused to be placated by the dismissal of the incompetent Minister of War or the banishment of his brother-in-law, Mahmud, who as Grand Master of Artillery had been responsible for the failure of supplies. The words had not actually been spoken, but it had been implied that the Padishah himself was to blame for this disastrous war. To-day, for the first time, Abdul Hamid feared for the safety of his throne, and was ready to sue for peace on any terms, not so much because he feared the Russians as because he feared his people. Friendless and alone, trusting neither his ministers nor his secretaries, he turned to Henry Layard in much the same way as thirty years earlier a lonely neglected child had turned to Stratford Canning in the garden of the Old Seraglio.

A week later, Lord Beaconsfield was writing from Downing Street to his confidante, Lady Bradford, 'You will be glad to hear that the Sultan has solicited our kind offices for peace with Russia and that Her Majesty's Government has accepted the trust.'

The fall of Plevna had roused the British people from their apathy and the majority of Lord Beaconsfield's colleagues in the Cabinet were beginning to see eye to eye with their chief. But with the cautious Lord Derby at the Foreign Office, the correspondence between London and St. Petersburg was conducted in such a dilatory fashion that the Russians were able to advance on Adrianople before they had even committed themselves to negotiate. Turkish resistance had crumbled and, in one of the most brilliant feats of the war, the Russian army had succeeded in crossing the snowbound Shipka Pass of the Balkan Mountains and in surrounding a large Turkish army at Shenova. By the end of January, Abdul Hamid was reduced to such a state of despair that he sent a personal telegram to Queen Victoria, pleading for her intercession with the Czar.

Throughout the war the sentiments of the Queen had been in open conflict with her Cabinet. Time after time she had called on her ministers to abandon their policy of weak-kneed neutrality, threatening to abdicate, 'rather than remain the Sovereign of a country which was letting itself down to kiss the feet of the great barbarians.' The proudly worded telegram which she dictated to Alexander expressing the hope 'that having always declared himself desirous of peace, he would now accelerate the negotiations', made no attempt to pander to the vanity of the victorious Czar, and in terms which she denounced as being both rude and vulgar, he replied: 'That the commanders in chief of his armies in Europe and Asia alone knew the conditions on which a suspension of hostilities could be granted.' By compelling the Turks to negotiate directly with the military commanders in the field the Czar was effectually preventing the interference of any outside power and Abdul Hamid who, to the very end, had hoped that England would be dragged into the war, now saw her fail him even in her peace efforts.

Meanwhile the sound of the Russian guns re-echoed across the hills of Thrace. On clear, frosty days they could be heard on the shores of the Marmara and every hour brought a fresh influx of refugees fleeing from the Russian terror. Their accounts of Cossack atrocities, of pregnant women disembowelled before their husbands' eyes, of Moslem virgins branded with the cross, brought panic to the over-crowded town where fifty thousand homeless people bivouacked inside the walls, seeking shelter in the old Byzantine vaults and cisterns, huddling for warmth at the gates of the *medreses* which could no longer house them. The Sultan handed over some of his palaces on the Bosphorus, the rich pashas followed his example, but there was no proper organisation to cope with the refugee problem, and to add to the general chaos came the first stragglers from the front, conscripts from Asia returning to their homes, starved and rapacious for pillage.

In this atmosphere of demoralisation and defeat, Abdul Hamid accepted the inevitable and sent a peace delegate across the Russian line. None of the foreign envoys were taken into his confidence, for the first condition exacted by the Russians was that the negotiations should be conducted in secrecy. The British Ambassador who kept an observant watch on the Sultan's movements and suspected, without actually knowing of the negotiations, writes of the amazing self-control shown by Abdul Hamid in these days of crisis. When his frightened courtiers kept begging him to cross over to Asia and to establish his court in the safety of Bursa, he replied that like the last of the Paleologi, he preferred to die in the ruins of his city rather than to live in exile: brave words when coming from a man whose nights were haunted by imaginary terrors. He may still secretly have hoped to retrieve by diplomacy what he had lost in battle, for he deliberately abstained from investing his delegates with full powers to negotiate so as to secure an immediate armistice while leaving the peace terms in the balance. But the Russians were to prove harder than the Sultan had anticipated. Once the Turkish delegates had crossed the line there was no news of them for over a week and, in spite of the promised armistice, the armies continued to advance, to the alarm and consternation of Europe.

On February 7, 1878, Lord Beaconsfield wrote:

> This has been a terrible day of excitement. Last night there
> came news from Constantinople that all the wires were cut
> by the Russians, so that our intelligence had to reach us via
> Bombay, that the Russians were on the very point of reaching
> Constantinople and Gallipoli and the city was at their mercy.

The British people, so slow to rise in anger, now voiced
the indignation of their Queen. In face of public opinion Lord
Derby resigned from the Foreign Office and the British fleet
was ordered into Turkish waters. Meanwhile Austria had
begun to mobilise her armies, fearing that a victorious Czar
might be tempted to ignore the promises he had made at
Reichstadt. But the joint action taken by the Great Powers
had come too late. By the time the British ships entered the
Dardanelles, the Turkish delegates, threatened and brow-
beaten into submission, had accepted the Russian terms. All
Abdul Hamid's diplomatic skill and evasive promises were of
no avail when pitted against the arrogant, uncompromising
attitude of the Russian generals. With his capital in the shadow
of the enemy guns and the Russian tents pitched at San
Stefano, only seven miles away, the Sultan did not even dare
to grant a *firman* for the passage of the British ships, though
not a single Turkish shot was fired in protest when on February
15 th British iron-clads forced the Dardanelles and sailed
into the Marmara to anchor outside the Golden Horn.

From the heights of Yildiz, Abdul Hamid watched through
a telescope the manoeuvring of the British ships and, for the
first time in many weeks, saw a faint ray of hope. Here was a
solution to the Treaty of San Stefano, the crippling, humiliating
treaty which the Russians had forced him to accept at the point
of their bayonets and which virtually abolished the dominion
of the Ottoman Empire in Europe by giving complete independence to Rumania, Serbia and Montenegro and creating
a greater Bulgaria stretching from the Black Sea to the Aegean.

The terms were still officially secret, but by making his Greek
doctor his confidant Abdul Hamid had ensured that the clauses
most harmful to English and Austrian interests in the Mediterranean and the Balkans would reach their respective Embassies.

Doctor Mavroyeni's carefully calculated indiscretions were invaluable to the Sultan on these occasions, and by the end of February both Layard and his Austrian colleagues were in possession of the preliminary draft.

The ships anchored off Seraglio Point were England's answer to the Treaty. Ostensibly the fleet was there to safeguard British nationals and British interests in case of trouble, but the sailors themselves gave a truer version as they washed their decks in view of the Russian camp, whistling the refrain of the popular music hall tune *'We don't want to fight, but by jingo if we do, We've got the men, we've got the ships, we've got the money too ... The Russians shall not have Constantinople.'* Abdul Hamid laughed for the first time for many days when Mavroyeni translated to him the words. This was the spirit of the England he remembered, the solid complacent England of the 1860's, the steadfast spirit of the Queen who had refused to give way to the mass hysteria aroused by Gladstone's fulminations and who, when told that the Russians were encamped on the shores of the Marmara, had replied simply and to the point, 'Then they must get out!'

Abdul Hamid knew his capital was safe so long as the two former antagonists in the Crimean War faced one another across that narrow strip of water. The Czar had arrived at San Stefano to visit his troops, but he would return to the orange groves of Livadia without attending Mass in Aya Sofia. Ignatieff with his Pan-Slavism was in disgrace for, in spite of all the bullying and threatening of Turkey, the bribery and cajoling of the Great Powers who each in turn had been offered a share of the spoils, Russia would end by giving way and submitting the clauses of San Stefano to the decision of a European Congress.

For six months the British fleet and the Russian armies lay within firing range of one another, without the Russians attempting to enter the city or the British attempting to land. The Sultan's favourite relaxation on these first spring days was to partake of his coffee and *chubuk* on a terrace, from where he could watch the armed might of the Great Powers ranged outside his capital which, beautiful as a mirage conjured from the water, coveted yet unattainable, lay between them. His country might be bankrupt and defeated, his lovely city riddled by misery and corruption, but he was still master of the greatest water highway of the world and his very weakness gave him the strength to hold the balance in the rivalry of the Powers. It was no longer the time for dramatic gestures. The pride and courage so characteristic of the Turkish people and which as their Sultan he had done his best to emulate, had resulted in nothing but humiliation and defeat. Patience and astuteness alone could save his empire, coupled with the ability to profit by the weaknesses of others.

He knew that it could only be a question of months before the turbulent people of the Balkans turned against their Russian liberators, before Slav and Greek hated one another as bitterly as they hated any Turk. From now on Abdul Hamid vowed to keep his empire at peace, to let others do the fighting on his frontiers and by fostering their dissensions, to help them to destroy each other. But before he could hope to carry out his policy, he had to be master in his own capital. Parliament must be dissolved and those interfering lawyers from the provinces sent back to their own homes.

One day in early spring the Sultan came down from Yildiz to Stamboul to attend what he alone knew to be the last session of the short-lived Ottoman Parliament. There was nothing in his manner to betray his intention. Attentive and apparently acquiescent, he listened to a long speech of a deputy from Erzerum, suggesting the cutting down of his Civil List. Only those who knew him best would have recognised the ominous gleam in the dark eyes, the hectic flush on his usually sallow face. The President of the Chamber paid tribute to the unexpected visit, little suspecting that at the end of the day's session each deputy would return to his lodging to find an Imperial *firman* ordering him back to his own province. The Sultan had struck, choosing a time when the average Turkish citizen was living in daily fear of the Russians and too concerned over the rising price of bread to give much thought to his political liberty. Only a handful of deputies dared to disobey their master's orders and instead of returning to their provinces, to follow Midhat into exile. The Ottoman Constitution and Parliament, so warmly heralded in the European

Press, was allowed to die unnoticed, for the Great Powers were too busy wrangling for precedence at the coming congress, too concerned over the balance of power in the Near East, to give a thought to Turkish liberty; and only a month after the signing of the Treaty of San Stefano, Abdul Hamid was left unchallenged to win his first victory over his own people.

Chapter XVIII

TWO MEN STILL worried the Sultan, haunting his days and nights: the one was his mad brother in Cheragan, the other was Midhat Pasha, whose warm reception in Europe and recent articles in the English Press pleading his country's cause had angered Abdul Hamid far more than if he had turned traitor and gone over to the Russians. The *djournals* compiled by the palace spies never failed to contain some reference to him. Playing on the Sultan's weaknesses and fears, they made Midhat responsible for every disturbance in the city, till the desire to get him back into his clutches became so much of an obsession with Abdul Hamid that he instructed his Grand Master of Ceremonies, Kiamil Pasha, who in the past had been on friendly terms with Midhat, to start corresponding with the ex-Vizir. Hearing that Midhat was in financial difficulties, the Sultan ordered Kiamil to send him the gift of a thousand pounds as proof of Imperial clemency, while at the same time Midhat was given to understand that, should he ever feel inclined to return to his own country, suitable employment would be found for his talent. But though the Sultan's gift was acknowledged with all due courtesy and gratitude, it was not until a year later that Midhat walked into the trap, homesick for his country, his work in Europe finished once the Eastern question had been settled at the conference tables of Berlin, and Europe, in particular England, had come to accept Abdul Hamid as a benevolent despot who, in the words of Lord Beaconsfield, 'was neither dissolute nor a tyrant, neither bigoted nor corrupt.'

An event occurred during this year which rendered Midhat's situation still more dangerous, for Abdul Hamid persisted in holding him responsible for the abortive revolution which broke out in the spring of 1878. Hunger and poverty had fostered discontent, preparing the ground for demagogues and agitators. Rumours were no longer confined to the reports of the palace spies. The Sultan could read for himself the signs of disaffection in the roughly written slogans that began to appear on the walls of Yildiz and of Dolmabagche. Who was responsible for these slogans which called on 'the usurper to renounce his throne and restore it to Murad the rightful owner'? Were they the crazy outpourings of homeless refugees or the rallying cry of an organised conspiracy? The police were at a loss to find the answer in a town to which a floating population of over fifty thousand had been added in the last months.

So general was the discontent, it was difficult to tell the agitator from the grumbler and the ravings of an out-of-work schoolteacher called Ali Suavi passed unnoticed. There was a time when Ali Suavi had enjoyed Imperial patronage. A native of Bokhara, he had come to Constantinople and through his own talents had risen to the position of professor at the secular school of Galata Saray. Here he had attracted the Sultan's notice and been appointed as tutor to his eldest son, Prince Selim. His troubles began the day he fell in love with and married an English governess, a woman of doubtful reputation, who both dominated and betrayed him, filling his head with dangerous Western notions hardly compatible with his position as tutor in the Imperial household.

Conscious of what he called his abysmal ignorance, Abdul Hamid had approved a modern and progressive education for his sons, but his enthusiasm for progress did not go so far as to allow them to learn their history from French and English text-books which extolled the virtues of constitutional government and excused the people who beheaded their king. No sooner was Ali Suavi suspected of revolutionary tendencies than he was summarily dismissed—a dismissal all the more disastrous in that it ended his academic career, for neither Galata Saray nor any other school would employ a teacher dismissed from the palace. Deserted by his wife who had found protection with a rich Armenian merchant of Pera, the unfortunate Ali became a homeless wanderer, frequenting the courtyards of the mosques where the refugees camped around the fountains, airing his rhetoric on those who like himself had nothing to lose and everything to gain by a change in the régime. The bitterness of frustrated ambitions encouraged his delusions, prompted by the whispering of Russian agents who, disguised as refugees, encouraged revolt in the poorer quarters of the city: 'Murad, the legitimate sovereign, still lived as a prisoner in Cheragan. Abdul Hamid was no more than a regent who had usurped his powers and involved his country in a disastrous war.' Poor Ali Suavi, in his threadbare coat, was the perfect tool for their propaganda. Seeing himself in the role of liberator and king-maker, he recruited his tattered followers from among those who, as desperate as himself, were ready to risk their lives in a hopeless cause.

May 18, 1878, was a holiday and the grounds at Yildiz were open to the public, one of the few concessions made by Abdul Hamid to the role of a democratic monarch. In the warm, sunny weather, rich and poor flocked from the teeming streets to the green lawns and rose arbours of the Sultan's gardens. The Imperial *bostandjis** were on guard to pick up the offending piece of paper or punish the malefactor who as much as touched a flower, but there was no one to control the comings and goings in the park, no one to notice that, shortly before noon, at the hour of mid-day prayer, little groups of men disappeared into the shadow of the trees and wandered down the paths which led to the bridge and aqueduct spanning the main road from Constantinople to Bebec and leading from the grounds of Yildiz to the gardens of Cheragan.

Cheragan slept in the drowsy heat of noon: not a living soul stirred in the gardens, even the soldiers on guard were asleep, and the heavy silence was broken only by the harsh discordant notes of a piano. The sound of this mad, uncontrolled music should have served as a warning to the men slowly creeping across the bridge, but, drugged with Indian hemp to give them courage, they were deaf to any note of warning: all they saw was the empty road, the unguarded bridge. Ali Suavi and his three hundred desperadoes had entered the grounds of Cheragan before the first shot was fired.

Still drowsy with sleep, soldiers and eunuchs fell before their wild assault, women screamed in terror of their liberators, while the piano continued its sad jarring notes, leading Ali Suavi direct to Murad's room. He had hoped for so much, only

*Bostandji—A gardener.

to find a helpless imbecile with drooling mouth and frightened eyes, who cowered behind the piano when he saw him and resisted with force when he tried to drag him from the room.

Meanwhile the alarm had been given. The Sultan's Albanian Guards were streaming down the hillside and Ali Suavi was among the first to fall to their bayonets. There were those who maintained he was already dead by the time the Albanians had arrived and who claimed to have seen the distracted Murad running from room to room, firing a pistol in the air—a pistol which had belonged to Ali Suavi.

It was a tragic, abortive revolution in which eighty rebels lost their lives while the rest were taken prisoner. Its importance was in the effect it had on the Sultan's character. In the first years of his reign Abdul Hamid had mixed with his people more than any of his predecessors. The citizens of Constantinople had become used to seeing their Sultan riding through the streets, or being rowed in a *caique* to the Sweet Waters of Asia. But now not only his habits but his whole mentality underwent a change. From the time of Ali Suavi's revolt he shut himself up in Yildiz which year by year, as his fear of the outside world increased, became more of a fortress and less of a palace. The park was closed and his only public appearances were at the Friday *selamlik*, or on certain ceremonial occasions when tradition forced him to visit the palace of his ancestors.

Henry Layard goes so far as to say: 'Ali Suavi's revolt had the effect of bringing out in Abdul Hamid the germ of insanity he and all the other members of his house had inherited from their ancestor, Sultan Ibrahim.'

The fact that the conspiracy had failed in no way allayed the Sultan's fears. He refused to believe that Ali Suavi had acted on his own initiative and insisted that the attack on Cheragan had been part of a conspiracy to assassinate him, financed by Russian gold and instigated by Midhat Pasha. The terror that had dominated his childhood came back to haunt him in the long and sleepless nights. The morning after the rising he got up convinced that the Grand Vizir, Sadik Pasha, was one of the conspirators, and in spite of there being no evidence of any kind, the unfortunate minister was instantly dismissed.

Even the faithful Said came under suspicion when in order to save his master unnecessary excitement he tried to prevent him from assisting at the interrogation of the prisoners. Invisible behind a grille, Abdul Hamid would listen for hours to the confessions extracted under torture by the secret police, always hoping to hear an avowal of the complicity of Midhat. The nervous strain of listening to these interrogations left him in such a state of mental and physical exhaustion that for a short time there was fear for his sanity. At a secret meeting of the Grand Council, the question of a regency was under discussion, and for two weeks he was too ill even to attend the Friday *selamlik*, during which time his Greek doctor and his foster-mother virtually ruled his empire.

Layard describes a strange nocturnal interview with Abdul Hamid at which Mavroyeni acted as interpreter. He had been summoned to Yildiz early in the evening and on arrival had been told that the Sultan was in the harem and would receive him later. Dinner was prepared for him in a small pavilion overlooking a lake, and in solitary state he sat down to partake of innumerable courses, waited on by silent servants. The rich, indigestible food, all served half-cold owing to the kitchens being at the other end of the park, was compensated for by the beauty of the setting. It was a night of full moon, the air was heavy with the scent of jasmine and the bulbuls sang in the hedges. But though Layard was a romantic by nature and fully alive to the beauties of Yildiz, he was tonight concerned with more terrestrial matters. The Sultan's breakdown could not have come at a more unfortunate moment. There were vital subjects to be settled before the congress opened at Berlin. By despatching Indian troops to Malta and sending her fleet into the Marmara, England had taken the lead in forcing the Czar to submit the treaty of San Stefano to a European congress. At Easter the Russian armies had retreated to Adrianople, while the British ships had retired to Besika Bay. But the British Empire was no charity institution. If Lord Beaconsfield espoused Turkey's cause, even to the extent of offering her help in the future, he counted on some guarantee or compensation in return and secret negotiations were already in progress when this abortive revolution had succeeded in demoralising the Sultan to such an extent that he was incapable of taking any decision.

An ambassador accredited to the Sublime Porte required a good constitution and endless patience to stand up to the intrigues and vacillations of the palace. Layard liked the Turks and had sympathy with Abdul Hamid, but tonight the atmosphere of Yildiz, the monotonous splash of the fountains, even the singing of the nightingales, combined to get on his nerves. It was already past eleven o'clock when Said came to fetch him for his audience and, judging by the strained anxious look on the usually arrogant face, it seemed as if even the indispensable Said was in doubts about his future. In silence they walked across the moonlit park to the unpretentious house surrounded by a walled garden which housed the Sultan's harem and which was connected by a conservatory to a small building known as the Little Mabeyn, the Sultan's private apartments. It was the first time a foreign ambassador had ever crossed the threshold and Layard could sense the disapproval of the two black eunuchs on guard at the gates. Here Said was dismissed, being told that His Majesty wished to see His Excellency alone, and Layard was led through a conservatory full of exotic flowers and rare birds to a small room giving out onto a garden where he found the Sultan lying on a sofa with his doctor standing beside him.

At first sight it was obvious that Abdul Hamid was not in a normal condition. His eyes shone with an unnatural brilliance, his cheeks were flushed and he addressed Layard in a voice shaking with emotion. Dispensing with all formality, he plunged straight into the subject which was on his mind, telling him that he possessed positive information of a plot against his life which was to be put into execution the following day and that, as he had only a few hours to live, he had called on the ambassador of the only friendly Power to give proof of his friendship by protecting his wife and children.

Mavroyeni acted as interpreter and his interpretation proved him to be a subtle Greek of the *phanar**. Harems were frowned

* *Phanar*—Phanariote, a descendant of one of the Byzantine families of Constantinople.

on in Victorian England and, in deference to the Queen's susceptibilities, a Christian ambassador was always accredited to her court. So the doctor now spoke of the Sultan's foster-mother and his wife, rather than of the four *kadins* and the latest favourite, a sloe-eyed Georgian girl, who had just presented His Majesty with a son.

Layard attempted to calm and reassure the Sultan, but he was not to be influenced by argument or reason, 'insisting on maintaining that the conspiracy against his life' which Layard appeared to doubt, 'had far-reaching ramifications—that the late Prime Minister and some of the highest personages in the State were implicated—that even his closest attendants were united against him and were determined upon his death.' As he spoke, Layard could hear a rustling from behind a screen and the stifled sound of women sobbing. No wonder Abdul Hamid's plaintive tones drew tears from his women; even Layard was moved to pity when he asked him, 'why he had lost the affection of his people when he had done all in his power to help them', adding, 'I have granted them a Constitution. I have willingly consented to any reforms and am ready to do so again. But they now hold me responsible for the war with Russia, and after the horrors they have witnessed and gone through, can they do other than hate me, though I am as much to be pitied as any of them.'

Towards the end of the interview the Sultan became calmer, as if his nervous excitement had spent itself in talk, and Mavroyeni, who accompanied Layard to the gates of Yildiz, held out hopes of a quick recovery. His Majesty, he said, had been subject to delusions ever since his early youth; at one time he imagined he was dying of heart-failure. But those hallucinations and periods of depression only lasted for a short time and if His Excellency would be patient, he would see that within a few days His Majesty would be able to attend to affairs of state. Meanwhile all one could do was to humour him in every whim. Looking at the doctor's smiling, cynical face, Layard wondered how much Abdul Hamid confided in him and whether Mavroyeni ventured to give political as well as medical advice. If the secret negotiations were satisfactorily concluded and the island of Cyprus was ceded by the Sultan in return for a guarantee by England to defend his Asiatic provinces against any further Russian encroachment, it would be largely due to the efforts of two phanariote Greeks, the Turkish Ambassador in London, Musurus, and the Sultan's banker, Zarifi. In the circumstances it might be wise to enlist the services of yet another Greek by gaining the goodwill of the Sultan's physician.

But did England really want Cyprus? Layard was in two minds about it as he stepped into the launch which was to take him across the moonlit waters to the summer Embassy at Therapia. He himself would have preferred a concession on the Persian Gulf, such as the Shatt El Arab at the mouth of the Euphrates. But that great imperialist who now ruled the destinies of England looked upon Cyprus 'as the key to western Asia'. Thirty years ago Disraeli was already envisaging the island as a British possession, in the days when as a young man he wrote his novel *Tancred* and quoted as the gossip of the Jerusalem bazaars, 'the English want Cyprus and will take it as compensation.'

Chapter XIX

O N MAY 5, 1878, Lord Beaconsfield wrote to Queen
Victoria,

> If Cyprus is conceded to your Majesty by the Porte and
> England at the same time enters into a defensive alliance with
> Turkey, guaranteeing Asiatic Turkey from Russian invasion,
> the power of England in the Mediterranean will be absolutely
> increased in that region, and Your Majesty's Indian empire
> immensely strengthened.

In this letter the author of *Tancred* used the language of
power politics. To guard against future Russian encroachment in Asia, England needed a base, 'where without disturbing the peace of Europe, she could accumulate material of
war and if necessary the troops for operating in Asia Minor
and Syria.' Cyprus had the advantage of being near to both
Asia Minor and Syria and of not being sufficiently important
to arouse the jealousy of the other Powers.

Six months before, the Porte had already hinted to the
British Government that the Sultan would be willing to sell,
or lease, certain territorial possessions, and the leasing of Cyprus
to England would have presented no difficulty had not the new
Foreign Secretary, Lord Salisbury, insisted 'that if a defensive
alliance is to be worth while and not be hampered by divisions
at home, the Porte must give specific assurances of good
government to Asiatic Christians.'

It was these 'specific assurances' which irritated and alarmed
Abdul Hamid, jealous, as always, of any foreign interference
in the internal administration of his empire. At the time of Ali
Suavi's revolt the question of Cyprus was still in the balance
with the Sultan refusing to commit himself to any agreement.
In exasperation, Lord Salisbury wrote to Mr. Layard that 'in
his present state of weakness and vacillation, the Sultan would
be better off with Janissaries, Pretorians or even Varangian

Guards, anything so as not to be exposed to the intrigues and
passions of Stamboul.'

Abdul Hamid's nervous collapse came as a blessing in disguise, for Mr. Layard found an unexpected ally in Doctor
Mavroyeni who as a child had met some of the survivors of
the massacres of Chios and was ready to use all his influence
in persuading the Sultan to sign an agreement which would
benefit his co-religionists in Asia. Removed from the reactionary counsels of the *mollas* and pashas of Stamboul, Abdul
Hamid was won over by the plausible tongue of his Greek
doctor and, to Layard's relief, the Sultan's recovery was
marked by the signing of the Cyprus Convention, which took
place at Yildiz on the evening of June 4, nine days before the
opening of the Congress of Berlin.

The text, which was short and showed trace of the haste in
which it was construed, contained only one operative clause,
by which

> Great Britain engaged to join the Sultan in defence of his
> Asiatic dominions against any further Russian attack while
> the Sultan promised in return to introduce the necessary re-
> forms there in consultation with his ally. In order to enable
> the latter to fulfil her engagements he assigned to her the island
> of Cyprus to be occupied and administered by her as a place of
> arms in the Levant, on payment of an annual tribute, calcu-
> lated by the average surplus of the revenue of the five previous
> years and on the understanding that a Russian evacuation of
> her recent Asiatic conquests should be followed by a British
> evacuation of Cyprus.

In spite of a few rumours largely due to Mavroyeni's indis-
cretion, nothing was known of the details of this secret treaty
until a month later when its publication took the diplomatic
world assembled at Berlin by surprise and was denounced by
England's enemies as yet another proof of 'the perfidy of
Albion'. At the time it was considered to be a great personal
triumph for Mr. Layard, but it cost him the Sultan's confidence. Having bought England's alliance, Abdul Hamid
expected her to defend his interests not only against Russia
but against all the other Powers, and Layard was to be held

responsible for every real or imaginary slight inflicted on the Turkish delegates at Berlin.

The Ambassador's difficulties were increased by the fact that when Abdul Hamid emerged from retirement ten days after Ali Suavi's revolt, he showed signs of an abnormality which had not been apparent before. From now on he lived in a world where every man's hand was against him and the constitutional malady he had suffered from since birth and which had become aggravated by his recent experiences made him the victim of strange delusions which were to increase with the years. Fear made him cunning, watchful of the slightest sign of disaffection, unwilling to accept advice whether it came from a foreign ambassador or a devoted servant.

Outside events contributed in undermining Abdul Hamid's health and nerves. With feverish anxiety he watched the game of diplomatic chess which was being played out at Berlin. Forewarned that Turkey would have to sacrifice large tracts of territory in Asia, he had sent the Greek Carathéodory to represent him at the Congress, judging it better for a Christian, rather than a Moslem, to suffer the indignity of signing away Turkish territory. But though Carathéodory was a man of decided ability, described by Lord Beaconsfield as 'the perfect Greek of the Phanar, good-looking, full of finesse, yet calm and plausible,' he was not of a stature to stand up to the bullying of a Bismarck or a Gortchakoff. Europe's most brilliant statesmen were assembled at Berlin and, with the exception of Lord Beaconsfield who was sufficiently an Oriental to sympathise with Turkish pride and susceptibility, the majority either bullied or ignored the Sultan's delegate.

A certain impulsive and warm-hearted Berlin hostess was so disgusted by this churlish behaviour that she urged Carathéodory to show a greater assurance, whereupon he replied with a Turkish fable of the hen who was asked by the cook whether she preferred to be eaten with a sweet or a sour sauce, for this was roughly Turkey's position—in either case she was going to be eaten.

The delegate's position was made more difficult by the Sultan's innate distrust of all his diplomats. It was Abdul Hamid's habit to leave his delegates without definite instructions so as to give him the opportunity of going back on their decisions. Later he was to realise these were the wrong tactics to have adopted at Berlin and he openly admitted his mistake in an interview given five years later to *The Times* correspondent, Henry de Blowitz.

De Blowitz had had the temerity to say that, in his opinion, Turkey made her greatest mistake in being represented at the Congress by men who, however devoted and well-intentioned, had no instructions to act on and trembled before Prince Bismarck, to which the Sultan replied that he realised this when he saw that the Greeks and Roumanians had been admitted to the Congress though they had no right to be there, and that his plenipotentiaries never dared to protest. He added, 'We were in a painful position. The enemy was at our gates and we could not reckon much on the equity of Europe.'

These words spoken five years later still reflected Abdul Hamid's bitterness at the decisions taken at Berlin. It was galling to his pride to see the casual manner in which the European statesmen, few of whom had any knowledge or even acquaintance with the regions under discussion, carved up his Balkan provinces. Through the efforts of Lord Beaconsfield the greater Bulgaria created at San Stefano had been reduced to a relatively narrow strip between the Danube and the Balkan range, while south of the Balkans an artificially created province to be known as Eastern Rumelia was restored to Turkey. But whatever gratitude Abdul Hamid might have had for England in restoring to him two-thirds of the territory he had lost at San Stefano, was offset by the British delegates insisting on the governor of Eastern Rumelia being a Christian, chosen and approved by the European Powers.

Another cause for bitterness was the occupation of Bosnia and Herzegovina by the Austrians. The dual monarchy had played an equivocal role throughout the war. By promising her neutrality at the secret Treaty of Reichstadt, Austria enabled Russia to concentrate the whole of her armed forces against Turkey. But when Russia's combined successes began to threaten her own *Drang nach Osten*, then Austria turned her coat and mobilised her armies in the Carpathians. Now she claimed as her share of the spoils the occupation of the provinces promised her at Reichstadt, insisting not only that Turkey should cede Bosnia and Herzegovina, but that she should beg her as a favour to take them—a piece of sophistry so blatant that even Lord Salisbury was roused to sympathy for the Turks, writing to Layard:

> The poor Turks make a wry face—submit to a cession—
> yes—they would say Kismet—ask for an occupation—yes—
> they can even make up their minds to that. But to ask to be
> allowed to cede a rich province to a country who has done
> nothing for them is more than they think their *softas* will
> understand.

Nevertheless it was England's policy to preserve the Concert of Europe and the turcophile Layard had the unpleasant duty of persuading the Sultan that the defence of European Turkey against Russia must in future mainly depend on Austria, and that an Austrian occupation was the best means of preventing a chain of Slav states from stretching across the Balkan peninsula. Abdul Hamid refused to be convinced and there was a series of dramatic scenes at Yildiz in which Layard was accused of treachery and disloyalty. England, according to the Sultan, had let him down. Her acquisition of Cyprus, her growing interest in Egypt, and Lord Salisbury's concern over the treatment of his Christian subjects, all went to disprove the altruistic attitude which England adopted at Berlin.

With the exception of Germany, none of the Great Powers was entirely disinterested. France threw out hints of a future occupation of Tunis; Italy made vague references to Tripoli; while the smaller countries, such as Greece, Serbia and Montenegro, not content with being recognised as independent, already sought to extend their frontiers at the expense of the Ottoman Empire. Races as well as nations sought a hearing at Berlin. Particularly ill-advised was a deputation of the Sultan's Armenian subjects, who presented their grievances and aspirations to the Congress at a time when Abdul Hamid was particularly sensitive on the subject of Armenia, of which large tracts had been conquered by the Russians.

Both Abdul Hamid and his immediate predecessors had treated the Armenians with tolerance and justice. Their treachery at the time of the Crimean War had been forgotten and many of them occupied important positions both in the Porte and the palace. Owing to the aversion of the average Turk to any form of commerce, most of the business of the Empire was in the hands of either Greeks, Jews or Armenians and it was among the Greek and Armenian brokers and bankers of Galata that the young Abdul Hamid made his first friends. His interest in every form of finance was so contrary to the tradition of the well-bred Turk as to revive the rumour of his mother's Armenian origin and, at the beginning of his reign, the Armenians were favoured to the point of being referred to as the *millet sadika*—the faithful nation.

But now this so-called faithful nation, encouraged by Russian agents and the American Mission Schools, claimed their independence, presenting themselves at Berlin as a persecuted people. The European statesmen, in particular the humanitarian Lord Salisbury, lent a sympathetic ear, and the clause, already inserted by the Russians in the Treaty of San Stefano, 'giving the Powers the right to superintend the reforms which the Porte had promised to carry out in the provinces inhabited by Armenians,' was solemnly ratified at Berlin. It was the clause which Abdul Hamid resented the most and the English added to his resentment by insisting on the right of appointing military consuls to see that the reforms were carried through.

Layard, as usual, had the unpleasant task of inducing Abdul Hamid to abide by the decisions of Berlin, and the relationship between the Sultan and the Ambassador suffered in consequence. There were certain critical moments when Layard had to remind His Imperial Majesty that it was largely through England's efforts that thirty thousand square miles of territory, including the whole of Macedonia, Epirus and Albania, had been restored to his empire.

The dinners at Yildiz were still as frequent and Abdul Hamid's professions of personal attachment both to the Ambassador and to his wife were as flattering as ever, but gradually the rift grew wider, till Layard began to dread the invitations which before he had been so proud to accept. On hot summer evenings when he was at his happiest in his own garden at Therapia, he would suddenly be summoned to Yildiz to spend half the night in a small stuffy room (for the Sultan never ventured out of doors at night) listening to endless complaints followed by gloomy warnings for the future. Europe would live to regret the decisions of Berlin and Abdul Hamid referred with bitterness to those famous statesmen who had divided up the Balkan peninsula without regard for or knowledge of its inhabitants. Greeks would refuse to become Bulgarians, Albanians would resist being incorporated in Montenegro and the Austrian army of occupation in Bosnia was already being stoned by the population it had come to liberate.

Layard had good reason to believe that a certain amount of the opposition in Bosnia was being directly financed from Yildiz. But when the Sultan spoke with tears in his eyes of the sufferings of his people and of how out of his own privy purse he was planning to settle large numbers of Bosnian refugees on farms in Palestine, the Ambassador could only declare himself to be touched by His Majesty's good intentions.

As he listened hour after hour to that slow, deep voice inveighing against the decisions of Berlin, Layard began to realise the hopelessness of his task. Thirty years ago, his great predecessor Stratford Canning had insisted that 'Turkish reform can only be achieved by a force from without keeping a steady continual pressure on the Sultan's government.' But he had neither the strength nor energy of Stratford Canning and in Abdul Hamid he had a very different man to deal with than the weak and gentle Medjid. Beneath that frail exterior, those dark melancholy eyes, was a will of iron bent on preserving a crumbling empire against foreign encroachment. Even when tormented with nerves and haunted by hallucinations, he still remained as inflexible as ever. And though Layard had seen the Sultan in a hundred different moods and each mood only represented a part of the real man, dominating all was the ambition to preserve his position, not only as Sultan of Turkey but as Caliph of Islam and no amount of foreign pressure would ever get him to grant a concession or reform which went against the dictates of the Koran or of the Sheriat, or in any way estrange him from the three hundred million Moslems whom he looked upon as his spiritual subjects.

Chapter XX

TWO YEARS HAD GONE by since the Treaty of Berlin, and without travelling beyond the suburbs of his capital Abdul Hamid had made himself into an absolute monarch, controlling the destinies of an empire which even in its present mutilated state was still larger than the whole of Austria, Germany and France together. He had made no attempt to revive the Parliament so summarily dissolved at the end of the Russian War, and the Sublime Porte was now completely subject to the palace. The Secretariat of Yildiz worked day and night, filing petitions and reports from all parts of the Empire, for no law or regulation, even of the most trivial kind, could be made without passing through the Sultan's hands. Henry Layard relates how at a time of crisis, when Abdul Hamid was overwhelmed by anxiety and work, he still found time to read through the files which dealt with the regulations of the *cafés chantants* of Pera. The Sultan's distrust of his advisers was such that he did not dare to leave to them the smallest decision and every day the dossiers of his spies, who thrived on his credulity, poured further poison into his system.

It was a sad, lonely life which the Commander of the Faithful and God's Vice-Regent upon Earth led within the precincts of his fortress palace, rarely venturing out except for the Friday *selamlik*. His subjects had no more than a brief glimpse of his pale face and melancholy eyes looking out of the windows of a plain green carriage, or driving swiftly past in an open landau; the simplicity of his carriage and his clothes contrasting with the elaborate uniforms of the ministers and generals who followed on horseback and on foot. Since the days of Ali Suavi's revolt he lived in continual fear of assassination and when driving to the Imperial mosques he was usually accompanied by one of his sons, for he knew no Turk would dare to shoot at the risk of killing a child. Yet in spite of the terrors which assailed him on venturing abroad, he continued

Sultan Abdul Medjid,
Abdul Hamid's father
(Mansell Collection)

A harem lady. There is
no known picture of the
little Circassian dancer
who was Abdul Hamid's
mother, but during his
early years in the harem
he would have been
surrounded by women
like this.   *(Popperfoto)*

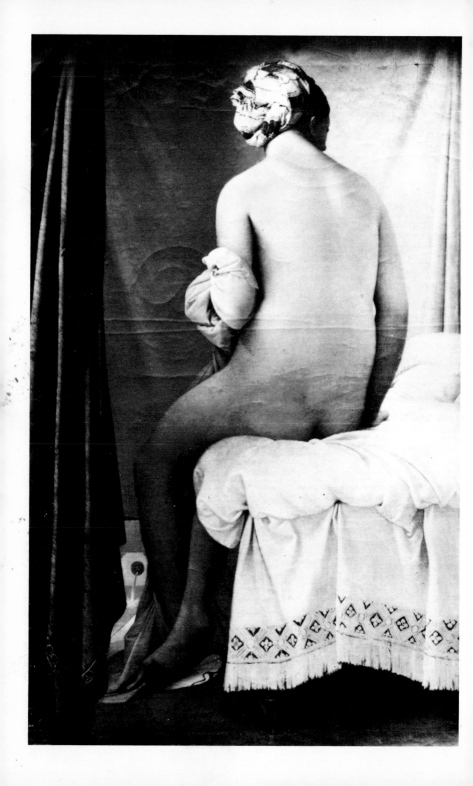

Facing page: Baigneuse by Ingres
(Mansell Collection)

The chief of the White Eunuchs
(Mr. Brinsley Ford)

Abdul Aziz, Abdul Hamid's
uncle who became Sultan in 1861.
At first a reasonable and
unassuming ruler, he ended up
a tyrannical megalomaniac.
(Mansell Collection)

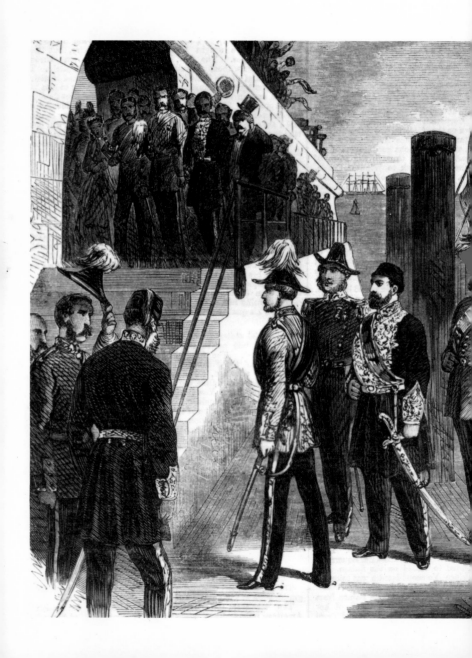

A drawing which
appeared in the *Illustrated
London News* of Abdul
Aziz and his companions
landing at Dover
(Mansell Collection)

Sultan Murad V, Abdul Hamid's brother and predecessor whose reign lasted only three months before he was deposed on grounds of insanity *(Popperfoto)*

Midhat Pasha, the Turkish statesman who led the movement for reform in the 1870s. He subsequently became Grand Vizier but Abdul Hamid got rid of him in 1877 *(Mansell Collection)*

Facing page: Abdul Hamid just after he became Sultan *(Hayat Magazine, Istanbul)*

The interior of Topkapu palace—the circumcision
room (*State Information Archives*)

View of Dolmabagche palace from the sea *(State Information Archives)*

The impressive main entrance of the Dolmabagche palace *(State Information Archives)*

Yildiz kiosk, the fortress home surrounded by high walls which became Abdul Hamid's favourite retreat *(Popperfoto)*

View of Istanbul showing the entrance to the Bosphorus *(Mansell Collection)*

Said Pasha, several times Grand
Vizier to Abdul Hamid
(*Popperfoto*)

Henry Layard, the British
Ambassador to Turkey during
the critical years of the Russo-
Turkish war and the Congress
of Berlin
(*Mansell Collection*)

Facing page, top:
The signing of the peace treaty
between Russia and Turkey at
San Stefano in 1878
(*Mansell Collection*)

Facing page, bottom: The
Congress of Berlin
(*Mansell Collection*)

Two cartoons which appeared in Punch in 1879 satirizing Abdul Hamid's reluctance to introduce the liberal reforms wanted by the British Government *(Punch)*

Facing page, top: Abdul Hamid driving through Istanbul on his way to Hamide Mosque *(Popperfoto)*

Facing page, bottom: Kaiser Wilhelm II's visit to Turkey in 1898 *(Thomas Cook & Son)*

Enver Bey, one of the
leaders of the July
Revolution of 1908
(Popperfoto)

Abdul Hamid in old age
(Mansell Collection)

to maintain the traditions of his ancestors and the humblest of his subjects had the right to present their grievances in person to the Sultan.

In Abdul Hamid's strange, contradictory nature the good battled with the bad, and the bad was largely instigated by fear. The very mention of Murad was sufficient to make his face turn ashen, his eyes dilate in rage. But when following Ali Suavi's revolt he could easily have had his brother murdered or kidnapped without incurring any direct responsibility, all he did was to have him removed for greater security to Yildiz. Even then, he sent him back to Cheragan as soon as he heard that the separation from his mother and his harem was affecting his health.

If Abdul Hamid ruled as a tyrant it was because he genuinely believed that his people were not yet ready for parliamentary government. At one of the last stormy sessions of the Turkish Parliament he openly admitted 'I have made a mistake in wishing to imitate my father, Sultan Abdul Medjid, in seeking reform by persuasion and liberal institutions. From now on I shall follow in the footsteps of my grandfather, Sultan Mahmud, who understood that it is only by force that one can move the people with whose guardianship Allah has now entrusted me.'

Convinced of his divine right, he admitted no opposition to his will and the number of liberal-minded Turks who sought refuge in Europe increased with the years. These exiles were a constant source of worry to the Sultan, who feared the adverse criticism abroad, and the greatest care was taken to prevent political suspects from obtaining passports, no easy task in a country where the underpaid official was usually amenable to bribery.

Abdul Hamid was particularly sensitive to foreign opinion and one of his first duties on getting up in the morning was to read through a translated summary of the reports of the European Press. One unfavourable comment was sufficient to ruin his day, and the unfortunate translator of the offending article would be summoned to his presence and every word would have to be re-transcribed before he was satisfied of the truth.

Both translators and secretaries led an exhausting life under a master who, summer and winter alike, rose between four and five in the morning. By six he was already in his study, drinking his first cup of coffee, ground and made in front of him by his *kahvedji-bashi*, smoking his first cigarette, rolled and prepared by one of his eunuchs from tobacco reserved for his use and which he preferred to the traditional *chubuk*. Every morning the Chief Secretary presented him with a report of the principal affairs of state, which was read aloud to him while he drank his coffee. Sometimes the Sultan interrupted to ask some detail about a certain matter mentioned in the report. If the detail was not of a nature to satisfy him he would order it to be examined afresh. As soon as the daily report was finished, a second secretary appeared, bringing him a summary of the news contained in the despatches from abroad. The Grand Vizir was then summoned and given his orders for the day. No kind of discussion was allowed in the royal presence, only replies to questions. If a minister had anything to say, he said it in a few words, and a sign of approbation, perhaps no more than a nod of the head, was accepted as an Imperial *irade*.

Apart from being a heavy smoker and inveterate coffee drinker, Abdul Hamid was frugal, almost austere, in his habits, and his meals, so different to the elaborate banquets of his predecessors, rarely consisted of more than one dish. His tastes were simple and he preferred a good pilaff or the humble stuffed marrow and cucumber to the elaborate concoctions prepared by his Greek chef. But however simple might be the food eaten by the Sultan, the most elaborate precautions were taken in its preparation. His milk came from a model farm at Yildiz where the cows were guarded day and night: his cooks cooked his meals in special kitchens with barred windows and iron doors, and, before it was served, each dish had to be tasted by the Chief Chamberlain, Osman Bey, who, as Superintendent of the Kitchens and Guardian of the Sultan's Health and Life, occupied one of the highest positions in the palace.

At certain hours of the day visitors to Yildiz might see the curious spectacle of His Majesty's meals being transported from the kitchens to the Little Mabeyn. First came two officials in gold-embroidered uniforms wheeling between them a trolley, covered by a carpet, which contained the Imperial dinner service: next came a lackey carrying the various dishes on an enormous silver tray, the whole covered by a black cloth hermetically closed and sealed: then followed a second lackey carrying a bread basket, also covered and sealed, and lastly came the water-carrier bearing in a sealed bottle the precious water of Kiathane, the only water Abdul Hamid had touched from the day when a gipsy foretold him a long and prosperous reign provided he only drank from the springs of Kiathane. The same kind of procession, though somewhat less elaborate, could be seen at the same hour in various parts of the palace gardens. Three thousand people fed from the Sultan's kitchens and there was a constant stream of liveried servants carrying covered trays from which exuded the savoury aromas of pilaff and roasted meat.

Other even stranger sights could be seen by the initiated, and among the most curious and, at the same time, the most pathetic, were the little cafés distributed in various corners of the park where, on his solitary walks, Abdul Hamid would stop and take refreshments, paying for his coffee like any ordinary mortal and thereby giving himself the illusion of freedom, even though the coffee was always prepared by one of the *kahvedji-bashi*'s staff. There must have been times when in his lonely grandeur Abdul Hamid regretted the days when he frequented, *incognito*, the cafés on the Bosphorus and there was no need to fear that the coffee might be poisoned. His tastes were those of a normal young man. He enjoyed riding and shooting, rowing and swimming, but in his fear of the outside world all his activities were now confined within the precincts of his park. Riding along the carefully tended paths of Yildiz must have seemed very tame in comparison with those early morning gallops in the forest of Belgrade: rowing on an artificial lake in the company of a veiled Circassian, veiled for fear that a gardener might see the beauty reserved only for the Sultan's eyes, had none of the charm of the moonlight excursions at Therapia.

His happiest time was spent in his harem in company with

his women and his children, and it was here that Abdul Hamid showed himself at his most human and his most lovable. The whole tempo of the harem was modulated to suit his mood. If he was gay, the rooms re-echoed to the sound of music and of laughter, his slightest witticism was acclaimed as brilliant. If he was sad, the youngest of his odalisques drooped in gentle melancholy. No one knew him better than his foster-mother, who had dedicated thirty years of her life to the study of his whims and moods and who now ruled over his harem with as strict a discipline as any Mother Superior in the running of her convent. The temperamental scenes and hysterics which had appealed to his father's vitiated tastes were frowned on, for Abdul Hamid came here not so much to be stimulated and excited as to be nursed and soothed.

Mrs., or rather Lady, Layard—for her husband had been knighted after the Treaty of Berlin—was a frequent visitor to the Imperial harem and she has left us a description of those rooms where the influence of East and West, a mixture of the beautiful and of the gimcrack, mingled in an incongruous whole. Plush-upholstered furniture from Paris and Vienna, most of it in the worst of taste, contrasted with exquisite carpets and embroideries; worthless bric-à-brac and Swiss cuckoo-clocks flanked priceless porcelain vases, the gifts of Chinese Emperors, while a mouse-trap, the Sultan's latest gadget from England, could be found on a silver table next to an agate, jewel-studded cigarette box. The same incongruities reflected in the women's dresses which varied from the beautiful old-fashioned Turkish court costume with the embroidered velvet jacket, the loose *entari* and emerald-studded belt worn by the Valide, to the over-ornate European tea-gown favoured by some of the younger *kadins*.

Abdul Hamid's foster-mother is described as 'a small fair woman still bearing traces of great beauty' who received her guests with the air of an empress, wearing the finest jewels of the Seraglio, and whom everybody, including the Sultan, treated with the greatest respect. Even the reigning favourite, the beautiful Georgian, Djemile Sultana, took second place, while the elder *kadins*, two women already middle-aged, remained in the background, rarely taking any part in the conversation.

All one knows of life in the Imperial harem comes from the letters and memoirs of foreign visitors, but not all of them were as privileged as Lady Layard, who had won the Sultan's gratitude when she nursed his soldiers during the Russian War. She was the first woman ever to be invited to dine at his table and he trusted her to the extent of allowing his children to go to tea with her at the British Embassy. She continued to enjoy his friendship to the end, even when the frictions and misunderstandings which followed on the Treaty of Berlin had brought her husband into disfavour. Many years later Professor Vambéry was surprised to find in the Sultan's private study the photograph of an Englishwoman. On asking, he discovered it to be Lady Layard, 'a lady for whom,' said the Sultan, 'I have the highest regard, for during the war she looked after my wounded soldiers with great self-sacrifice and I shall always be grateful to her.'

Lady Layard was one of the few who persisted in maintaining that by nature Abdul Hamid was of a kind and gentle disposition and that his character was only warped by the circumstances and tragedies of the beginning of his reign. She tells many charming anecdotes of the dreaded Sultan in his family circle, mending a broken clockwork doll for one of his daughters, taking a childish delight in the pianola which played the tunes of his favourite Offenbach, recounting for her benefit some old Turkish fable with the gestures and mimicry of a born actor or, in a more serious mood, discussing the problems of female education, his plans for a new girls' school at Scutari, where the daughters of good Turkish families would be educated on European lines with a special curriculum designed not to offend Moslem susceptibilities.

On one occasion the Sultan pointed to the pretty little slave girl who acted as interpreter and whose fluent Periot French had already intrigued the Ambassadress, saying, 'If this girl is better educated than the rest, it's because she lived as a small child in the house of a Belgian *modiste* of Pera, a highly intelligent and educated woman.' Lady Layard was surprised to hear the Sultan referring in this way to Flora Cordier whose sudden disappearance had provided endless gossip for the diplomatic tea-tables of Pera, and even more surprised by the indulgence with which he treated the girl, allowing her to sit down in front of him and to chatter incessantly, never correcting her when she interspersed her own comments in a way not always respectful to her mistresses.

In the rigid hierarchy of the Imperial harem, the pretty little slave girl was a law unto herself, neither the *kadins* nor the eunuchs dared to correct her and, at the time of Lady Layard's visit to the harem, the protégée of Flora Cordier seemed well on the way to follow in her footsteps. All would have been well had her eyes not strayed in the direction of the Sultan's elder son, Prince Selim, who at eighteen was already established with a household of his own, living in a kiosk adjoining the Mabeyn. The young prince, who had already shown the erotic tendencies of his ancestors, is said to have fallen for the charm of the pretty slave girl and with the help of a complacent eunuch to have met her at dusk in secluded corners of the park. But it was not long before the vigilance of His Highness the Kizlar Agasi detected the romance. For the prince it meant banishment from his father's presence; for the little slave the punishment was death by drowning. Abdul Hamid might talk of progress and reform, but the medieval harem laws were still inflexibly carried out, and the Bosphorus received another victim to add to that sad army of ghosts who haunt by night the fishermen brave enough to venture round Seraglio Point.

Perhaps Abdul Hamid was at heart as kind as Lady Layard would have us believe. But in his eyes, as in the eyes of any other despot, the drowning of a little slave girl was as necessary and as inevitable as the drowning of the twenty *softas* who had incited their colleagues to revolt against the decisions of Berlin. The Sultan might sympathise with their over-zealous patriotism, but by rebelling they were setting themselves up against his authority and, like his grandfather, Sultan Mahmud, he was determined to rule by force and crush the slightest opposition. There were many curious anomalies in Abdul Hamid's character and among the most curious was the fact that the man who later earned the title of the Red Sultan could rarely, if ever, be persuaded to sign a death warrant. It was sufficient for him to say in front of his servants that he prayed that Allah might punish a certain individual who was robbing him of his sleep and the man in question would disappear.

There was one person whom Abdul Hamid would willingly have killed with his own hands and that was Midhat Pasha. When the Powers pressed for concessions and reforms in Syria and Anatolia, he prevailed on Midhat to return to the country and accept the post of Governor-General of Syria—a gesture calculated to please Europe and to bring about his downfall. In Syria, as in his former posts, Midhat devoted all his energy to the cleaning up of a corrupt, inefficient administration, and before long Christians and Moslems were unanimous in praise of the new *vali*. But when Midhat wrote to Constantinople, insisting on the need for further reforms and the dismissal of certain corrupt officials, his letters remained unanswered. The Sultan had not recalled his arch-enemy in order to make him the most popular man in his empire, and in the autumn of 1879 he viewed with a jealous eye the British Ambassador's journey through Syria and his meeting with Midhat Pasha in Damascus.

Of all the signatories to the Treaty of Berlin, England was the one most determined to see that the terms were properly carried out. Russia and Austria were for the moment content with their spoils, France was intriguing in Tunis and Prince Bismarck had allowed it to be known that Germany would not be a party to any coercion of Turkey in the execution of the promises embodied in the Treaty. Only England, acting partly out of humanitarianism and partly because Lord Salisbury rightly believed the Eastern question to be ultimately concerned not only with the European, but also with the Asiatic provinces of Turkey, insisted on the right of imposing on the Sultan the obligation to introduce reforms in the provinces inhabited by Armenians. With his suspicious mind, Abdul Hamid was convinced that the British Ambassador's journey to Damascus and his visit to Midhat Pasha was in order to plot reforms over which he was not to be consulted.

On his return to Constantinople, Layard found the Sultan

at his most intractable. England's decision to appoint military consuls to supervise reforms in Syria and Anatolia was regarded by Abdul Hamid as an insult to himself and his Empire, though on second thoughts he saw in it a useful weapon with which to arouse the jealousy of the other Powers, who ever since the Cyprus Convention had suspected England of planning to establish a protectorate in Asia Minor. Lord Salisbury's policy was on the whole a mistake, for not only did it alienate the Sultan and disrupt the Concert of Europe, but it encouraged the Armenians to believe that the English were in some way pledged to their assistance and that they had only to provoke incidents to receive British intervention; a dangerous illusion for a people who lived in the heart of Asia, surrounded by hostile Moslem tribes.

Layard was among those who realised the danger of his country's policy and all his efforts were concentrated on persuading the Sultan to make concessions of his own accord and to employ experienced Europeans in the higher administrative posts—a difficult task, in view of Abdul Hamid's rooted objection to intrusive Europeans whose presence alone had a disturbing effect on the submissiveness of his subjects. There were one or two Englishmen on whom Layard pinned his hopes: one was Abdul Hamid's old friend Mr. Thomson, who still continued to enjoy the Sultan's confidence, the other was Major-General Baker Pasha, who as a young man had served in the Crimean War and who, after a much-publicised scandal, had been forced to leave the British Army.

For the last two years Baker Pasha had been employed in organising the new Turkish gendarmerie and so great was the Sultan's confidence in him that at his own discretion he had been allowed to recruit twelve young English officers to help him with his work.

Like most of Abdul Hamid's friendships and enthusiasms, his relations with Baker Pasha gradually cooled. There was too much jealousy at the palace, too many intriguers profiting by the Sultan's weaknesses to permit any foreigner to retain his ascendancy for long. But in the winter of '79-'80, Baker Pasha was still in favour, his genial wit and sound common sense introducing a breath of fresh air into the hot-house atmosphere of Yildiz. Thus, after many months of vacillation and procrastination, Sir Henry had the satisfaction of writing to Lord Salisbury, 'His Majesty has consented to appoint Baker Pasha as Inspector-General of the reforms in Asia Minor.' This, however, was to be his last achievement as Ambassador. In April, 1880, the Conservative Government in England fell from power, and William Ewart Gladstone, the man who had poisoned the first months of Abdul Hamid's reign by his campaign against Bulgarian atrocities, became for the second time Prime Minister of Great Britain, and one of the first acts of the new government was to recall Sir Henry Layard from his post as Ambassador to Constantinople.

Chapter XXI

THE RIGHT HONOURABLE George Goschen, Member of Parliament for Ripon, who succeeded Sir Henry Layard as Great Britain's envoy to the Porte, was of a very different calibre to his predecessor. To begin with he was not a career diplomat, but a politician whom Mr. Gladstone, having found difficult to fit into his Cabinet, had sent to Constantinople entrusted with a special mission—to see that the terms of the Treaty of Berlin were properly carried out. Knowing that he was not going to stay for long, Mr. Goschen had none of the hesitations of an ordinary ambassador over bullying and coercing the government to which he was accredited. His views were fundamentally those of his chief—namely that the Eastern question would only be settled, 'once the Turks were bundled bag and baggage out of Europe'. Questions which had been left unsettled at Berlin and in which the other Powers had lost all interest now became matters of primary importance in the policy of the British Government. Only Great Britain and, in particular, Mr. Gladstone, seemed to care whether the rectification of the Greek frontier included an extra slice of Epirus or Thessaly, or whether Montenegro extended her coastline to include the ports of Antivari and Dulcigno.

Apart from his policy and opinions, Mr. Goschen was personally objectionable to Abdul Hamid on account of his previous connections with Egypt. When in 1876 the extravagance of the Khedive Ismail resulted in the suspension of payment on treasury bills, Mr. Goschen had been sent to Cairo on behalf of the English bond-holders and the report presented by him and his French colleagues had resulted in the Khedive being forced by the Great Powers to submit to the institution of a Commission of Public Debt and to the appointment of two foreign controllers to supervise his finances. The Sultan who, according to Sir Henry Layard, was particularly jealous of any interference in the financial affairs of his empire, 'was now obsessed with the idea that Mr. Gladstone's Government had the intention of reducing him to the condition of the Khedive and to place him under a kind of tutelage with Mr. Goschen in control.'

The fall of the Conservative Government in England had shocked and frightened the Sultan. However much he may have complained against England in the past two years, he had always known the Sultanate was safe so long as Disraeli remained in power and Great Britain pursued an Imperial policy whose keystone rested on the preservation of the Ottoman Empire. Sir Henry Layard, who within recent months had been the chief object of his suspicions, became once more on the eve of his departure the Sultan's dearest friend.

Abdul Hamid expressed the greatest indignation over the Ambassador's recall, which he described as an insult to himself. He went so far as to say that he would refuse to receive his successor, until Layard prevailed on him to adopt a more reasonable attitude. Not only the Sultan, but all his entourage, from the imperturbable Said, who came in and out of office according to his master's moods, but whom the Sultan could never do without for long, to the Greek banker Zarifi, who acted as the chief intermediary between the palace and the British Embassy—all expressed sorrow at the departure of an ambassador who had liked their country and respected their customs. When Sir Henry Layard left Constantinople he left with the esteem both of the Sultan and of his people and, as a proof of the Sultan's affection, he carried in his luggage the magnificent Bellini of Mahomet the Conqueror. Unfortunately indiscretions at home were later to destroy the pleasant impression he had made in Constantinople, adding his name to the long list of those whom the Sultan regarded as having betrayed his trust.

Meanwhile Abdul Hamid had to reckon with Mr. Goschen, a man whose tactlessness and over-impulsiveness even succeeded in getting on the nerves of his own staff. Acting against the advice of his chief dragoman, he insisted on inserting criticisms of the Sultan's régime and words of warning from

his government in the speech he was to make at his first public
audience. When news of this reached Abdul Hamid through
the medium of his spies, the Ambassador was immediately informed that His Imperial Majesty was 'ready to consider any
observations that Mr. Goschen might think it necessary to
submit to him in a private audience, but he absolutely declined
to receive a lecture in public, offensive to his dignity and which
would lower him in the eyes of his subjects.' Mr. Goschen had
therefore to withdraw his speech and substitute it by the usual
complimentary phrases. But the courtesy did not last long.
As the champion of small nations, Mr. Gladstone elected to
support the claims of Montenegro, the smallest, and in his eyes
one of the most deserving, of the Balkan Principalities. When
the Albanian inhabitants somewhat naturally refused to hand
over the villages allocated to Montenegro by the Congress of
Berlin, England suggested to the signatory powers that in
place of these Albanian villages, the Porte should cede to
Montenegro the Adriatic seacoast towns of Antivari and
Dulcigno.

Abdul Hamid's reply was that so long as he lived he would
never consent to such a sacrifice. His reply was all the more
firm since his experience on the question of Armenian reform
had taught him that the Concert of Europe was not united.
In this he proved to be right, for when a naval demonstration
instigated by England, consisting of men-of-war belonging to
the various nations, appeared in the Adriatic, and Turkey still
refused to yield, the other Powers gradually withdrew their
ships till England was left alone to bully the Porte into submission. Optimism reigned at Yildiz: it was considered that
this time England had over-reached herself. She would never
dare to act alone, and her Ambassador would be recalled in
disgrace. The Sultan was even seen to smile in conversation
with his Foreign Minister. But the optimism of the palace
found no echo in the offices of the Sublime Porte. Carathéodory
had taken the measure of Mr. Goschen and recognised him as
a vain, ambitious man determined to make his mark. The
Government had given him full power to act and he was the
kind of man who would run the risk of war rather than go
back on his decisions.

Two days after the last of the Austrian ships had sailed away, Mr. Goschen asked for a private audience with the Sultan, as he had an important message which had to be delivered personally. The message was no less than an ultimatum. 'If His Majesty refused to give way, British ships would occupy an important, but unnamed port, in His Majesty's dominions.'

It was a tense moment as Sultan and Ambassador faced one another across the room. Even his dragoman noticed that the usually calm and self-confident Ambassador was trembling with emotion. The sinister atmosphere of Yildiz, the oppressive silence of rooms where no one dared to speak above a whisper, where servants and ministers stood with bowed heads, their hands folded across their chests in the presence of the Padishah and the only sounds were the number of clocks ticking in various cadences—all combined to upset the nerves. Crouched in an enormous golden chair was the Sultan, his feet resting on the sacred carpet no other foot could touch, his small nervous hands playing with the amber beads of his *tesbieh*. At first there was no intimation that he even heard the words spoken by Mr. Goschen, for it was fully five minutes before he answered, minutes which dragged like hours. Only the eyes from under their heavy lids blazed with a yellow, angry light. The lines round the hooked nose grew deeper, the full underlip pushed forward and the whole face became set and sullen. This must have been the moment when Abdul Hamid regretted the days when his ancestors committed a presumptuous ambassador to the prison of the Seven Towers, and not a single country had the power to raise a voice in protest.

When he spoke, the answer came clear and loud. Once more it was a definite 'No'. But Mr. Goschen was not going to allow himself to be intimidated and bluffed by a sick man dressed up in the trappings of the past. That very evening a message was signalled to the British fleet at anchor in the Adriatic to be ready to sail under sealed orders. No sooner was this message intercepted by the Turkish authorities at Dulcigno than it was transmitted to Yildiz, where the scene was very different from the previous morning.

Chaos and hysteria reigned supreme, dragomans came and went, white-faced ministers sat about in ante-rooms waiting for their orders, while soft-footed eunuchs passed in and out of the Sultan's rooms, the whites of their eyeballs showing in fear. The effort of controlling himself in front of the British Ambassador had been too much for the Sultan's nerves, he had now given way to a paroxysm of rage alternating with despair. At one moment he was heard to say that he would be happy if London were destroyed, as if he had only to give the word for the legions of Janissaries and the fleet of Suleyman to carry out his orders; at the next moment he was lamenting that his religion prevented him from giving up the heavy burden of his throne, for he would rather be a wandering dervish than be held responsible for the ruin of his empire. Neither his ministers nor his foster-mother were able to appease him and it was only after Mavroyeni had administered a sedative that he recovered sufficient control to read with calm the message from Dulcigno.

The British meant action. They were prepared to go ahead and occupy one of his own ports. He was probably astute enough to guess that the port in question would be Smyrna. Out of the past came memories of that windy day at Spithead with the great ironclads riding the waves, firing their guns in mock battle. Then it had been part of a show to impress the foreign visitors, but now these guns would be fired in earnest, shelling the fortifications of his finest harbour. Dawn was breaking when Mavroyeni, who had been spending the night in a room adjoining the Sultan's, was told to summon the Chief Secretary. A few hours later, in the glittering mid-day heat of the Adriatic, when the British ships were about to sail the Admiral was informed that a boat flying the Sultan's flag was coming from the shore with a man frantically waving a piece of paper. The paper contained the message that Abdul Hamid had given way.

Mr. Goschen had won his victory, but in those few hours he had succeeded in destroying all the good will his predecessors had so laboriously and in face of so many difficulties struggled to maintain between their country and the Porte. From that day all direct communications ceased between him and the Sultan. He was never again received in audience and the negotiations over the rectification of the Greek frontier which ended in the Porte ceding some land in Thessaly were conducted between him and the Foreign Minister.

Shut up in his palace, Abdul Hamid spent his days in brooding over the map of his empire. Carefully in his own hand he had marked out the losses suffered at Berlin. Thrace and Macedonia, Crete, the islands of the archipelago and the artificially created province of Eastern Rumelia, were all that remained of the great empire which once threatened the existence of Vienna. Even these torn and partitioned territories were only preserved through the jealousies of the Great Powers.

Abdul Hamid's principal bitterness was directed against England and this bitterness came to a climax when the Liberal Government made public in Parliament one of Sir Henry Layard's private despatches intended only for the eyes of the Queen and of the then Conservative Cabinet. Though most of the personal references to the Sultan were cut out, it nevertheless contained such frank and open criticism of Abdul Hamid, his ministers and his régime as to rouse him to a pitch of frenzy. The Turkish people were equally indignant, while the foreign ambassadors, and in particular the Russian, M. Nodikoff, were delighted at the opportunity of scoring off a former colleague of whose success they had always been jealous. No one was more indignant than Sir Henry Layard at what he regarded as a breach of trust, and it led to his permanent estrangement from the Liberal Party and to his premature retirement.

The parts of the despatch which the Sultan resented the most, were the references to Midhat Pasha as 'the one man who might have saved his country, if he had not been continually obstructed by the palace *camarilla*.' It had been shortly after Layard's visit to Syria that Midhat, seeing his efforts at reform systematically discouraged, had sent in his resignation as Governor. The Sultan, who suspected Layard of being instrumental in his having taken this decision, had at the time refused to accept it and Midhat was appointed to the post of Governor-General of the Vilayet of Smyrna.

Abdul Hamid had not yet made any concrete plans for ridding himself of his ex-Vizir when, in March 1881, two separate events far removed from one another finally decided his actions.

In Russia, his old enemy, Alexander II, was assassinated by Nihilists and the murder of a fellow monarch was sufficient to reduce the Sultan to a state of abject terror. In his eyes revolutionaries and constitutionalists were the same thing and the fears which had been dormant since the time of Ali Suavi's revolt once more obtained the mastery. For days he would only touch food prepared by his foster-mother or go to bed at night after the woman who shared his bed had searched every cranny for a hidden bomb. He was in this abnormal frame of mind when he welcomed Abdul Aziz's former minister, Mahmud Nedim, on his return to Constantinople after many years of banishment. For though Mahmud more than anyone else had been responsible for his country's financial ruin, he had the one great asset of being Midhat's bitterest enemy.

The Sultan was only too ready to listen to Mahmud's story of how the late Sultan Abdul Aziz had died not from self-inflicted wounds but at the hands of a gang of assassins hired by Midhat and His Majesty's brother-in-law, Mahmud Djelaleddin, and that there were living witnesses who could prove the truth of this assertion. His Majesty had only to visit the ex-Valide now living in retirement at the Old Seraglio and he would find that Pertevniyal Sultan was of a very different opinion than when in the first moment of distracted grief she had believed herself to be guilty of her son's death.

It was a cold March day and an icy wind was blowing from the Black Sea. Under sunless skies the cupolas of Stamboul seemed to crush the city under their weight of lead while the cypress groves hung a heavy pall over the cemeteries which stretched down to the Golden Horn. It was a bleak, depressing day and the Sultan shivered in his sable-lined coat as he drove through the narrow cobbled streets which led from the Galata Bridge past the offices of the Sublime Porte to the gates of the Topkapou Palace. The gardens were silent and deserted, only the wind stirred the dead leaves no one had troubled to brush away, whistling among the tangled rose bushes and broken tiles of neglected courtyards. Everything about the palace, and in particular the harem quarters, had the same air of hopelessness and decay. But no sooner had the Sultan passed through the former 'Gates of Felicity' than the whole of a dying world suddenly came to life. Here were gathered together the survivors of three reigns, toothless old hags who had known the caresses of the great Mahmud, middle-aged women still bearing the traces of the beauty which had attracted the fickle Medjid, others still young and fresh from the harem of Abdul Aziz, living in hope of a marriage to some sheikh or pasha of the Sultan's choice; but he came so rarely to the Old Seraglio and there were already so many superfluous women in his own harem at Yildiz.

The wave of excitement rose to a crescendo at the Padishah's approach. Even the oldest turned to their mirrors and put on their finest jewels, but he passed through the courtyard looking neither to right nor left, and the chill of his indifference communicated itself to young and old. ·

Pertevniyal Sultan lived apart, as befitted her position of ex-Valide. Abdul Hamid had offered her her own palace, but she had preferred to retire to the familiar scenes of her youth, to these gardens to which Mahmud had brought her from the mean streets of Stamboul. Even in retirement she had still the opportunity to intrigue and in recent weeks her former protégé, Mahmud Nedim, had been seen hanging around the courtyard of the Mahmudieh Mosque during her hours of prayer. She had been only too ready to believe the story which exonerated her from any share of guilt in her son's death and soon she was fully convinced that a gardener and an ex-wrestler, both acting under Midhat's orders, had been introduced into the palace of Cheragan, where they had succeeded in murdering her son. Mahmud Nedim's story was both skilfully and ingeniously told and Pertevniyal was a garrulous and imaginative old woman. By the time of Abdul Hamid's visit she fully believed that when the holy men were preparing her son's body for the tomb she herself had noticed a tiny mark above the heart, which could only have been the wound of a stiletto.

It was not often that she had the honour of the Sultan's visit and the black eyes in the fat, waxy face gleamed with pleasure as Abdul Hamid bent low over her crinkled peasant's hand, begging her forgiveness at having to resurrect such painful memories. It was characteristic of him to listen rather than to talk, to let others weave the webs in which to ensnare his enemies, and he listened patiently to that hoarse old voice describing in every detail the story he had already heard.

He was in a good mood when he left the Topkapou Palace and the eunuchs were ordered to distribute the contents of a bag of gold among the horde of clamouring women. As the gates closed behind him, the last flicker of hope was extinguished, the finery was discarded and the inhabitants relapsed once more to their peevish quarrelling. The Sultan returned to Yildiz and the same evening Mahmud Nedim was summoned to his presence and invested with his new appointment as Minister of the Interior. Six weeks later it was publicly announced that Midhat Pasha, the Sultan's brother-in-law Mahmud Damad Pasha and the former Sheikh ul Islam, Hayrullah Effendi, together with two aides-de-camp and an ex-wrestler and gardener, all attached to the service of the late Sultan, had been arrested and were to be put on trial for the murder of their sovereign.

Chapter XXII

THE WEEK OF THE opening of the State Trial coincided with Mr. Goschen's departure from Constantinople on what he himself regarded as the successful conclusion of his mission, though not all the members of the British Cabinet appear to have shared this view. In spite of Mr. Gladstone's personal feeling towards the Turks, Great Britain's foreign policy still adhered to the principle of preserving the Ottoman Empire and to help in healing some of the unnecessary wounds inflicted by the Hon. Member for Ripon. Queen Victoria now appointed as her Ambassador to the Porte, the Earl of Dufferin, one of the most brilliant and experienced of her great pro-consuls. As a young man Lord Dufferin had gained his first experience in the East when Lord Palmerston sent him to conduct an investigation into the massacres in the Lebanon and he had already then shown that extraordinary tact and flair in dealing with men of different races and religions which were to distinguish him in after life. He was not only a man of great ability, but of enormous charm, and he was to require all his tact and charm in the job which now awaited him in Constantinople.

At the time of Lord Dufferin's arrival, the forthcoming State Trials were the one topic of conversation both in the drawing-rooms of Pera and the coffee houses of Stamboul. Young men who had come to believe in a constitutional government and the liberty of the Press now read with disgust the newspaper articles directly inspired by Yildiz, denouncing as guilty, men who had not yet been tried; while in their *yalis* on the Bosphorus the rich pashas shook in their shoes, for the Sultan had not hesitated to send his own brother-in-law to the dock and no one knew whose turn would come next.

Great pains had been taken to give the impression that the trial was being conducted legally, and both the embassy dragomans and the representatives of the foreign Press were

invited to be present. For greater security it took place not in
the ordinary law courts in Stamboul, but in one of the kiosks
of Yildiz, where Midhat and Mahmud were already imprisoned. The improvised courtroom was packed throughout
the proceedings, and witness after witness, starting with the
two self-confessed murderers—the wrestler and the gardener
of Cheragan—was called on to reconstruct the story of the
ex-Sultan's murder. Piece by piece the evidence compiled
by Midhat's enemies mounted to a gigantic indictment
against him, till finally it was the turn of the defence. Arrogant
to the end, the Sultan's brother-in-law refused to say a word
in his defence, but Midhat put up a brave and spirited fight until
he realised there was to be no cross-examination and that the
verdict was a foregone conclusion. With the exception of one
courageous *ulema*, all the judges declared the prisoners to be
guilty and condemned them to death.

Later it was asserted that the courts were packed and that
the judges were in the Sultan's pay. But to this day it has never
been entirely proved that Midhat had no part in Abdul Aziz's
death.

Three days after the conclusion of the trial an impartial
observer, Lord Dufferin, wrote to his friend and cousin,
Sir Clare Ford:

> Taking the most indulgent view, this trial seems to have been
> very clumsily conducted, even as regards the less important
> prisoners, and Midhat s condemnation was quite unjustified by
> the meagre evidence advanced against him. Many seem to
> believe there has been no murder at all, and that the whole
> thing has been trumped up by the Sultan with a view of
> getting rid of Midhat and discrediting his predecessor Murad.
> It is impossible to form an absolute opinion from the scanty
> reports of the proceedings furnished by the pashas and the
> dragomans. Doctor Dickson in very clear and precise language
> demonstrated to me the other day that it must have been
> suicide but I have great doubts on the point. I am inclined to
> think that most of the accused are guilty and I should not be
> surprised to learn that Midhat had been mixed up with it, but
> for the present it is a clear matter of conjecture and I am going
> to endeavour to prevent the execution of the capital sentence,
> which would be scandalous in the circumstances.

Lord Dufferin was not alone in appealing for clemency. This time the Concert of Europe acted together and prevailed upon the Sultan to reduce the death sentence to banishment for life. Abdul Hamid was magnanimous but his clemency cost him nothing. Men condemned to banishment in the Arabian Desert very soon welcomed death, and when Midhat and his fellow prisoners were sent to Taif, in the neighbourhood of Mecca, their friends and families had little hope of their return.

The Sultan had remained invisible throughout the trial, leaving his people to judge the criminals who had dared to conspire against God's Vice-Regent upon Earth. The proceedings were never even referred to in his presence, but his doctor noticed a sudden improvement in his health and nerves from the moment he heard that Midhat had arrived in Taif. For a short while he gave the impression of being at peace. The *djournals* of his spies were relegated to the files, and on one or two occasions he even ventured beyond his palace gates and was seen in public at popular resorts such as the Sweet Waters of Europe or of Asia. This amiable mood was reflected in his foreign policy. He appeared to have settled his differences with England, and Lord Dufferin was received with the exquisite politeness he could command at will. The fact of Lord Dufferin being an Irishman seems to have recommended him in the Sultan's eyes. Having visited England in the year of the Fenian Rising, Abdul Hamid was under the illusion that an Irishman would be less intransigent in upholding England's interests. And for a few months, Sultan and Ambassador set out to charm one another till the storm clouds gathering over Egypt destroyed this idyllic relationship.

Egypt had always been regarded by the Ottoman sultans as the fairest jewel in their crown from the days when Selim I conquered the country and, by defeating the Mameluke sultan and deposing and pensioning off the last of the Abbassid caliphs, established his own claim to the Caliphate. It had been a bitter day for Ottoman pride and prestige when the presumptuous vassal, Mehmet Ali, obtained by force the hereditary pashalik of Egypt, though officially the Sultan still remained the suzerain or overlord. Under the irresponsible

Abdul Aziz, the Khedive Ismail had been able to extend his authority by judicious bribes and extravagant presents, but the vast sums spent in buying his independence and in making Egypt into a modern state contributed to his financial ruin. The Khedive's bankruptcy brought European control to Egypt—a control resented in Cairo and almost equally resented in Constantinople. Abdul Hamid had come to the throne determined to win back the rights of suzerainty forfeited by his predecessor. It was not only his temporal powers, but his spiritual powers as Caliph, which were at stake. Cairo was one of the great centres of the Islamic world. Some of the oldest shrines of worship were in the Libyan Desert. When in 1879 the Khedive Ismail staged a *coup d'état* and dismissed the European ministers forced on him by the Great Powers, his rash, unpremeditated action is said to have been secretly supported by the Sultan. But Ismail had played his last card; the Powers, in particular England and France, were prepared for action. The Valley of the Nile had become too important for them to leave it in the hands of a wildly extravagant despot, and backed by the various foreign bondholders, they now insisted on the Khedive abdicating in favour of his son Tevfik.

Abdul Hamid was in a quandary. To allow England and France to nominate one of his own vassals would lower him in the eyes of his subjects and millions of Moslems throughout the world: to act independently and revert to the old Ottoman laws of succession by appointing the Prince Halim, the last surviving son of Mehmet Ali, as Khedive would involve him in a quarrel with the Powers. Fortunately for the Sultan, Carathéodory was still his Foreign Minister and the subtle, accommodating Greek persuaded him that the only possible solution was to act immediately and to send a telegram to Tevfik conferring on him the right of succession and at the same time to notify this decision to his ambassadors in Paris and London. In this way there would be no loss of face and his people need never learn that he had again been forced to submit to the dictation of Europe.

England was not yet committed to any definite policy in Egypt and was ready to welcome Abdul Hamid's co-operation and to treat him as the lawful suzerain. France, on the other hand, was opposed to anything which might tend to enhance the Sultan's prestige in North Africa. As for Abdul Hamid, he distrusted France and England equally and to disentangle the devious threads of his Egyptian policy we must look behind the official façade of Yildiz, the elaborate dinner parties served *à la franca* gleaming with Sèvres and golden plate, attended by prominent Levantines and ministers with a gloss of Parisian culture. We must penetrate beyond those mirrored halls with the rows of stiff gold chairs, to the twisted corridors and small cell-like rooms inhabited by men who fostered prejudice and superstition, sheikhs and *mollas*, dervishes and astrologers, all who, in a lesser or greater degree, enjoyed the Sultan's confidence and by professing to guide his soul, controlled his political actions.

The fact that Abdul Hamid was not really religious at heart, but wished to give the impression of being so, made him particularly susceptible to religious influences. And in the past two years his ministers had been watching with a growing distrust the comings and goings of a tall young man with the transparent eyes of a visionary, wearing the green turban of a descendant of the Prophet. A native of Aleppo, by name Abul Huda, he had arrived for the first time in Constantinople towards the end of the Russian War and, through the aid of one of his compatriots, had gained access to the Sultan. Mysticism and theology were in his blood, for he could claim descent both from the Prophet and from the famous twelfth-century mystic, Al Sayid Al Rifai, the founder of the Rifai, or Dancing Dervishes, one of the most esoteric and fanatical of all the hundred sects of Islam. He came to the palace with a mission, determined to be heard, and in Abdul Hamid he found a man who was already prepared for his message.

He spoke to the Sultan not only in the name of the Arab world, but in the name of the whole of Islam. What were a few lost provinces in Europe when in the teeming ports of the Indian Ocean and the farthest Pacific island millions of pious Moslems still looked to their Caliph for guidance? In his soft insidious voice Abul Huda conjured up in the Sultan's imagination the great dream of Pan-Islam; of a vast spiritual empire opposed to the material forces of the West.

The idea had been vaguely germinating in Abdul Hamid's mind since the early days of his accession. Providing he paid lip service to his Caliph any itinerant scholar from Bengal or Mongol chief from Turkestan could always be sure of finding food and lodging at the Sultan's expense. In conversation with certain ambassadors, in particular the British, Abdul Hamid had on more than one occasion referred to the great religious forces at his command. But it was Abul Huda who first brought the dream into the realm of power politics, and in 1881, at the time of the Egyptian crisis, he was among the Sultan's closest and most intimate counsellors, though officially his post was merely that of religious connotator and lecturer on Moslem beliefs and traditions.

The story of the Arabi revolt in Egypt and its consequences is familiar history. It was mainly a nationalist movement directed against European control and the turcophile or Circassian pashas. With the slogan 'Egypt for the Egyptians' it swept the country, till England and France found themselves committed either to interfere in the internal affairs of the country, or else to abandon all they had worked to accomplish in the past five years and run the risk of causing a financial panic in Paris and London. But though the Powers knew that in the end they would have to come to the help of the weak and helpless Khedive, they could not agree as to the means by which intervention was possible. England (and this time even Mr. Gladstone) seems to have considered that, as suzerain of Egypt, it was the Sultan first and foremost who should be called in to re-establish the authority of the Khedive, whereas France, with her interests in Tunis and Algeria, was at all costs determined to prevent Turkish troops from reappearing in North Africa. This fundamental difference between the two policies was to be largely responsible for the shaping of events. If the Khedive, backed by England and France, had been allowed to appeal openly to the Sultan, Abdul Hamid would in all probability have seized this opportunity of reasserting his authority and gone to the assistance of his weakened vassal. But this full co-operation was not asked for till six months later and in these intervening months the sequence of events all tended to confuse the situation even more.

Unable to resist the popular movement, the Khedive had been forced to accept Arabi as his Minister of War. There had been the usual note of protest from England and France, a note which not only committed them to future intervention, but succeeded in antagonising all classes of the Egyptian population. There had been the usual appeal to the Concert of Europe, where both Prince Bismarck and the Czar had shown an exceptional benevolence towards the principle of Anglo-French intervention; Prince Bismarck because he hoped it might distract France from concentrating on Alsace-Lorraine and eventually cause friction between her and England, and the Czar because he was relieved to see that England was concentrating her Eastern policy in the direction of the Suez Canal rather than the Straits. Still faithful to the policy of dual control, an Anglo-French fleet staged a naval demonstration in front of Alexandria which led to rioting throughout the country. Meanwhile the French Government had fallen. Monsieur Gambetta, the protagonist of joint intervention, had been succeeded by Monsieur Freyceynet, who in common with the majority of his countrymen did not believe that France was in a position to indulge in Eastern adventures. On June 1, 1882, he announced in the French Chamber: 'that under no circumstances would his country be committed to any military intervention in Egypt.' A few days later the French ships set sail from Alexandria, leaving the Royal Navy to deal alone with a situation which was rapidly developing into anarchy.

It was only after the desertion of France, the failure of an Ambassadors' conference in Constantinople, a conference, incidentally, which the Turks had refused to attend, only after the British fleet had bombarded Alexandria and Europeans were being massacred in the streets, that the Sultan was invited in the name of the Concert of Europe to send troops into Egypt. One can hardly blame Abdul Hamid if in the circumstances he hesitated in taking a decision which might prejudice his position as Caliph.

When, at the very beginning of the trouble, the Khedive had suggested that the Sultan should send a commission to enquire into the situation, Abdul Hamid had very characteristically sent not one, but two, commissioners, the one openly credited to the Khedive, the other secretly accredited to Arabi. Unknown to his ministers, he even corresponded with the nationalist leader. Underestimating the strength of the movement, he had been optimistic enough to believe that Arabi might be persuaded to play the role of the champion of Islam and to win back Egypt for his Caliph. It was only when the nationalists started a purge of the Turkish elements in the country that Abdul Hamid was finally persuaded that there was no advantage to be gained from supporting the rebels.

After the failure of the conference of Ambassadors, the Egyptian problem became mainly a British concern. An expeditionary force was already on its way, but to the very end the Liberal Government adhered to the principle of Anglo-Turkish co-operation. The ambiguity of Abdul Hamid's attitude necessitated certain guarantees. First it must be made quite clear that once his troops had entered Egypt, they would neither join forces with Arabi nor, once the Khedive's authority had been restored, refuse to leave the country, and in order to avert these dangers, the Sultan was to be asked to sign two documents. The first was a proclamation denouncing Arabi and his followers, the second was a military convention, which was to define the scope, duration and conditions of the Anglo-Turkish occupation.

Assisting Lord Dufferin in these intricate and delicate negotiations was his young secretary and brother-in-law, Arthur Nicolson, and, in his brilliant biography of his father, Sir Harold Nicolson has described those eventful days of August-September 1882 during which Abdul Hamid made the greatest mistake of his career which eventually led to the British occupation of Egypt.

Sir Harold writes:

> The Sultan hesitated to sign either of these documents. He was afraid that if he publicly repudiated Arabi, he would lose his prestige with the Islamic world. He was afraid that if he signed with Great Britain a convention, limiting his right of intervention in Egypt, all hope of re-establishing his direct authority over his vassal would be gone for ever. Abdul Hamid was correct in both these apprehensions. Where he made his

mistake was in not realising that the British Government were at last determined on action, and that when once the wheels of action are set moving in England, they are exceedingly difficult to stop.

It was with the utmost difficulty that Said Pasha persuaded the Sultan to accept the idea that joint-intervention should be subject to certain agreed conditions. Even when he finally accepted the idea, he still continued to procrastinate and vacillate, changing first one document, then the next; offering to sign the one while refusing to sign the other; listening to a multitude of counsellors who all gave him contradictory advice: summoning Valentine Baker to the palace as the one Englishman he could really trust and, no sooner had he left, receiving whoever was the most opposed to the principle of Anglo-Turkish co-operation. Meanwhile Turkish troops were assembled in Crete, waiting to proceed to Egypt the moment the convention was signed. Time was running short. A British force was already in Egypt and Arabi had declared a *jehad* or holy war. On September 6, Abdul Hamid ordered a completely false version of the draft proclamation to be published in the papers and Lord Dufferin, justifiably enraged at this 'inconceivable lack of good faith', refused to accept the apologies of the Porte. Seeing that his master had gone too far, Said now begged the Sultan to come to a decision and finally, on September 15, Lord Dufferin was informed that both the convention and proclamation had, except for a few details, been agreed to in their final form.

Sir Harold Nicolson recounts that at 3 p.m. on that day the Ambassador, together with his secretary, proceeded to Yildiz for a last interview with the Sultan. Further conditions were raised and Abdul Hamid suggested that these conditions should be negotiated with his ministers.

For five hours Lord Dufferin used all his powers of persuasion, those powers he had inherited from his great ancestor Sheridan, to induce the Turkish ministers to agree to the convention in the only form in which he himself would consent to sign. The brilliant summer day faded into twilight and still they were unable to come to a decision. At nine o'clock the ministers left to hold a second interview with the Sultan, while the Ambassador and his secretary were served with elaborate refreshments and coffee in jewelled cups. At ten o'clock the discussions were resumed and by midnight there was hope of the Sultan's signing before dawn. Once more Said and the Foreign Minister, Assim Pasha, disappeared behind the mirrored doors which led to the Sultan's study. The hundred palace clocks struck 1 a.m. and at 1.15, what Nicolson describes as 'the sinister figure of the Sultan's astrologer was seen creeping across the anteroom towards his master's room.' It was Abul Huda, who throughout the negotitaions had been using all his influence to prevent the Sultan from signing a proclamation which would damage him in the eyes of the Arab world. To the diplomats of Pera he was nothing more than an astrologer, an agent in the pay of the anti-British party, and they knew that his appearance meant the negotiations had failed.

Twenty minutes later Said and Assim reappeared. 'His Majesty was unable to approve the compromise agreed to and further discussions would be required.' It was now 1.45 a.m., and for nearly eleven hours Lord Dufferin and his secretary had been sitting on stiff gilt chairs, hoping to the end that wisdom and moderation would prevail in the Sultan's councils. Now the Ambassador's patience was at an end, even Said's last desperate appeal failed to move him. Tired and discouraged, he drove down to the Bosphorus where a launch was waiting to take him back to the summer Embassy. Here to his surprise he found the lights still blazing in the chancery. A secretary was waiting on the quay with a ciphered telegram in his hand. It was a telegram which had arrived nine hours before and which, for some unknown reason, the head of the chancery had failed to send on to Yildiz. It told Lord Dufferin not to sign the convention without further instructions as that very morning of September 15, British forces had completely defeated Arabi at Tel El Kebir.

Late that afternoon Said Pasha arrived at Therapia to say that his master was now anxious to sign. In his quiet, almost diffident fashion, Lord Dufferin replied that it was now too late. He knew only too well that no explanations or assurances would ever make either Abdul Hamid or his ministers, or even his diplomatic colleagues, believe that he had ever been anything more than playing with the Sultan, till the British troops had obtained a single-handed decision. With a rueful smile he added, 'His Majesty's hesitation of yesterday has made my reputation as a diplomatist but ruined it as an honest man.'

Chapter XXIII

THE ENGLISH OCCUPATION of Egypt was a blow from which Abdul Hamid was never to recover. All the assurances as to the temporary nature of the occupation and the acknowledgement of his continued suzerainty failed to convince him of the sincerity of England's intentions. From now on he feared her more than he feared Russia, hating while admiring her statesmen for their duplicity and guile, talents of which they themselves were quite unaware. He did not dare to show open hostility and in public still spoke of England as a country whose friendship he had always sought and done his best to maintain, but he was delighted whenever an occasion arose of acting against her interests, and the French Ambassador found him a willing ally in fomenting the intrigues by which France, jealous of England's success in Egypt, was trying to undermine her authority. Both Lord Dufferin and the British India Office were aware of the secret encouragement given by the Sultan to the rebellious Pathan tribesmen on the North-West Frontier, of the vast sums spent on religious propaganda in Egypt and the Sudan, of the strengthening of the Turkish garrison in the Sinai Peninsula and the Persian Gulf—all pinpricks—some of them dangerous, some of them merely irritating, directed against Britain's Imperial interests.

Abdul Hamid made no attempt to find a scapegoat for the failure of his policy in Egypt, for the one man who might have been held responsible had made himself too indispensable to be dismissed. With his knowledge of the Arab world and its religious institutions, Abul Huda was able to place the Sultan's agents in every important *tekke** and *medressé* of the Empire and to act as a link between his master and the sheikhs of Syria and Arabia. In a short space of time he had established himself as a kind of *Grey Eminence* whose position it was impossible to define and whose influence it was difficult to gauge

* *Tekke*—A monastery.

and for over ten years he continued to dominate the secret counsels of Yildiz, until he was finally supplanted by the Arab, Izzet, whom he himself had introduced into the palace.

Whether Abul Huda was genuine or a charlatan, his conception of Pan-Islam bore the hallmark of genius. In spite of its anti-European bias, it was primarily a defensive movement, its object being firstly to enhance the prestige of Abdul Hamid, both within and beyond his frontiers, and secondly to cause embarrassment to Powers possessing Moslem subjects, whenever they tried to adopt a policy inimical to Turkish interests. It was only later, when German influence began to increase in the Ottoman Empire, and still more so when the young German Kaiser became Abdul Hamid's only European friend and protector, that Pan-Islam became more aggressive in policy, and by then it was Izzet rather than Abul Huda, who inspired the decisions of Yildiz.

In the 1880's Abul Huda was at the height of his fame and honours and decorations showered on him. Believing in his visionary powers and gifts of prophecy, the Sultan would summon him at all hours of the day or night, either to interpret a disturbing dream or to define a difficult passage of the Koran. The pashas of the Porte were justifiably indignant when important decisions were postponed to the day which Abul Huda declared to be auspicious, but the person who resented him even more was the Sultan's doctor. In Mavroyeni's opinion, all these exalted dreams and visions, this dabbling in the occult, had a disastrous effect on his nervous and unstable patient. Abdul Hamid's health was once more causing concern, for the brief improvement which had followed on Midhat's banishment had lasted only a few months. The Egyptian crisis had brought on again those paroxysms of rage alternating with melancholia which resulted in ever-recurring fainting fits and nervous disorders which reduced him to little more than a skeleton.

It was not only the Sultan's physical, but also his mental, condition which was worrying Mavroyeni. He had taken again to the reading of those pernicious *djournals* with their accounts of revolutionary conspiracies and attempted assassinations foiled by the efforts of those who called themselves his loyal servants. The enmity for England he did not dare to show brought other hated images to mind; political fears degenerated into private ones, for the barred gates of Cheragan could not prevent certain rumours from leaking out. It was said that the ex-Sultan Murad's health was gradually improving, and that he now enjoyed long periods of lucidity, periods which might have been even longer had it not been for the champagne and *raki* so lavishly supplied from the cellars of Yildiz. It was several years since Abdul Hamid had visited Cheragan, but the memory of a sad and vacant face came back to haunt him in the sleepless nights and, while Murad haunted his nights, Midhat began to obsess his days. The protracted martyrdom of his imprisonment in Taif could no longer satisfy the Sultan's passion for revenge; in his imagination Abdul Hamid already saw the English plotting Midhat's escape, perhaps even planning to employ him in Egypt. Who knows as to what secret agreement Midhat and Layard may have reached in Damascus on that journey which the British Ambassador had assured the Porte had been purely one of archaeological interest? These suspicions gradually assumed such alarming proportions in the Sultan's mind that Mavroyeni wondered as to whether Midhat's death might not be the only way of curing his patient.

Others less scrupulous than Mavroyeni were of the same opinion. Abdul Hamid was in the habit of confiding in his eunuchs whom he trusted in a way he never trusted any normal man, and they, in return for these confidences, made it their business to interpret and carry out his most secret wishes. He had only to lament the wickedness of Midhat and wonder why Allah allowed such wretches to survive, for His Highness the Kizlar Agasi to record these words and transmit them by secret code to the Turkish authorities at Taif. On May 18, 1883, a telegram arrived at Yildiz announcing that on the previous night their Highnesses Midhat Pasha and Damad Mahmud Pasha had both succumbed to an epidemic of typhoid fever.

The Sultan had been well served, but the servants had been over-zealous in carrying out his orders. A double death aroused suspicion and in private Abdul Hamid was heard to complain that, as usual, the fools had blundered. It was a mistake to have included Mahmud, though his brother-in-law's death was hardly to be regretted. During the war he had shown himself to be both a traitor and a coward and the news caused the Sultan no more than a temporary irritation. All that really mattered was that Midhat was dead and that at last he could feel secure upon his throne. That night there was no need for Dr. Mavroyeni to administer a sleeping draught, for his patient slept as peacefully as a child.

The news of the deaths at Taif was received with scepticism both in Turkey and abroad. But it was not until many weeks later that a letter written by one of Midhat's fellow prisoners, reached his family, saying, 'His Highness did not succumb to the illness from which he was suffering. The truth is that in the same night, and at the same moment, both Midhat and Mahmud Pasha were strangled.'

There is another story which asserts that Abdul Hamid was not entirely satisfied as to the proof of Midhat's death till the day when a mysterious case, labelled *'Japanese Ivories—to be personally delivered to His Majesty, the Sultan'*, arrived from Taif, which on being opened was found to contain the embalmed head of Midhat Pasha. It is as ghoulish and fantastic a story as any out of the *Thousand and One Nights*, and in all probability, just as fictitious, for had he believed it to be true Midhat's son could never have been persuaded to make friends with Abdul Hamid. Only a few years after his father's death, one hears of Haidar Midhat not only being received at Yildiz, but actually accepting favours from the Sultan.

Nevertheless the story of the Japanese ivories was all too readily believed in those later years when the germ of insanity bred by fear had developed in the Sultan's brain to an extent where he was able to contemplate in cold blood the massacre of thousands of his subjects.

But in the early 1880's those mental aberrations which were gradually to warp his character and distort his mind could still be defined as eccentricities. The hallucinations of the night had not yet become the realities of the day, and to his European visitors Abdul Hamid gave the impression of a man moderate and balanced in his judgment and open to friendly criticism. He was sufficiently in touch with modern times to give interviews not only to Ambassadors, but to any foreign visitor whom he thought likely to influence public opinion in his country. Unfortunately, his ignorance of Europe and of European personalities put him at the mercy of the various Levantines who served as liaison between the palace and the foreign embassies. The visitor to Constantinople who wished to have an audience with Abdul Hamid found that he had a far greater chance of success by cultivating the friendship of these sometimes dubious characters, rather than by producing a letter of introduction for the Grand Vizir who, whether he happened to be Said or one of his rivals, was usually far too nervous of his master to risk getting involved with foreigners.

The Times correspondent, Henry de Blowitz, who arrived in Constantinople as a passenger on the first train from Vienna, gives an amusing account of the machinations and intrigues which preceded an audience with the Sultan. He had not been in the city twenty-four hours before he discovered that it was easier to enter Yildiz by the back door rather than by the front, that neither letters of introduction to the Grand Vizir, nor the recommendation of his ambassador were of any use and that the men who, for some reason or other, enjoyed the Sultan's confidence were to be found in the back streets of Pera and the counting-houses of Galata, rather than in the great *yalis* on the Bosphorus. Ironically enough it was one of the despised Armenians—the editor of the Sultan's newspaper *Vakit*—who after a week of incessant lobbying and intrigue finally procured him an invitation to assist at the Friday *selamlik*, which was to take place in the newly completed Hamidieh Mosque; and the first intimation he received of this being more than the normal polite gesture extended to any distinguished foreigner was when Said Pasha broke his silence and invited him to his house on the same day.

In the later years of his life, Abdul Hamid's fears rarely allowed him to venture beyond the small white mosque adjoining the barracks of Yildiz, from where de Blowitz now watched the ceremony of the Sultan going to prayer. It was an impressive sight, with the blue uniforms and scarlet fezzes of the infantry contrasting with the green and silver of the cavalry, the flowing cloaks and turbans of the zouaves with the white *fustanella* and embroidered jackets of the Albanian Guards—the men and horses so superbly disciplined as to remain almost immobile throughout the ceremony.

The whole hillside was alive with people—little family groups squatting on the grass (for no good Moslem dared to prevent his wives and children from assisting at the ceremony), all waiting for the moment when the gates of Yildiz would open and the Sultan, seated in an open landau, come slowly down the hill preceded by two closed broughams carrying the chief ladies of the harem. It was only a matter of minutes before he disappeared into the mosque, minutes in which the pent-up excitement of the crowd broke out in loud, enthusiastic cheering.

But was the Sultan really at prayer? de Blowitz asked his neighbour, Dr. Mavroyeni, as they shared a window seat in a drawing-room which was part of the guard-house. Once in this room one automatically became the Sultan's guest, and an *irade* had just reached de Blowitz, ordering him to be ready to proceed to Yildiz as soon as the *selamlik* was over.

'No, the Sultan was not at prayer,' Mavroyeni hastened to enlighten him on what was merely one of a thousand European errors. The mosque was not entirely consecrated to prayer; many things were discussed there, and the *selamlik* existed for no other reason than to give the people the opportunity of seeing their Sultan once a week. It was not merely by chance that de Blowitz had the Sultan's doctor for a neighbour. Mavroyeni was not only there to enlighten this foreigner on Turkish customs, but to bring the subject round to the much discussed question of his master's health. Certain unpleasant rumours had to be discredited and, giving the impression that he knew nothing of the invitation to Yildiz, he regretted that de Blowitz had not seen the Sultan, for then he would have been able to discount the stupid untruths which were told about him. He would have judged for himself how sound his mind was, how just he was and how healthy too. People said he had all kinds of diseases—that he had scrofula and was subject to fainting fits. It was infamous, considering that he who was the Sultan's doctor had never seen him ill. In fact, he could describe himself as his master's most expensive luxury.

One can detect the irony behind the sycophantic words which Mavroyeni can never have expected to be believed. Yet, for all their exaggeration, they seem to have made an impression, for when the *selamlik* was over and de Blowitz found himself in the Sultan's presence, he saw him as a man still young in years, virile both in voice and gesture and in his description of Abdul Hamid, written only a few weeks after Midhat Pasha's death, there is no trace of the trembling neurotic who murdered out of fear.

The Sultan, who received him in a small room furnished in European fashion, greeted him with a charming informality. In this close proximity the journalist was able to note every detail of Abdul Hamid's appearance: 'the brown skin, warm and dry looking, the short thick well-groomed black beard, the mouth which seemed sad but resolute, the wide straight forehead slightly furrowed, which made him look older than his years, and the large black eyes set deep in their sockets, their expression not gentle, but thoughtful and penetrating.' His voice was louder than that of the majority of his subjects, each word distinct, each sentence spoken without the slightest hesitation.

Mavroyeni had set out to impress the foreign visitor by giving him a rosy picture of the Sultan's health. Abdul Hamid now spoke in defence not only of himself, but of his country, 'the sick man of Europe, whom so many judge to be incurable but who, to the annoyance of his enemies, was rapidly recovering.' De Blowitz had been at Berlin and had been able to judge for himself not only the mistakes committed by the Turks (and Abdul Hamid was the first to acknowledge these mistakes) but the lack of generosity on the part of the Great Powers.

There was pathos in the Sultan's tone when he spoke of the humiliations imposed on him at Berlin, the sacrifices from which he was still suffering, 'As if Bulgaria and Thessaly were any happier at present than they were before their separation.'

But the mistakes committed at Berlin belonged to the past. Egypt was now the vital question and throughout the interview, whatever was under discussion, whether it was a question of education or of financial or political reform, Abdul Hamid always managed to bring the conversation round to Egypt. 'Was the British Government disposed to evacuate, and when?' It was an awkward question, and de Blowitz could do no more than hint that public opinion, which had to be stimulated, when England was obliged to go alone into Egypt on a costly and dangerous expedition, might be against immediate evacuation but that in spite of this Turkey could continue to have confidence in the friendship both of England and of France.

'And in the meantime, neither France nor England has hesitated to violate my rights.' The Sultan was referring not only to Egypt, but to the French occupation of Tunis. For though he was ready to collaborate with France in her anti-British campaign in Egypt, he could not forgive her for denying his right of suzerainty in North Africa. Encouraged by the Sultan's frankness and simplicity, de Blowitz reminded him of Turkey's terrible blunder in refusing to send troops into Egypt. But this time he had gone too far. Abdul Hamid had been ready to acknowledge the faults committed at Berlin, to listen to his criticisms of absolute government, and even to accept his suggestions for reform, but in attacking Turkey's Egyptian policy, *The Times'* correspondent was attacking him in person. The subject was changed abruptly, and by asking his visitor how long he intended to stay in Constantinople, the Sultan intimated that the interview was over. Even so he remained the *charmeur*, assuring his visitor that he valued his opinion and would be grateful for his friendship, asking him to write to him on topics of current interest and promising to answer unless decisions of State prevented him from doing so. On saying goodbye, he accompanied him to the door, taking his hand in his and holding it for a few moments, one of his favourite gestures when he put himself out to please; for the sacredness of his person was so deeply ingrained in his nature that he regarded it as one of the highest honours if he as much as touched a hand.

It had been a fascinating experience for the journalist to see the legend of Yildiz materialised in a simple, unassuming man. For the Sultan it had been an interlude, pleasurable on the whole, giving him the opportunity of employing all his talent of charming, impressing, perhaps even of convincing. It had been a brief escape from boredom, from the eulogies of sycophants, the frightened acquiescence of his ministers. One side of his curious, complex nature rebelled against the loneliness of his position and yearned for friendship and for understanding. In speaking to *The Times'* correspondent, he had adopted an attitude of pride and self-defence, but underlying the pride was a last plea for England's friendship, a friendship he wanted on his own terms and which, when offered in all sincerity, he had failed to accept. Confused, misled and betrayed by the conflicting elements in his entourage, he was gradually to turn to Germany as the one country which had asked nothing at Berlin and from where he thought there was nothing to fear.

Chapter XXIV

I T WAS THE END of October 1889 and Constantinople was
preparing for an Imperial visit; the town re-echoed to the
hammers of stonemasons and the crashing of timber, roads
were being repaved, broken walls rebuilt, crumbling ruins
patched up with plaster and with paint, for it was not every
day that the Sultan received the visit of a fellow sovereign.
It was all the more flattering, as the young Emperor of
Germany had barely been a year upon the throne and had
insisted on this journey in face of Prince Bismarck's disapproval.

Abdul Hamid remembered one other Imperial visit when
the beautiful French Empress had been welcomed by his uncle
in the fantastic setting of a palace panelled in mother-of-pearl.
But Beylerbey was on the Asiatic shore and in the past year
it had become an ordeal for him even to cross the Bosphorus,
so he considered it both safer for himself and more flattering
to his guests to lodge them in his own domain, and the
'Merasim' Kiosk, a palace rather than a pavilion, with a
banqueting hall large enough to seat one hundred and twenty
guests had been specially built in Yildiz Park in honour of the
visit. The Sultan had supervised every detail of the furnishing,
even to the length of carving with his own hands some of the
exquisite woodwork which decorated the doors and screens.
He took a great pride in his craftsmanship and, having heard
that the young Emperor dabbled in the arts, he was anxious to
impress him not only as a statesman, but as an artist and a
man of taste.

The unfortunate Master of Ceremonies was summoned to
the palace at all hours of the day and night to discuss the preparations for the reception. The list of guests for the state banquet was being constantly revised and the names of several
important pashas belonging to the Russo-French party had
been eliminated. With his prodigious memory the Sultan recalled every item of the menus he had partaken of twenty

years before at Buckingham Palace and the Tuileries and the French chef, specially imported for the occasion, had been ordered to include in his menus Windsor soup, as a compliment to the Emperor's grandmother Queen Victoria. In honour of his guest the visit was to be celebrated by a public holiday, with illuminations in the streets and fireworks on the Bosphorus, in spite of the fact that the Sultan loathed fireworks and was terrified at the very sound of an explosion. At times he would lament in private to his doctor that this visit would be disastrous for his health, but no sacrifice was too great to please his new friend, who had insisted on coming, against the advice of his great Prime Minister, to pay him homage not only as a European sovereign, but as Caliph of Islam.

What appeared to be a completely spontaneous gesture was in reality the result of years of careful planning on the part of Germany's astute Ambassador, Count Hatzfeldt, who at the time of the Egyptian crisis realised that England had forfeited the privileged role she had occupied at Constantinople since the days of Stratford Canning and that Germany was the only Power in a position to take her place.

Neither Count Hatzfeldt nor his successors aspired to the role of the 'Great Elchi'. Eschewing politics, their main object was to secure a market for German goods and to establish a German sphere of influence in the Near East. Slowly and methodically Germany began to infiltrate into Turkey in every walk of public life. If the Sultan had need of doctors to fight the epidemics which ravaged his country, of engineers to construct his railways or of technicians to work his mines, Germany was ready to supply them. And Count Hatzfeldt's greatest triumph was when Abdul Hamid accepted the German Government's loan of the services of the famous scholar-soldier General von der Goltz to train and equip the Ottoman Army on modern European lines.

In the wake of the generals and technicians who gave Germany her prestige, came an army of commercial travellers, and gradually the trade mark *Made in Germany* began to appear on household objects in cottages and *khans* from Salonica to Baghdad. Unlike some of their aristocratic colleagues, the German ambassadors to the Porte were never too proud to take an interest in commerce and German businessmen in Turkey could always rely on the backing of their Embassy.

Thus began quietly and unobtrusively Germany's *Drang nach Osten* and even the most suspicious of Sultans could feel nothing but gratitude for those quiet and efficient technicians who seemed so ready to help his country and asked so little in return.

The financial chaos which followed on the war had shown Abdul Hamid that it was impossible for his country to survive without the assistance of Europe. He had always been jealous of outside interference, particularly in the financial sphere, but when his Treasury was reduced to hand-to-mouth borrowing from private banks, he was forced to act on Said Pasha's advice and invite the representatives of the various foreign bond-holders to discuss the question of the Public Debt. This meeting in Constantinople resulted in the establishment of the 'Council for the Administration of the Ottoman Debt', by which a small group of financial experts from Great Britain, Germany, France, Austria and Italy were assigned certain important state revenues, such as the taxes on salt, silk, tobacco and spirits, to administer in payment of the interest due to the foreign bond-holders.

This new department was a success from the very beginning and the chief credit for its success goes to Said Pasha who succeeded in allaying his master's fear of foreign interference by persuading him to make the Council into a Turkish institution, so that its members would be the Sultan's servants rather than his tutors, acting solely in the interests of Turkey and of the Turkish bond-holders.

By the time of the German Emperor's visit it had been in existence for over seven years and the building known as 'Le Palais de la Dette' had become one of the landmarks of the city. The revenue, fairly collected and assessed for the first time in history, had so increased that two-thirds of the surplus funds were able to be paid direct into the Turkish treasury. Abdul Hamid's suspicions had given way to reluctant admiration of the way in which a small group of foreigners had made their department into the most efficient and best administered in the Empire. Thanks to their efficiency, Turkey's creditors were once more beginning to have confidence in the country, and the invasion of German businessmen, like swallows heralding the spring, was a sign of this renewed prosperity.

For the past ten years the Empire had been gradually recovering from the aftermath of war. Refugees from Bosnia and Circassia had been settled in Palestine and Syria. Hospitals and schools had been built both in Constantinople and the outlying provinces. In spite of his reactionary tendencies, the Sultan realised that if his country was to succeed in the modern world the people required a more progressive education than that provided by the religious schools and he was directly responsible for the creation of the technical and administrative colleges where young men were trained for the public services, while the new medical school at Scutari was built and endowed out of his private income.

The 1880's may be said to have been the golden age of his reign, when he had at last the time to put his house in order. The Treaty of Berlin had convinced him that, at whatever cost, it was vital for Turkey to preserve her neutrality, and to the surprise of Europe he made no attempt to intervene when trouble broke out in Bulgaria only a few years after the Russian forces had left the country. The Treaty gave him the right to protect Eastern Rumelia by force, but not a single Turkish soldier was mobilised when, after a bloodless revolution, the people of that province proclaimed their union with Bulgaria. His ministers and generals urged him to assert his authority, but he was clever enough to realise that a united Bulgaria under Alexander of Battenberg was a very different proposition from the great Slav state Russia had planned at San Stefano. The Czar's young cousin was showing a greater loyalty to his adopted country than to his illustrious relative and the Russian officers appointed to guide his steps in loyal subservience to the Czar had all been summarily dismissed.

In these circumstances Bulgaria was less dangerous to Turkish than to Russian, or even to Austrian interests, and the Sultan accepted the accomplished fact and appointed Prince Alexander to be *vali* of Eastern Rumelia, but he made no attempt to support his vassal when a few weeks later Serbia, incited by Austria, declared war on Bulgaria and Prince

Alexander appealed to his suzerain for help. Resenting the very existence of these peasant states created out of the debris of his European empire, Abdul Hamid was only too delighted to see them at each other's throats, with Austria forced to intervene to save Serbia from an humiliating defeat and Russia intriguing to get rid of a prince she herself had placed upon the throne. Nor did he try to profit by the situation when, in one of the most nefarious of all their Balkan intrigues, the Russians organised the kidnapping of Prince Alexander and then forced him to abdicate.

The Sultan knew that Eastern Rumelia was now irretrievably lost, that it could only be a question of years before the last shadow of his suzerainty vanished, therefore it was a matter of comparative indifference to him whether a Battenberg or any other foreign prince ruled in Bulgaria. Beyond a few formal protests at the illegality of the proceedings, he made no attempt to intervene during the stormy elections which in the end brought Ferdinand of Coburg to the Bulgarian throne.

At the time Abdul Hamid's refusal to act was interpreted as a sign of weaknesss, but he was far cleverer a diplomat than the majority of his critics, and his experience of Berlin had shown him that his only chance of survival in Europe was to treat the Balkan states as a gigantic cock-pit where, by constant intrigue and manipulation, Serb and Bulgar, Greek and Albanian could be pitched into sanguinary conflict and Russia and Austria maintained in perpetual rivalry.

For the next twenty years his whole policy in the Balkans was to be based on the principle of *divide et impera*. So much of what appeared to be weakness and vacillation was part of a carefully concerted plan to keep the rival states at loggerheads with one another and to prevent Turkey from becoming involved in a European war. Little did Abdul Hamid foresee that the visit of the German Emperor, by which he hoped to consolidate his neutrality, was to be the first link in a long chain of events which would end in dragging his country into a disastrous war and finally in destroying the Sultanate.

On November 2, 1889, Constantinople woke to the sound of the guns announcing the German Emperor's entry into the

Marmara and at Yildiz a tired, anxious man rose after a sleepless night to confront the ordeal of an Imperial visit. To-day of all days he wanted to appear young and vigorous, but the face reflected in the looking glass was that of a man prematurely old. Six years ago de Blowitz had described Abdul Hamid as being still in the prime of life, but these six years of constant nervous strain had robbed him of the last vestiges of youth. He was only forty-seven, but his beard would have been already grey had it not been for the constant attention of his foster-mother who dyed it with a special concoction of her own brewing, while his body was so emaciated that he even denied himself the luxury of the *hammam* for fear of losing an ounce of flesh.

The elaborate ritual of the Sultan's toilet, which in the old days vied with the royal levée at Versailles, had been simplified by Abdul Hamid to the extent that it rarely took him more than half an hour to dress. The few who were privileged to assist at his toilet were men who, however humble and unworthy in themselves, wielded more power than his ministers. There was the feared and hated Lufti Aga, a former slave, who by his talent for gossip and intrigue had attained such an ascendancy over his master that he employed him to spy on his own son; there was the eunuch Bahram Aga, whose honeyed tongue extracted dangerous confidences which were duly repeated in the intimacy of the Sultan's dressing-room, and the most inconspicuous, though perhaps the most important of them all, was the Sultan's foster-brother Ismet, who, as Keeper of the Imperial Wardrobe, was in constant attendance.

A curious, almost affectionate relationship existed between Abdul Hamid and the son of his Albanian wet-nurse—an intimacy strengthened by a physical resemblance, which enabled Ismet to be fitted for all his master's suits and uniforms and even on occasion to impersonate him at certain public ceremonies. He was the only man in Yildiz Kiosk who for thirty years maintained what was accounted as the highest privilege of all—the right of entering unannounced into the Sultan's presence. And today he was present, humble and unobtrusive as usual, to put the last touches to his master's toilet, girding the sword around the shrunken body, pinning the diamond stars and medals on the coat.

The Sultan was dressed, but he had still to visit the harem before he was ready to face the world, for only the Valide and the *kadins* were allowed to share the secrets of the dye-pot and the rouge which gave him the illusion of immortality.

It was nearing midday by the time the S.S. *Hohenzollern* rounded Seraglio Point. Even the weather had conformed to the Sultan's wishes and the autumn sun blazed with a summer radiance on Stamboul, turning its leaden domes to silver, its cypresses to bronze, gilding its crumbling ruins with the vanished gold of Byzantium.

The Emperor William was sufficiently imaginative to appreciate the beauty of the scene. Sailing across the Aegean, past islands wreathed in legend, coasting the shores of Troy, he had seen himself in turn as each of Homer's heroes, as noble as Hector, as brave as Achilles, even if necessary as cunning as Ulysses, for was he not here to prove himself a better diplomat than Prince Bismarck would allow him to be? He knew little about his Turkish host and that little was contradictory. Hatzfeldt and Bismarck considered the Sultan to be a man of talent, a far shrewder statesman than his ministers. Von der Goltz on the contrary found him narrow-minded and obstructive, jealous of German influence in the staff college and refusing to give either him or any of his foreign colleagues a real executive command. According to the General the Turkish soldier was among the finest in the world, but the Sultan was a neurasthenic and a coward who forbade revolver practice at military reviews and kept his warships bottled up in the Golden Horn because he could never forget that the navy had played an important part in the revolt against his uncle Sultan Aziz.

A Prussian general had no pity for a neurasthenic, but the Kaiser, who remembered his own frustrated childhood when he had had to overcome the physical defect of his withered arm, felt a certain sympathy for Abdul Hamid and was ready to make allowances for the whims of a sick man.

To the booming of guns and the hooting of sirens, the German sovereign entered the Bosphorus. The sun glittered on the marble palaces and white yachts of Pera, flashing across the water to the domes and minarets of Scutari. Linked in a chain of light Asia and Europe joined in welcome. Bands played, a thousand men lining the shores presented arms and from every public edifice the star and crescent and the German eagle fluttered proudly side by side.

The Sultan accompanied by his Grand Vizir, Kiamil Pasha, was waiting on Dolmabagche pier. For the first time since his accession Abdul Hamid had to meet a European sovereign on equal terms. As a diplomat and statesman he was flattered by the Kaiser's visit, but there was another side to his character which secretly resented it, longing back to the days when his ancestor Suleyman could say to Europe, 'There is a man called Charles who calls himself Emperor. Does he not know that I am Emperor and there is only one Emperor upon earth, just as there is one God, whose name is Allah.'

The decision to receive his guest as a European sovereign had caused him many a sleepless night. Even now he was not sure as to how the more orthodox Moslems would react to his driving through the streets with the German Empress at his side, or whether the Sheikh ul Islam would openly voice his disapproval at sight of the Padishah kissing a Christian woman's hand. But his last-minute doubts and hesitations vanished the moment the Emperor came on shore. To all outward appearances William of Hohenzollern seemed the very incarnation of youth and strength, even the warmth and vigour of his hand clasp was reassuring, for it was only later the Sultan realised that the iron grasp which nearly crushed his delicate fingers was deliberately assumed to cover the infirmity of a paralysed left arm and that all this ostentatious display of strength masked a nature as unsure and as neurotic as his own.

For their part the German sovereigns were delighted with their host. A recent visit by the Shah of Persia had given the European courts an unfortunate impression of the habits of Eastern potentates. A story was told of how the Aubusson carpets of Schönbrunn had been strewn with asparagus stalks when the Austrian emperor followed the Shah's example and behaved as if it were the most normal thing in the world to throw chewed asparagus stalks onto the carpet.

But no one could have been more courteous or more polished in his manners than the Sultan as he bent low to kiss the Kaiserin's hand before escorting her to the state carriage. The simplicity of his manner made even the most elaborate of Eastern compliments sound sincere and served as manna to the vain young Kaiser. '*Chok Yasha*', cried the soldiers lining the road to Yildiz, their bayonets forming a shimmering hedge of steel, and William noted with satisfaction that within a few years General von der Goltz had been able to train these primitive Asiatics into the semblance of Prussian grenadiers. When he commented on this to his host the Sultan smiled in acquiescence, but the eyes under their heavy lids smouldered in anger. Didn't the upstart Hohenzollern realise that these men were the descendants of the Turks who had once threatened the existence of Vienna? But the moment of anger passed. For all their tactlessness his guests were so eager to please and his capital had never seemed so beautiful as when seen through their eyes.

'*Padishah Chok Yasha*', roared the crowds pressing forward between the double file of bayonets, for though the troops had been ordered to include the German sovereigns in their cheers, to the ordinary man in the street there was still only one Emperor, one Padishah supreme upon this earth. And with his small gloved hand Abdul Hamid acknowledged the acclamations of those who still recognised him as the Shadow of God on Earth.

Chapter XXV

FOR FIVE DAYS the German sovereigns lived in what the
Empress Augusta described as a 'dream of the Arabian
Nights', waited on by slaves and eunuchs, served upon
golden plate, while every morning a messenger from the
Sultan brought some rare costly gift.

Abdul Hamid took pride in showing his guests the wonders
of Yildiz, his menagerie of wild beasts, collected from all over
the world, whose yearly upkeep cost the Imperial treasury
thousands of pounds; his superb arab stud said to be the finest
in existence, and his aviary of exotic birds. The Kaiserin, like
most of the female visitors to Yildiz, was touched by the
Sultan's love of animals and flowers, and still more touched,
when, on a visit to his famous rose-gardens, Abdul Hamid presented her with a bouquet in the middle of which was pinned
an enormous diamond.

The treasure house of the Seraglio was opened to their
astonished eyes and William had only to admire a jewelled
sabre which had once belonged to Selim the Conqueror for
the sabre to be his. No wonder the Empress found it all quite
fabelhaft. It was so very different from the hum-drum, bourgeois atmosphere of Potsdam where the Emperor himself
supervised the household account books. Abdul Hamid had
succeeded in impressing his visitors and he in turn was flattered
by their praise. The interest the Kaiser took in the new schools
and colleges, particularly in the military training college at
Pancaldi, and the enthusiasm with which he spoke of Turkey's
military resources had reassured the Sultan as to the wisdom of
his policy.

Russia would never have embarked on the war of 1877
without the tacit assent of the Central Powers, and Turkey
had a far greater chance of maintaining her independence now
that she had Germany for an ally. This added sense of security

was reflected in the geniality of the Sultan's manner. The visit dictated by political expediency had turned out to be far pleasanter than anticipated and a mutual respect and understanding had grown between him and his guest. He admired the young Kaiser for his exuberant vitality, his refusal to submit to the dictation of Prince Bismarck, while to the Kaiser he represented the mysterious and intangible East, the mystical power of the Caliph holding sway over three hundred million Moslems.

Germany had come into the field too late to obtain more than a secondary share of colonial spoils. In the scramble for Africa, England and France had secured the lion's share. Russian ambitions blocked the way to the Far East and the only road for the *Drang nach Osten* lay through the Sultan's empire. The Ottoman Empire was dying not from poverty but from neglect, for it possessed some of the richest and as yet unexploited territories in the world—territories which, if properly administered, would bring endless wealth both to the Sultan and his German ally. Economic necessity had brought the Kaiser to Constantinople. Turkey provided not only an outlet for Germany's growing population and a market for her manufactured goods, but she was rich in all the raw materials of which Germany was short. In certain districts of Mesopotamia the soil was so abundant in oil that the roads were made out of its solidified lava, but the inhabitants were as yet unaware of the invention of the petrol engine and of the importance of oil in the modern world.

The Kaiser's imagination took flight. German technicians and engineers would breathe life into a dying land and revive the empires of Babylon and of Syria. A vast network of canals and railways would bring the Arabs of the Persian Gulf within reach of Constantinople and artificial fertilisers would enrich the impoverished earth of Arabia. His was a nature to whom dreams became reality, and even a sceptic like Abdul Hamid was fascinated when the Kaiser suggested they should undertake together the revival of western Asia.

'I know that your Majesty speaks French.' In this one sentence the Kaiser managed to dispense with interpreters and break down the barrier which till now had existed between

Abdul Hamid and his foreign visitors. Neither the Sultan's nor the Kaiser's French was fluent, but it was sufficient for them to understand one another and they spent hours closeted together while the palace *camarilla*, the Sublime Porte and the foreign embassies were all busily surmising what might be the consequences of this new friendship.

'It is believed that no political questions were discussed,' wrote the British Ambassador, Sir William White, who, unlike the majority of his colleagues, viewed with a benevolent eye the budding friendship between Germany and Turkey. For the moment England had nothing but goodwill for Queen Victoria's grandson and signs of his breaking loose from the traditional alliance with Russia were warmly welcomed at Downing Street. Sir William White was the ablest envoy England had accredited to the Porte since the days of Stratford Canning, but circumstances made it impossible for any British Ambassador, however able, to regain the Sultan's confidence in his country. Personally Abdul Hamid both liked and respected Sir William, even on occasion referring to him with affection as 'Baba', or 'Father', White, but the continued occupation of Egypt and the British Government's insistence on the Sultan's carrying out the promised reforms—a matter on which Lord Salisbury and Mr. Gladstone saw eye to eye— had resulted in Abdul Hamid hating England even more than he hated Russia. As Count Hatzfeldt told Sir William, 'Russia does not worry the Porte with questions of reform as you do. She goes to war sometimes and takes a morsel of land, but then leaves them to repose. You do not take the land, but you destroy the repose.'

For the past years Russia had been adopting a more conciliatory attitude towards the Porte and the British Foreign Office saw with concern that Abdul Hamid was beginning to respond to the Czar's advances. This made the German visit doubly welcome to the English, for not only did it annoy the Czar, but as Sir William White wrote, 'Abdul Hamid is shrewd enough to realise that there is no friendship lost between Germany and Russia and will profit by the situation to maintain his independence and resist the Russian efforts to inveigle him into an alliance.'

At the State Banquet given on the night of the German sovereigns' arrival, the British Ambassador observed with pleasure the absence of the pro-Russian pashas, though as he mentioned in a despatch:

> this does not mean that the Sultan will do anything openly to offend the Czar. There are even some vague rumours that he would like to see the latter pay him a visit at Constantinople from the Crimea next year, and judging from his character I should not be surprised that he would show very considerable courtesy to Russia, just at the present moment, so as to remove every suspicion that he had joined the Triple Alliance.

The banquet was of a magnificence such as had not yet been seen at Yildiz. All of the hundred and twenty guests were served on massive golden plate and drank out of crystal goblets encrusted with gems. The food prepared by the French chefs was so far above the usual standard that it was commented on in the diaries and memoirs of the various envoys, used to half-cold, indigestible meals prepared by the Sultan's Levantine cooks. A dinner at Yildiz was usually an ordeal rather than a pleasure and the oppressive silence of the Turks, who did not dare to speak in their master's presence and who drank nothing but sherbet and water, was not calculated to add to the gaiety. But tonight the Sultan had given orders for conversation to be general, and his own apparent good-humour, the ease with which he conversed with the German Empress, albeit through an interpreter (for in front of his subjects he never admitted that he spoke French) helped to relax the atmosphere. But in spite of his excellent spirits it was noted that he did not touch any of the exquisite dishes prepared by the foreign chefs, and pleading a régime, contented himself with a simple pilaff and eggs prepared in his private kitchen.

After dinner the ambassadors and their wives were invited to accompany the royal party to a room from where there was an excellent view of the illuminations on the Bosphorus, and to each in turn the Sultan paid the unwonted honour of enquiring after their health and that of their families.

This however was the only State Banquet held during the German Emperor's visit and none of the ambassadors, with the exception of the German, Count Radowitz and his wife, was invited to the private dinners, where the guests ranged from Said Pasha, now Foreign Minister, and still the Sultan's most intimate councillor, to Herbert von Bismarck, appointed by his father to put a curb on the young Kaiser's impulsive actions; from the Sultan's banker Zarifi to Colmar von der Goltz, whom the Sultan feared and disliked for his influence on the Turkish Army, but who was nevertheless too useful to be dismissed.

Of the various guests, the one whom the Kaiser treated with the greatest courtesy and to whom he was always ready to listen was the German engineer, von Pressel, who for the past twenty years had been employed in the Ottoman service.

Von Pressel was a genius who throughout his life had cherished a dream which was nothing less than to link the whole of Asiatic Turkey by a chain of railways stretching from the Bosphorus to Baghdad. The idea had not originated with him. Already in the middle of the century an English ordnance officer named Francis Chesney had obtained a concession to construct a railway from Alexandretta on the Mediterranean to Kuwait on the Persian Gulf, but lack of interest both on the part of the British Government and of the City of London, had forced him to abandon the project. And it was the Turks themselves who, in the reign of Abdul Aziz, brought von Pressel from Germany to construct what was to become the first link in one of the most famous and disputed railways in the world.

Then followed nearly twenty years of frustration for von Pressel. The financial chaos resulting from the Russian War forced the Turks to sell those ninety-one precious kilometres of railway running from Haydar Pasha on the Bosphorus to Ismit on the Sea of Marmara. An Anglo-Greek company was the buyer, but after eight years of procrastination not one more kilometre of railway track had been laid and, with an inconceivable short-sightedness on the part of the English who already possessed other railway concessions in Turkey, the company sold out to representatives of the Deutsche Banke.

No sooner were the Germans in control than things began to move. Six months before the Kaiser's visit, the Deutsche Bank, in cooperation with the Bank of Stuttgart, had launched a company known as The Imperial Ottoman Railways of Anatolia and had secured the concession to extend the railway as far as Angora.

Von Pressel was never to see the realisation of his dream, but in William of Hohenzollern he found an enthusiastic disciple ready to carry on his work. From now on von Pressel's railway became the Kaiser's railway, and in all future discussions the representatives of the Deutsche Banke received strong diplomatic support not only from their Embassy, but from the Kaiser himself, who, when necessary, was always ready to intervene with telegrams to his friend the Sultan. Abdul Hamid favoured von Pressel's plan, for part of the policy of Pan-Islam was to bring all the Moslems of the Empire within reach of Constantinople and their Caliph. But being a sceptic and a realist he knew the Turkish treasury could never stand the strain of financing railways in Asia, while to be financed by Europe usually ended by being almost as expensive. The railway linking Vienna to Constantinople controlled by the Oriental Railway Company, an enterprise dating from his uncle's reign, had cost the Empire some of the richest forest land of Eastern Rumelia. By distributing *baksheesh* in the right quarters, the Austrian financier Baron Hirsch had succeeded in obtaining a concession with kilometric guarantees, which were so abused that the construction of the Rumelian railways has come down to history as one of the major financial scandals of the nineteenth century.

His experience of European financiers had taught the Sultan to be wary. Baron Ostrorog, a Frenchman who served Abdul Hamid for many years, wrote, 'The Sultan was charmed but not intoxicated by the Kaiser. He was fascinated but not convinced.' Abdul Hamid needed Germany's collaboration in the revival of his empire, but he had no intention of turning Asia Minor into a German colony. The Kaiser, however, had been warned of the Sultan's suspicious nature and he was careful to play down his own ambitions and praise the achievements of his friend.

Visits to museums and mosques, to schools and archaeological sites were all fitted into five crowded days, but Abdul
Hamid never accompanied his guests on these excursions for
every step taken outside the gates of Yildiz was an ordeal and
he limited himself to two drives to Dolmabagche, one on the
day of their arrival, the other on their departure.

While the Kaiser visited the mosques, the Kaiserin escorted
by His Highness the Chief Eunuch and the Sultan's married
daughter, Princess Zekiye, paid a state call on the Imperial
harem. The visit was not an unqualified success. Augusta was
shy and reserved and the Sultan's foster-mother, wearing the
elaborate Turkish court costume, blazing with jewels and surrounded by a bevy of beautiful young women, each dressed
more richly than the other, was a somewhat unnerving spectacle
at eleven o'clock in the morning. Unversed in Turkish etiquette,
the Empress made no attempt to kiss the small jewelled hand
held out to her but gave it instead a vigorous handshake which
labelled her as uncouth in the eyes of women to whom manners were an essential part of life.

The Princess Zekiye acted as interpreter, while her fourteen-
year-old sister Naime, who was already an accomplished
musician, played German tunes on the piano in honour of the
guests.

When the Empress left the harem after partaking of an
enormous meal of fifteen courses, watching a series of exotic
dances and listening to an endless flow of compliments painfully translated by the young princess, the Sultan's youngest
daughters, two pretty little girls of five and three, accompanied
her to the gates where they solemnly presented her with a
bouquet entirely fashioned out of precious stones. Once more
Augusta resorted to her only simile. 'It was just like something
out of the Arabian Nights.'

The five days passed all too quickly and though the British
Ambassador was right in asserting that no important political
questions were discussed during the German visit, in that short
space of time a friendship was cemented which was to have
dangerous consequences. Abdul Hamid felt strengthened by
the Kaiser's visit, encouraged by his praise, and from now on
his policy and actions were determined by the fact that he had

Germany for an ally. A moving ceremony took place on the last evening, when the Emperor decorated the Sultan with the collar of the family order of the Hohenzollern, and stooping to receive it, Abdul Hamid took off his fez, showing himself for the first time in public with his head uncovered. At the last luncheon which took place at Dolmabagche on the day of his departure, the Kaiser spoke of Germany's unalterable friendship for the Sultan and the Turkish people. And when the time came to say goodbye, Abdul Hamid, to his intense embarrassment, found himself enveloped in a warm embrace with William's waxed moustaches scratching his cheeks.

But in spite of his embarrassment the spontaneity of the embrace warmed his lonely heart, and he found himself missing the human companionship of the past few days as he drove back to Yildiz through the cheering crowds to whom he was a symbol rather than a man.

There was a sudden stir in the crowd, as a heavy parcel came hurtling across the double file of bayonets to fall at the Sultan's feet. For a second Abdul Hamid thought 'This is the end—this is the bomb I am always waiting for.' The people screamed in terror as one of the Albanian Guards flung himself across the floor of the open carriage to protect his master. But on examination the parcel turned out to be not a bomb, but a newborn baby whom some indigent mother had entrusted to her Padishah. A wave of relief passed over the crowd and for once the people saw their Sultan smile as with a gentleness of which he was capable at times, he stroked the baby's head. The child sent him by Allah to protect, came as a good omen and was a fitting climax to the German visit. On his return to the palace he ordered it to be sent to his harem and brought up at his expense.

Chapter XXVI

THE FESTIVITIES WERE over and Abdul Hamid had returned to the crowded emptiness of Yildiz where no one dared to look him in the face or contradict his word. On the table of his study were the usual files of reports and petitions from the provincial governors, reports which told of nothing but sedition and general discontent. The elaborate spy system maintained at a fabulous cost kept the Sultan informed of day-to-day events in the furthest parts of his empire, but it in no way contributed to his peace of mind to know that there was anarchy in Macedonia, open rebellion in Crete and the Yemen and that the revolutionary societies in Armenia were continually growing in strength.

Armenia was a particular thorn in the Sultan's side, for he had treated its people with humanity and justice till the time when, incited by Russian agents and encouraged by the democratic teachings of the American missionaries, they began to assert their rights to independence. A deputation had only to appear in Berlin for the Powers to espouse the Armenian cause. England, as usual, was only too ready to interfere in the internal affairs of Turkey, while at the time it suited Russia's policy to ferment trouble in the frontier provinces of Turkey by supporting the project of an autonomous Armenian State. At San Stefano Russia had been the first to stress the necessity for reform in the Sultan's Armenian *vilayets*. But at Berlin, Great Britain had stipulated that the Russian troops were to be evacuated from Turkish territory before the reforms came into effect, thus, inadvertently, and out of jealousy of Russia, rendering an invaluable service to Abdul Hamid who, once the armies had departed, was free to resort to his usual policy of procrastination and delay.

By 1881 the promises were still on paper and in this year the assassination of Czar Alexander II brought a complete reversal in Russia's Armenian policy. The new Czar, Alexander III,

was a rigid, narrow-minded autocrat opposed to all liberal influences. There was no longer any question of an autonomous
Armenia. The schools were closed, the use of the Armenian
language discouraged, while every effort was made to force
the people, the majority of whom were Gregorian Christians,
to adopt the Orthodox Faith. Alexander was a sovereign after
Abdul Hamid's own heart, with no intention of pandering to
revolutionary tendencies either in his own territories or in
those of his neighbours. The Russian consuls in Turkish Armenia, who had been busily financing secret societies on the
model of the Pan-Slav committees, were recalled and the Czar
personally assured the Sultan that 'he had no desire to interfere
in the affairs of Turkey, providing the Porte adhered to the
stipulations of the last treaty, particularly in regard to regular
payment of the war indemnity.'

Deprived of Russian help, the Armenians turned to the
Western Powers and in particular to England, where both Mr.
Gladstone and Lord Salisbury warmed to the cause of one of
the oldest and most persecuted Christian races in Asia. For the
past years the Sublime Porte and the various signatory Powers
at Berlin had been bombarded with notes from Downing Street
stressing the urgency of the Armenian question. With the
possible exception of France, who considered the Armenian
Catholics to be under her protection, Europe was no longer
interested and with a frank brutality Prince Bismarck told the
British Government, 'that Germany cared nothing for Armenian reform and the matter should be allowed to drop'. Nevertheless England persisted in upholding Article 61 of the Treaty
of Berlin and successive Ambassadors, from Sir Henry Layard
to Sir William White, had the unpleasant task of hectoring and
bullying the Sultan on the subject of Armenia. No wonder
that Abdul Hamid was now violently anti-British, in spite of
his personal liking for Sir William White, 'whose charm of
manner was so far removed from the policy he was forced to
adopt.'

The occupation of Egypt still rankled and in anger he had
refused to receive the special envoy sent by Lord Salisbury
to discuss the tenure and conditions of the occupation. After
intriguing in turn with the French, the Khedive, even with the

Mahdi in the Sudan, and expending vast sums from the Pan-Islam campaign funds on financing nationalist newspapers in Cairo, he had been forced to accept the unpalatable fact that the British were in Egypt and had no intention of getting out.

It is strange how a man whom Prince Bismarck considered to be one of the shrewdest diplomats in Europe, and who stirred the Balkan cauldron with such a mischievous and accomplished hand so as never to burn his own fingers, should yet have failed so lamentably in Egypt. On this occasion his anxieties as Caliph seem to have over-ruled his better judgment, allowing him to be swayed by his sheikhs and astrologers with their blind prejudices which led them to support any fanatical savage waving the green flag of the Prophet in preference to peaceful co-operation with the British.

Abdul Hamid recognised his failure in Egypt and this made him all the more sensitive on the subject of Armenia. He blamed Europe for the agitation which led the usually peace-loving Armenians to resist the tyranny of their Kurdish neighbours and take up arms against them. He blamed Europe and those pernicious Western doctrines, which in the name of liberty encouraged the nihilism already in the air and led wealthy Armenian merchants, who had emigrated to Europe and the United States, to finance the cause of their co-religionists in Cilicia and Kurdestan. What was Armenia? When a handful of Russian liberals envisaged an Armenian State on the confines of Russia and of Turkey, did they really imagine that the successful usurer and banker of Constantinople, the wealthy cotton merchant of Smyrna and Adana would emigrate to those mountain valleys to live among ignorant shepherds with whom they had nothing in common, other than their religion? The whole movement was the result of revolutionary propaganda and for this the Sultan blamed not only Europe, but America—those missionaries whom in the magnanimity of his heart his grandfather Mahmud had allowed to start schools and colleges in various parts of the Empire.

Abdul Hamid had always viewed these Protestant missionaries with distrust. Half the trouble in Bulgaria could be traced back to Robert College on the Bosphorus, where the Bulgarian nationalist leader Stambuloff had been a favoured pupil. He was convinced that these so-called respectable missionaries were implicated in the *Hintchak*, the Armenian secret society, which advocated a policy of violence as the only means by which Europe could be forced to intervene on their behalf. In the middle eighties the agents of the *Hintchak* were already at work, distributing arms among the young men and organising raids to resist the demands of the Kurdish *beys*, who flourished on an age-old system by which the Christian Armenian paid tax in kind to the local *bey* as the price of his protection against the depredations of rival tribes. The system was hard on the intelligent hard-working Armenian who in times of bad harvest suffered from the rapacity of his overlord. But until now he had submitted to the situation, finding little to choose between the exactions of the Kurd and the exactions of the local governor, who in many cases was the weaker of the two. For the *valis* and *kaimakams* appointed from Constantinople had very little authority over the wild mountain tribes of Kurdestan. When they came of their own free will to fight in the Sultan's wars it was usually in search of loot and to the citizen of Constantinople one of the most terrifying aspects of the Russian War had been the savage hordes of Kurds and Circassians on their way back from the front pillaging everything they could lay hands on.

But now the Armenians were showing themselves more independent even than the Kurds and there were armed clashes in the mountain villages of Eastern Anatolia. The local authorities began to fear for their lives and bombarded the Porte with reports of sedition and revolt, stressing the necessity for reinforcements. Because the Kurds were followers of the Prophet and known to be protected by the Sultan it was easier to put all the blame on to the Armenians, particularly as there had been instances in recent years when some well-meaning *vali* had sent a notorious Kurdish criminal in chains to Constantinople, only to find that after a few months in prison he had been quietly released.

By the time of the Kaiser's visit, the reports of disturbances in the Armenian *vilayets* were piled high on the Sultan's desk, and strengthened by the knowledge that he now had Germany for an ally, Abdul Hamid was determined to crush the Armenian rising by all the means at his disposal.

He was already a sick man at the time—sick both in mind and body, suffering from a chronic sleeplessness which Mavroyeni's sedatives could no longer cure. Women could still comfort him by day, but the woman who shared his bed at night would usually be dismissed long before the dawn, or wake startled from her sleep to find her master no longer at her side. The eunuchs and soldiers on guard were used to seeing the Sultan prowling from room to room, snatching an hour of sleep on some couch where the imaginary assassin would not think of finding him. Holding their breath in fear, they would watch him pass, not daring to make a sudden movement lest it might bring those nervous fingers to the trigger of the revolver which was always in his pocket and with which he was never known to miss. A young gardener had lost his life by inadvertently crossing the Sultan's path when he thought he was alone. A little slave girl who had strayed away from her mother and was found by Abdul Hamid playing with one of his jewelled firearms was shot dead in a blind moment of terror.

For a few days the solid, reassuring presence of William of Hohenzollern had chased away the shadows. Contrary to expectations, Abdul Hamid had been stimulated instead of exhausted by the visit and his entourage had never seen him in better spirits. But now the inevitable reaction had set in. Once more the shadows gathered dark and threatening and at night every gleam of light piercing the heavy curtain took on the shape of an Armenian knife. It was not as a normal man that Abdul Hamid judged the Armenian question, but as one who was crazed by terror, and the memoirs of Professor Vambéry, one of the few Europeans who came near to understanding him, help us to obtain a faint insight into his complicated and tortured mind.

After an absence of over thirty years the Hungarian scholar-traveller had returned to Constantinople to find himself welcomed by the Sultan as an old friend. The young scholar who had taught French to the Imperial princesses was now world famous, and Abdul Hamid took pleasure in hearing from the lips of a European who, disguised as a dervish, had travelled in the remotest parts of his empire, of the various customs and beliefs held in places neither he nor his ministers had ever visited. But already in 1890 Vambéry found that the one question which obsessed him more than any other was that of Armenia and what he termed 'the everlasting persecutions and hostilities of the Christian world.'

'By taking away Greece and Rumania,' said the Sultan, 'Europe has cut off the feet of the Turkish state body. The loss of Bulgaria, Serbia and Egypt has deprived us of our hands, and now by means of this Armenian agitation, they want to get at our most vital parts and tear out our very entrails. This would be the beginning of total annihilation, and this we must fight against with all the strength we possess.'

Of all the powers, Abdul Hamid blamed England most, and Vambéry regarded his anger as not entirely unjustified:

> For although in London good care was taken to keep publicly aloof from the disturbances in the Armenian mountains, the agitation of English agents in the North of Asia Minor was beyond all doubt. Not only [writes Vambéry] was the Sultan carefully informed of this most foolish and irresponsible movement, but whatever the Hintchakists and other revolutionary committees of the Armenian malcontents brewed in London, Paris, New York, or Marseilles, full knowledge of it was received in Yildiz, with the Armenians themselves providing the secret service.

It was characteristic of Abdul Hamid to continue employing Armenians in the palace. He was a past master at exploiting the frailty of human nature and now profited by the anxiety of the Armenian Civil Servant to keep his job, by employing him as an *agent-provocateur* with his own people. Armenians have never been good at keeping secrets and the chief culpability of the Sultan lies in the fact that, having been previously informed of every detail of the rising, he should have realised (had he not been blinded by fear and rage) that the number of genuine revolutionaries was comparatively small, that, given the necessary concessions and reform, the majority would have been only too ready to listen either to the advice of their

Patriarch or to the Protestant missionaries who, contrary to what he thought, had always deplored the use of violence. But Abdul Hamid would no longer listen to reason. The very name of Armenia had become anathema. And one spring evening in 1891, when he and Vambéry were peacefully sipping their after-dinner coffee, in the Chalet Kiosk at Yildiz, he suddenly said with an air of cold determination, 'I tell you I will soon settle those Armenians. I will give them a box on the ears which will make them smart and relinquish their revolutionary ambitions.' That night Vambéry retired to bed full of gloomy forebodings for the future and he lay awake till morning listening to the hooting of the owls, the heavy tramp of the guards outside his windows and the melancholy singing of the Koran-reciters at the palace gate. Two days later his forebodings materialised when an Imperial *irade* announced the formation of an irregular force of Kurdish cavalry to be known as the *Hamidieh*, the 'Sultan's Own,' to be used for operations against the Armenian rebels.

The die was cast. Armenians who had hesitated to ally themselves with the forces of violence now swelled the ranks of the *Hintchak*. Pamphlets calling on the people to resist their oppressors were circulated from house to house. From Trebizond to Zertun, from Adana to Diarbekir, the Armenian who had bowed his back for centuries prepared to fight. The Government responded by bastinados and wholesale arrests, by depriving the Armenian trader of the permits without which he was unable to move from one province to another, while the strictest censorship was applied to all news coming out of the disaffected *vilayets*. Secure in the protection of their Caliph, the Kurds became more aggressive and a small-scale massacre in the region of Lake Van heralded what was to come. Seeing the red light of danger, the foreign consuls on the spot entreated their embassies to intervene before it was too late, but in Constantinople the great battle for the railways had begun and the Powers had never been more disunited or Abdul Hamid more sure of himself.

Arthur Nicolson, who returned to the British Embassy in 1892, writes that, 'Venice in its darkest days was light and freedom compared to the Stamboul of today', while his new chief,

Sir Clare Ford, who had succeeded that great diplomatist Sir William White, had not been in Constantinople a week before he discovered 'he was in a hot-bed of political intrigue, where even a simple act of formality such as the form of investiture for the new Khedive cannot be allowed to pass without a tremendous fuss taking place.' The new Ambassador was a delightful and cultured aesthete whose talents shone in posts like Madrid and Rome, but who was completely out of his depth in coping either with the intrigues of the Sublime Porte or with those of his diplomatic colleagues. He arrived at the moment when Abdul Hamid, encouraged by France and Russia, was trying to retrieve some of his lost prestige in Egypt by wording the *firman* for the proclamation of Abbas Hilmi in such a way as to include the Sinai Peninsula in Turkish, rather than in Egyptian territory. Prompt action in Cairo on the part of the British Commissioner, Lord Cromer, put a stop to these manoeuvres, but they made the English aware that in the new French Ambassador Paul Cambon, they had a brilliant and dangerous antagonist, 'who will do everything in his power to destroy the last vestiges of English influence and rub salt into the Egyptian wounds.' The growing dissension between the diplomatic representatives to the Porte was particularly gratifying to Abdul Hamid who boasted to Vambéry that there was no lack of suitors for his country's favours. 'She was courted by all but was still a virgin and would not give her heart or hand to any of them.'

Recognising the new British Ambassador to be a social, rather than a political figure, Abdul Hamid set out to charm him and, to Arthur Nicolson's despair, his chief was completely won over by His Majesty's affability.

' I must say the Sultan is a most interesting personage,' wrote Sir Clare Ford after a series of dinner parties at Yildiz, at which he, his family and various distinguished English visitors had been lavishly entertained and presented with enamel or diamond-studded orders according to their rank.

In the Ambassador's opinion it would have been bad manners to spoil the pleasant atmosphere of these evenings by pressing for some sordid railway concession. Such matters were much better left in the able hands of Sir Edgar Vincent, Chairman of the Ottoman Bank, or of Vincent Caillard of the Public Debt. But while his chief was being entertained at Yildiz, listening to piano duets played by the Sultan's children, Arthur Nicolson raged to see his German colleague Prince Radolin quietly walking off with the concession to extend the Anatolian Railway from Eski-Shehir to Konya—and this despite the fact that the existing British railway groups in Turkey were now offering more favourable terms than those advanced by the Deutsche Banke; nor did it improve matters to know that Paul Cambon, after doing everything possible to fight against German mastery in the Levant, now threatened to leave Constantinople unless the Turks transferred to French control the Smyrna-Cassaba railway which till now had been owned by a British group.

Paul Cambon's own memoirs tell of his dealings with the recalcitrant Sultan, who possessed what he called *le génie du faux fuyant*. For the past years Abdul Hamid had grown to consider France as a secondary Power, to be used by and to make use of, as in the case of Egypt, but not to be really feared. In Cambon's opinion it was time for France to assert herself and occasionally to make the Sultan feel the steel within the velvet scabbard. One of his favourite ways of intimidating the Sultan was by threatening to get himself nominated to London where the Ottoman Empire would find in him a bitter enemy.

But even Cambon's high-handed policy could not prevent the Germans from obtaining the concession to extend the railway as far as Konya. As that astute and unscrupulous financier Baron Hirsch told Edgar Vincent, 'Only one power is ever trusted by Turkey at a given time. The others are negligible and undeserving of a financier's attention.' With Abdul Hamid it was not only a question of trust but of fear and when Russia vetoed the project of a German constructed railway running from Angora to Diarbekir and eventually to Baghdad, the German company began to find unexpected obstacles in their path.

The Sultan's caution was rewarded by Russia refusing to associate herself with England's demand for a commission of enquiry to report on conditions in the Armenian *vilayets*. Nor did she attempt to interfere when, in 1893, the notorious trial

of two Armenian professors attached to the American missionary college at Marsivan brought public feeling in Britain and
the United States to fever heat. The two professors, accused of
printing seditious leaflets, had been brought in chains before a
tribunal at Angora, by whom they were condemned to death.
But no sooner was the verdict known than there were mass-
meetings and demonstrations all over the English-speaking
world. And for the first time in history the Turks found they
had to contend with the reaction of public opinion, not only
in England, but in America.

The U.S. Minister at the time was a rough-hewn Texan
judge, particularly obnoxious to the Sultan on account of his
unpleasant habit of tobacco chewing, which he spat all over
the place. But now no time was lost in treating him to the
usual softening-up process reserved for impressionable diplomats and Nicolson, who had seen it work on his own chief,
noted in sorrow that 'the U.S. Minister has been nobbed by
the Sultan.'

After inviting the Minister and his family to dinner, and
placing his daughter next to his favourite son Burhaneddin,
Abdul Hamid sat and listened patiently for a whole hour to
Judge Terrell delivering an oration on the art of government,
'informing His Majesty that he was a plain man, unused to
courts, but confident that truth was a commodity that rarely
reached the ears of kings or sultans.' Terrell confided to Nicolson
that the Sultan hung his head and sighed and he thought he
had hit his mark. The net result of all this was that the hitherto
'incorruptible minister' was persuaded that the Sultan was the
'best man that ever breathed and only his agents were vile.'

Unfortunately for Abdul Hamid it was not so easy to seduce
the English. Sir Clare Ford was on leave and from Downing
Street Lord Rosebery sent the strongest instructions to Arthur
Nicolson who at a stormy interview with Said Pasha insisted
on the professors being released.

No wonder the Turks accused the English of fanaticism,
for strictly speaking the affair was none of their concern. The
College of Marsivan was American and the professors were
Turkish subjects. Both the Austrian and German Ambassadors
kept sedulously aloof, Cambon openly sided with the Turks

and the Russian Nelidoff was delighted to see the English so unpopular.

Backed however by liberal opinion throughout the country, Lord Rosebery did not hesitate to threaten and Abdul Hamid was once more forced to yield before British pressure. In silence he pocketed his humiliation. But this time he was determined to show at the earliest possible opportunity that he was master in his own house.

Chapter XXVII

I T TAKES VERY little to light the fires of religious fanaticism
and, in the mass of consular reports and blue books dealing
with the Armenian Massacres, the hand which ignited the
fuse, the incidents, trivial in themselves, which spread death and
devastation throughout the Armenian *vilayets* and soiled even
the streets of Constantinople with blood, tend to be overlooked
in the horror of the whole.

In a bald sentence one reads that in the summer of 1894
some agents of the *Hintchak* were captured in the mountains
of the Sassoun and, in the hope of capturing some more, the
local governor ordered out forces of the *Hamidieh* cavalry to
raid every Armenian village in the district. The Armenians in
these regions were hardy mountain shepherds who, with a
courage which belied their reputation, succeeded in beating
off the attack. In Constantinople the Sultan heard with rage
that Moslems were being killed by Christians furnished with
foreign arms and, in a *firman* addressed to his provincial
governors, Abdul Hamid invested them with full powers to
repress the rebellion.

The terror had begun and once begun there was no going
back. Age-old grievances and hatreds, jealousies and fears,
cupidity and lust allied themselves under the green banner of
the Prophet. Incited by their sheikhs and *imams*, men were free
to pillage and to murder, to rape and disembowel, all in the
name of Allah. Three thousand people perished before the
foreign embassies could lodge a formal protest. Even then there
were those who maintained that the reports were grossly
exaggerated, that the consuls on the spot had lost their heads,
and that anyway it was none of Europe's business as to how
the Sultan dealt with rebels in the outposts of his empire.

And while the foreign embassies wrangled over legalities,
the terror spread from the Sassoun to Van, from Bitlis to Diarbekir, from Trabzon to Erzerum. A cattle-raid or quarrel

(217)

in the bazaar, the shooting of a tax collector or the discovery of an arms dump, and the signal was given for the massacres to begin. Armed with bludgeons and with hatchets, with yataghans and knives the rabble poured out into the streets to murder indiscriminately any Armenian in sight. Churches, hitherto respected by Moslem law, were desecrated and at Urfa, the ancient Edessa, in one of the most horrible of all the massacres, over two thousand people including women and children were burnt alive when an infuriated mob set fire to the cathedral where they had taken refuge. Let it be said in fairness that it was usually the lowest elements which committed these outrages and that in almost every town there were some brave and pious Moslems, amongst them *valis* and *kaimakams*, who sheltered the Armenians at the risk of their lives. But all too often the European consuls were witnesses to the complete indifference with which the officers and other local authorities viewed the acts of savagery committed by the mob, contenting themselves by saying, that given the opportunity 'the Armenians would have done the same.' Nor were they altogether wrong in this assumption, for some of the acts of provocation committed by the *Hintchak* were as criminal as they were foolish, considering Armenia's geographical position and the fact that, in the words of Lord Salisbury, 'the British fleet could not sail across the Taurus mountains.'

In his more rational moments Abdul Hamid must have realised the danger of the forces he had unleashed, that sooner or later the civilised world would unite in horror against the excesses committed in Asia Minor. But he had either to condone these excesses or lose prestige in the eyes of the men who had acted on his orders. There are strange contradictory reports of his behaviour during these months, strange contradictory glimpses of a man who at times gave the impression that he was going mad, at others that he had never been saner or more master of himself.

While the *valis* in the disaffected provinces cried out for reinforcements, more and more soldiers were being drafted to the capital to ensure his personal safety. Arabs and Syrians were added to his Albanian Guards and their hatred of one another gave him an added sense of protection. The activity of the palace spies was redoubled; amusements as simple as a paper-chase in the Forest of Belgrade organised by the young Embassy attachés was regarded with the gravest suspicion and accompanied by agents of the secret police; at an operatic performance which inaugurated the opening of the new Pera Palace Hotel, there were as many spies as guests, and a ball, which was to be given by a rich Greek, was suddenly countermanded by order of the Grand Vizir on the excuse that it might serve as a place of gathering for Armenian conspirators.

Matters had come to a pass when even the ordinary citizen was beginning to suffer from the petty tyrannies which deprived him of his freedom. Any young man who frequented European society too much, became suspect to the palace. The laws for women had never been so severe. Not only were they forbidden to go shopping in the European quarter, or to employ Christian governesses in their households, but their very dress was subject to a special decree and no lady dare show herself in public except in the thickest of *yashmaks* and the plainest of *feradjes**. Woe betide the Turkish woman who, whether widowed or single, ventured to travel abroad, for she was likely to find herself banished for life from the Sultan's dominions.

The greatest tragedy of all was that no one suffered more from these petty tyrannies than Abdul Hamid himself who by nature had both wit and humour, taking far more pleasure in French farces and light opera, detective novels and the society of Europeans than in the grave preachings of the Sheikh ul Islam and the religious discussions of the learned *mollas* and *ulema* of his court. But having adopted the role of Caliph, recognising in that role the only chance of enhancing his personal prestige, he had set himself out to be as fanatical as the most fanatical of his sheikhs. There is a story told how at the beginning of the Armenian troubles, when the British Ambassador attempted to remonstrate on the injustice of having the whole male population of an Armenian village tortured and imprisoned because one Moslem had been killed, the Sultan looked at him with cold eyes, saying, 'But don't you understand, a Moslem has been murdered.'

*Feradje—A mantle.

He was particularly sensitive to anything which touched him in his position as Caliph and nothing is said to have annoyed, and yet impressed him more, than when Queen Victoria appealed to him on behalf of her Moslem subjects and the unnecessary hardships of the Pilgrimage to Mecca. The Queen's letter addressed to her Ambassador is a masterpiece of diplomatic tact.

> The Sultan knows [she writes], that the Queen Empress has Mohamedans constantly about her whose faithful devotion and good conduct are beyond all praise and that she has great respect for the Mohamedan religion. The Government of India have done all they can to provide for the comfort of the pilgrims as far as Jeddah. But after that and at Mecca and Medina, they are cared for by the Turkish authorities and have very little to eat and their sufferings are very great. The Queen would earnestly beg the Sultan to enquire into the state of affairs there, of the treatment of the pilgrims and of the great number who are allowed to go sick and uncared for; of the bad state the holy places themselves are said to be in. She would gladly help, but no one but those professing the Faith of Islam dare interfere and the Queen for the sake of her suffering subjects appeals to the Sultan.

The ghost of Disraeli might have dictated this letter, which led to the wholesale dismissal and disgrace of the Turkish authorities at Mecca and Medina and the building of a new caravanserai from funds supplied out of the Sultan's Civil List. It may have had even more far-reaching consequences, inspiring, in later years, what was to be the most successful project of Abdul Hamid's Pan-Islam campaign—namely the building of the Hedjaz or pilgrim railway running from Damascus to Mecca and constructed entirely out of the voluntary subscriptions of pious Moslems.

Piqued in his pride as Caliph, Abdul Hamid listened to Queen Victoria's appeal, but she was less successful when it came to intervening on behalf of his Christian subjects. A plea for clemency addressed to him at the height of the Armenian Massacres received a curt reply to the effect that the Sultan regretted that both Her Majesty and the people of

England were so ill-informed as to the truth of what was happening in Armenia.

Sir Philip Currie who, in 1894, succeeded Sir Clare Ford at the British Embassy did all in his power to bring his recalcitrant colleagues into line and force the Sultan to accept a scheme of reform to be applied under the supervision of European commissioners. Sickened by recent events, the Ambassadors were ready to sink their differences and even Paul Cambon dropped his intrigues in Egypt to ally himself with his British colleague. But while the Ambassadors got together, their Governments remained at loggerheads. The last thing Czarist Russia desired was the grant of autonomy to the Turkish Armenians, which would inevitably strengthen the demands of the Armenians of Transcaucasia for better and more liberal government. Nor would it have suited French policy in Syria to have a British fleet sail into Alexandretta. So the moment Great Britain threatened coercion both France and Russia withdrew their support and the Sultan realised he could continue with impunity to ignore the protests of the foreign Powers.

In England Mr. Gladstone came out of his retirement to brand him as the 'Great Assassin': in France M. Clémenceau denounced him as the *Monstre de Yildiz et le Sultan Rouge*', but from September 1895, when a mass demonstration of Armenians in the capital led to rioting and bloodshed at the gates of the foreign embassies, to the last days of August 1896, when Armenian revolutionaries made a desperate attempt to force the attention of Europe by wantonly attacking the Ottoman Bank in Stamboul—during the whole of these eleven months one massacre followed on another, till the rivers of Eastern Anatolia were polluted by rotting corpses and jackals and carrion birds were the only inhabitants of Armenian villages.

Thousands, even tens of thousands are said to have perished and the Armenian revolutionaries share with the Sultan the culpability for their deaths. There may have been cases when, by their avarice and treachery, the Armenians deserved the hatred of their Turkish neighbours, but once the fanatical passions of the mob had been unleashed there was no discriminating between the innocent and the guilty. In certain cases the massacres may have started as so many pogroms in Eastern

Europe were started, by a desire on the part of the local authorities to alleviate the discontent of the population by providing them with suitable victims. The Sultan himself was a past master in this art of government, but in Armenia his fears got the upper hand and having opened the Pandora-box he could no longer control the elements he had evoked.

One of his chamberlains describes how, at the end of a stormy interview with the British Ambassador, he found Abdul Hamid lying prostrate across his desk, his face buried in his hands, his whole body shaking with sobs. An English-woman visiting Constantinople at the time, described him at the Friday *selamlik* 'as the most wretched pinched up little sovereign—a most unhappy looking man with a look of absolute terror in his large eastern eyes, eyes which haunted me for days as of one gazing at some unknown horror.'

On the other hand Paul Cambon, who dined at Yildiz shortly after the massacres of Trabzon, in which over five thousand people died, writes of the Sultan as being in the best of humour, never even mentioning Armenia and only con-cerned with the question as to whether or not he should recog-nise the right of Ferdinand of Saxe-Coburg to the Bulgarian throne. According to Vambéry Abdul Hamid knew moments of remorse, when he regretted the rigorous measures he was forced to adopt, but from first to last he believed that these measures were necessary and that the only way of eliminating the Armenian question 'was by eliminating the Armenians themselves'. This cynical phrase was coined by his new secre-tary, Izzet Bey, the fellow-townsman of Aleppo whom Sheikh Abul Huda had introduced into the palace. The son of a pros-perous Arab landowner, Izzet had been educated at the Jesuit College at Beirut and thereby possessed a pliability and breadth of outlook denied to the more orthodox Moslem. But beneath the varnish of a Europeanised education lay the deep-rooted jealousy and hatred of the Arab for the Armenian usurer and merchant who controlled most of the trade from the Euphrates to the Mediterranean. More intelligent and even more unscrupulous than other members of the palace *camarilla*, Izzet now made himself into the instrument of Abdul Hamid's Pan-Islam policy and of the German alliance, fusing the political interests of the one with the economic interests of the other. Much of the Sultan's intransigence over Armenia can be traced to his growing influence: he persuaded his master that he had nothing to fear from Europe so long as he could rely on the Kaiser's support, that Armenia's geographical position made armed intervention virtually impossible, and that it was far more dangerous to submit to foreign dictatorship and risk antagonising his Moslem subjects by granting concessions to a rebellious minority.

During these months there was a general holocaust of all those who stood in Izzet's way, starting with the hitherto indispensable Said who, after attempting to persuade his master to change his policy, was dismissed from office and forced to seek refuge in the British Embassy. By the dismissal of Said, Abdul Hamid, in the words of Paul Cambon 'had succeeded in destroying his own Government,' yet never had his diplomatic talents stood him in better stead than during these eleven months in which he proceeded to eliminate the Armenian question in defiance of world opinion. While his *Hamidiehs*, whom he referred to as 'his faithful Cossacks' turned Eastern Anatolia into a giant graveyard, he continued to play with the idea of reform, consenting and then delaying, holding back only to strike the harder and managing to convince a confirmed cynic like the Russian Chancellor, Prince Lobanoff, 'that there was no reason to lose confidence in the goodwill of the Sultan.'

Only the Armenian revolutionaries seem to have understood that a policy based on fear could only be quelled by fear and, in the last days of August 1896, twenty desperate men, armed with bombs, succeeded in broad daylight in attacking and seizing the premises of the Ottoman Bank. It was a wanton and wholly unjustified attack in which innocent clerks and porters were blown to bits for no other purpose than to draw the attention of the Great Powers, and in particular of England, to the Armenians' political grievances.

Abdul Hamid and Izzet were only waiting for this opportunity. All the evidence goes to prove that they were forewarned of the attack, for at the very moment when the first bombs were thrown, armed bands appeared in various quarters of the city and, at a given signal, set out to attack and pillage every house inhabited by Armenians. So systematic was the attack that lists of the Armenian occupants must have been supplied by the authorities. And while wretched artisans and shopkeepers were being beaten to death, the twenty men entrenched in the Ottoman Bank continued to rain bombs on the soldiers and police, till in order to save the premises from being destroyed the foreign embassies negotiated their surrender on the promise of a safe conduct and permission to leave the country. The promoter of this cynical but essentially practical policy was the English Director of the Bank, Sir Edgar Vincent, who at the first alarm had crawled out of his office window and escaped to safety across the roof. All his influence and powers of persuasion had been brought to bear on convincing both the foreign embassies and the Sublime Porte that too many vested interests were at stake to risk the destruction of the Bank. So the twenty revolutionaries were escorted to safety on board Sir Edgar's yacht, while seven thousand of their compatriots lost their lives in a four-day massacre.

In a way they may be said to have succeeded in their object. Only a handful of Europeans had witnessed the carnage of Trabzon, the human bonfires of Urfa, but now diplomats and tourists were engulfed in the same wave of terror which swept over the European quarters of Constantinople. Dragomans and attachés literally waded in blood on their way to the Sublime Porte and saw with their own eyes some of the Sultan's elegant aides-de-camp stamping with their heels on the bodies of dying Armenians. Even the youngest of attachés must have felt that he and his country were partly to blame for these crimes, for the events of the previous year and the sanguinary fashion in which the police had broken up the Armenian demonstration of December 1895 had given the Great Powers ample warning of what would occur in the event of another act of provocation. Now at last they were roused to action. An open telegram written in French, signed by the signatories of the Treaty of Berlin including Germany, told the Sultan that 'the massacres must cease immediately and that if the situation continued it would imperil both his throne and dynasty.'

It was not so much the threat of the Great Powers as the reaction of his own people which alarmed Abdul Hamid. The excesses committed by the mob had revolted every law-abiding citizen and there had been many instances of Moslems protecting Armenians. Even the *imams* of the Holy Mosque of Eyoub had given shelter to fugitives who had rowed across the Golden Horn from the Armenian quarter of Haskeui. In many cases the situation had got so out of hand that the rabble had vented their hatred not only on Armenians but on their own private enemies, and two of the Sultan's chamberlains had been killed at the very gates of Yildiz.

In a collective note which, in diplomatic language, charged Abdul Hamid as having connived with the assassins, the Great Powers warned him that 'such a force, springing up under the eyes of the authorities and with the co-operation of certain of the latter's agents, becomes an exceedingly dangerous weapon. Directed to-day against one nationality in the country it may be employed tomorrow against the foreign colonies or may even turn against those who tolerated its creation.'

These words echoed the Sultan's fears at having conjured into existence a force more dangerous and more powerful than any rebellious minority, a force which in clever and adroit hands might attempt to challenge his authority, and on the evening of the third day of the massacres, Friday August 28, the order went out that the master had 'forbidden to kill.'

Chapter XXVIII

ALL EUROPE UNITED in condemnation of the 'Red Sultan', all except the Kaiser who chose this moment to emphasise his personal relations with Abdul Hamid by sending him a signed photograph of himself, the Kaiserin and their children, thereby showing that his Ambassador's signature to the collective note of protest had been no more than a formal gesture and that in private he condoned the actions of his friend.

The Sultan was in a particularly susceptible mood, seeing himself attacked not only by Europe, but by his own people, and his heart warmed to the fellow-sovereign who showed he understood what lesser men ignored—that in order to keep the body of an empire intact, one is sometimes forced to cut out the canker which threatens to destroy it. The outrages committed in the centre of his capital and the hooliganism of the mob, who in many instances had resisted the attempts of the police to disperse them, told Abdul Hamid that this time he had gone too far and that some effort must be made to placate public opinion both at home and abroad. Was he genuine in his remorse or merely a consummate actor when he received the foreign envoys with a grief-stricken countenance, assuring them that he would have renounced his throne rather than be a witness to the horrors of the past three days? Faced by those dark mournful eyes, even the most sceptical found it hard to doubt his sincerity and the blame for recent events was put on the palace *camarilla* rather than on the Sultan.

The only one who refused to be taken in, or even to pretend to be taken in, was the new British Ambassador, Sir Philip Currie, who by his bluff, straightforward manner had aroused the Sultan's antipathy from the moment of his arrival. Abdul Hamid would on occasion resort to the most childish tricks in order to annoy him, such as receiving him in an unheated room in the middle of winter. And while the Sultan in his warm sable-lined cloak prolonged the audience for over an hour, the unfortunate Ambassador would be kept shivering in his thin uniform, with the result that he would be confined to his bed for a fortnight. Time only served to accentuate this mutual dislike and Abdul Hamid held Sir Philip directly responsible for the threatening tone of the collective note and the decision of the Powers to reinforce their Stationnaire ships in the Marmara, so as to protect their nationals in the event of further trouble.

Throughout his life Abdul Hamid had cherished the ambition of freeing his country from what he regarded as the strangle-hold of the Capitulations. Those extra-territorial rights enjoyed by the foreign Powers had never weighed on him so heavily as during the past year when European journalists had been able to evade the rigid censorship on news coming from the interior by using the foreign post offices. It was with bitterness that he now found himself in the position not only of having to accept the tightening of the Capitulations but of actually allowing the embassy dragomans to help in restoring order in the capital. Eye-witnesses in those early days of September 1896 describe what was virtually the first step towards international control in Turkey, with the dragomans entering the churches where thousands of Armenians had taken refuge and persuading them to return to their homes, their safety from interference being guaranteed by the Powers and no Ottoman officials being allowed to be present.

But it was now, when the Sultan's prestige was at its lowest, when he was execrated abroad and confronted in his own country by a growing tide of discontent in every class; now when it seemed as if the whole edifice of his power was about to crumble, that the threat of a war with Greece brought every patriotic Turk rallying to his standard.

For the past year there had been a continual state of tension in Crete, which fifty years after the liberation of Greece was still chafing under Turkish rule. Sporadic attempts at rebellion by the Christian majority against the Turkish overlord had been so ruthlessly suppressed that on several occasions the Powers had been forced to intervene, but the reforms they had made the Sultan accept had been abrogated the moment their attention was turned elsewhere. And during the Armenian massacres Abdul Hamid took the opportunity of encouraging the Moslem minority by recalling the Christian governor of Crete, that same Alexander Carathéodory who had served him so loyally at Berlin, and appointing a Moslem in his place. Once more a wave of fanaticism swept over the island with the Christians rising in open revolt and appealing for help to their mother country, Greece. Under the pressure of public opinion, King George sent troops to the island and nothing could have been more satisfactory to Abdul Hamid than when the Great Powers branded Greece as the aggressor and, in the early days of February 1897, sent their warships steaming into Suda Bay, while in the various chancelleries of Europe the Armenian question was relegated to the files.

If the Powers had acted at once they might have prevented a war, but once more precious time was wasted in drawing up notes and ultimatums, while feeling in Athens rose to fever heat and the royal palace was besieged by hysterical crowds crying out for a crusade against the infidel. Neither the King of Greece nor the Sultan really wanted to fight. The one secretly hoped that the Powers would prevent hostilities at the last moment so that he could yield to their pressure without risking his position with his subjects, and the other was personally disinclined to embark on a war which might mean the end of the Turk in Europe and which, even if successful, would gain him nothing, for European public opinion would never allow Christians who had once been liberated to return under the Turkish yoke. Left on his own, Abdul Hamid would probably have adopted the same passive policy as in Bulgaria, flattering the Powers by provisionally yielding to their ultimatum and granting a large measure of autonomy in Crete, while secretly inciting the Moslem population against the Christian majority. It was only after Greece had refused to withdraw her troops and units of the Greek army on the mainland had crossed the Turkish border that the pro-war element headed by the General Staff gained the ascendancy in the councils of Yildiz.

Behind the young officers trained by von der Goltz and burning to come to grips with the enemy was another and more powerful influence. From Berlin the Sultan's august ally incited him to put his new army to the test and prove the efficiency of the Mauser rifles and guns supplied by Krupps. In his eagerness to see what kind of troops the Ottoman Empire could put into the field, the Kaiser ignored such sentimental considerations as the fact that his sister was Crown Princess of Greece. But still Abdul Hamid hesitated to commit himself and it was not until two months after the Greek forces had landed on Crete that Turkey finally declared war on Greece and the five old warships which had been bottled up in the Golden Horn for the past fifteen years sailed out into the Marmara, cheered by an enthusiastic crowd.

In this thirty-day war, which he had neither wanted nor provoked, Abdul Hamid found the unlooked-for opportunity of regaining his popularity. From first to last it was an unbroken series of Greek disasters. Their troops, though brave, were totally disorganised and in every way outclassed by the disciplined Turkish soldiers under their German-trained officers. It was only a question of days before the Turks advancing through Thessaly had captured Larissa, only a question of weeks before the bellicose feeling in the Greek capital had given way to panic and the Royal Family had been made the scapegoats for the failure of the war. So dangerous was the situation that before the month was up the Powers were again forced to intervene and to put an end to hostilities which threatened the collapse of a dynasty they had placed upon the throne.

In the full tide of victory Constantinople gave itself over to an orgy of rejoicing. Forgotten was the bitterness and discontent of the past months. Even the Young Turks had discarded their grievances and in the sunlight of public approval, Abdul Hamid drove through the streets acclaimed as 'Ghazi', the victorious one. Two months ago at the time of Ramadan he had hardly dared to venture out for fear of assassination. On the annual pilgrimage to Stamboul to pay homage to the Prophet's relics, he had been so overcome by nerves that at the last moment he had let his carriage go empty at the tail of the great procession while he went by water from Dolmabagche to the Old Seraglio, hardly a dignified procedure for a monarch paying his annual visit to his capital. But now the spontaneous cheering of the crowd, the confident bearing of his soldiers, injected new life into his veins. He had not wanted war, but when it became inevitable he had played a vital if unobtrusive part in ensuring victory. A judicious grant of bishoprics and schools to the Slav element in Macedonia had persuaded Serbs and Bulgars that there was more to be gained by remaining neutral than by espousing the cause of their co-religionists in Crete and thereby encouraging Greek pretensions in Salonica, while Turkey's conciliatory attitude towards the ultimatum of the Powers had contrasted favourably with Greek intransigence and was rewarded by an Austro-Russian note warning the Balkan courts not to intervene in the struggle.

The European Ambassadors had never seen him in a more amiable mood and his old enemy Sir Philip Currie even found him co-operative on the question of Armenian relief, stretching cynicism to the length of publicly thanking the British Relief Committee for their efforts in alleviating the sufferings of his Armenian subjects.

Queen Victoria's Jubilee gave him the opportunity of showing that his quarrel with England was not with the country, nor with the Queen, but only with certain of her politicians, and all his ministers from the Grand Vizir downwards were ordered to attend the Embassy party in honour of Her Majesty's birthday, while the five most important Christian functionaries of the Empire represented him at the Jubilee service in the Embassy chapel.

Certain sections of the British public found it hard to accept this sudden *volte-face* and relations were once more strained when Mr. Gladstone, whom all those working in favour of an Anglo-Turkish rapprochement would gladly have seen in his grave, threatened a hostile demonstration against the special mission sent by the Sultan to congratulate the Queen on her sixty-year reign. Fortunately Victoria was too much of a diplomat to allow her private opinion of Abdul Hamid to interfere with what she believed to be her country's interests, and she received his mission so graciously that good feeling was restored. As a token of his personal appreciation the Sultan sent sixty of the royal performers from his private theatre at Yildiz to entertain Lady Currie's guests at the Jubilee *fête* held in the grounds of the Summer Embassy at Therapia.

The reason for all this sudden amiability became clear when the peace conference opened at Constantinople and Turkey presented her claims, which included the cession of the greater part of Thessaly and the payment of a war indemnity of ten million pounds. It was generally considered that Abdul Hamid would never have dared to make such exorbitant demands had he not been backed by the Kaiser, who, in his anxiety to win the Sultan's friendship, continued to show a cynical disregard for the fate of his sister's country. The rest of Europe, however, was not prepared to see Thessaly return to Turkish rule and in the end the Sultan had to content himself with a purely formal rectification of the frontier and an indemnity of four million pounds.

Meanwhile the thorny problem of Crete was temporarily shelved by the Powers taking over the protection of the island. Here again Germany and her ally Austria disassociated themselves from the Concert of Europe by withdrawing their ships, leaving Great Britain, Russia, France and Italy to the ungrateful task of policing an island where both Christian and Moslem inhabitants were in open revolt against their authority.

Economically Turkey cannot be said to have profited by the war and her victorious soldiers had every right to resent the interference of the Western Powers. But as a leader, the Sultan had gained an immense prestige not only in his own dominions but throughout the Moslem world. Indian princes had subscribed large sums to the Ottoman War fund, and congratulatory addresses arrived at Yildiz from Moslem communities scattered throughout the Pacific and Indian Oceans. Till now the British India Office had been inclined to minimise the Caliph's influence on the Moslems of India, but it seemed as if Abdul Hamid's Pan-Islam propaganda was beginning to take effect, and at the traditional festival of Kurban Bairam—a ceremony no infidel was allowed to witness—Indian princes in full regalia stood beside Arab sheikhs to acclaim Abdul Hamid when he rode into the courtyard of Dolmabagche Palace to slay the sacred ram.

A young secretary of the British Embassy who was present at the diplomatic reception which followed on the ceremony, wrote home to his father, 'The Bairam celebration always impresses me with the immense power of the Sultan and how futile it is to bully him.' Eight months ago the same young man had seen Abdul Hamid threatened by the Powers in his own capital, several times during the past year he had heard rumours of an imminent rising on the part of the Young Turks and been told by sober-minded politicians that Abdul Hamid's reign could not last another year. Yet at the first threat of war every Turk had rallied to his standard and now on the eve of victory he was more inviolable than ever.

Even the most ambitious of Balkan princes had still to pay homage to the 'Old Man' in Yildiz Kiosk and among the princes and pashas present at the Kurban Bairam reception of 1897 was Ferdinand of Saxe-Coburg, come to thank his suzerain in person for his official recognition as hereditary prince of Bulgaria and *vali* of Eastern Rumelia. Vassal and suzerain were well matched in subtlety and cunning and Midhat and Stambuloff, the two men who had placed them on their thrones, had suffered the same fate. For even if Ferdinand had not actually connived at the assassination of his former minister and mentor, no serious attempt had been made to punish his assassins.

While the vassal was ready to flatter, the suzerain was ready to be gracious. It pleased the Sultan's vanity to receive the homage of a prince with Bourbon blood in his veins. And for all their mutual distrust Abdul Hamid and Ferdinand had a grudging admiration for each other's talents and took a certain pleasure in each other's company. In future conversation with foreign statesmen the Bulgarian prince always made a point of singing the praises of his Imperial suzerain, the Sultan of Sultans with whom he was on the best of terms and whom he declared to be '*un Potentat délicieux*'.

Constantinople was filled with visitors in this summer of 1897 and in spite of his increasing debility and chronic sleeplessness, Abdul Hamid took endless trouble in the receiving of his foreign guests. The frugality of his personal habits, his mania for saving, which went to the length of his once presenting a secretary with the model of a fez composed entirely out of bits of sealing-wax laboriously scraped off old letters, formed a curious contrast to the prodigality of his gifts, both to foreign potentates and to his favourites. A good deal of this generosity was calculated in order to impress public opinion with his munificence, but at times he was capable of being completely disinterested in his generosity and he was seen at his most chivalrous and charming when the ex-Empress Eugénie returned to Constantinople as an old lady in exile to revisit the scenes of her former triumphs, driving with a single aide-de-camp along the road in the forest of Belgrade, which had been made in her honour by Abdul Aziz over twenty-seven years ago.

At Yildiz she was received as if she were still a reigning sovereign, which was somewhat embarrasing for the French Ambassador, Paul Cambon, who remarked with malice that 'the Sultan standing beside the tall and willowy Eugénie looked like a black gnome or spider'. It was one of the rare occasions when Abdul Hamid showed himself to be not only chivalrous but magnanimous, remembering those receptions at the Tuileries, when Eugénie had concentrated all her charm on his brother Murad, addressing him no more than a few perfunctory words.

Murad was a name the old Empress had been warned never to bring up in conversation. Even the boatmen on the Bosphorus averted their eyes as they passed under the shadow of the walls of Cheragan, while the coachmen drove faster past the palace gates, for fear that one of the Sultan's spies might accuse them of loitering in the neighbourhood. After twenty years Abdul Hamid still lived in fear of the living ghost of Cheragan and no visitor or servant dared remind him of that hated presence. Once a month a board of medical examiners solemnly presented their report on the ex-Sultan's health, reports which were as much of a mockery as the annual publication of the statute of the Constitution of 1876, which the Sultan asserted he had never directly violated.

Chapter XXIX

IN OCTOBER 1898 the Emperor William paid a second visit to Constantinople on his way to Palestine, where he was to inaugurate the new Lutheran Church in Jerusalem. The visit could not have been better timed, coming in a month when the situation in Crete had embittered Abdul Hamid's relations with the four Protecting Powers who, whatever might be their differences in other parts of the world, continued to act in close co-operation in policing the island and in preventing the port from reinforcing its garrison.

When an outbreak of Moslem fanaticism in the British sector resulted in the British Consulate being set on fire and in the Vice-consul and his servants being burnt to death, the Admirals in charge finally lost patience and, in a Joint Note, called on the Sultan to withdraw his remaining troops from the island, leaving only a small token force to protect an emblematic Turkish flag.

It was a bitter pill for Abdul Hamid to swallow at the end of a victorious war, but his Navy was in no condition to defy the warships of England, Russia, France and Italy combined, and he had no alternative but to accept the situation in which he retained only the nominal suzerainty of the island and, as a crowning humiliation, had to accept a Greek Prince as Governor. In these circumstances Germany appeared to be Turkey's only friend. By withdrawing his ships from Crete and refusing to be associated in the Concert of Europe the Kaiser had added to the Sultan's debt of gratitude. In conversation with those who, like Vambéry, openly opposed the German alliance, Abdul Hamid would say: 'It is useless to cavil at my friendship with the German Emperor, for the Germans do me as much good as they are permitted to do, while the rest of Europe do me as much harm as they can. Whatever material benefits they reap are but a just return for

the services they render to the material future of Turkey.'
He was under no illusion as to the profits the Kaiser intended
to derive from his friendship and he was shrewd enough to
realise that this visit was not merely dictated by religious
enthusiasm, for the inauguration of the new Lutheran Church
in Jerusalem did not necessitate the presence in the Royal
Suite both of the Foreign Secretary, Prince von Bulow, and of
Dr. Siemens of the Deutsche Banke. The time had come for
William to present him with a bill for services rendered and
the concession for the Baghdad Railway was to be the chief
item on the bill.

In spite of the active support of the new German Ambassador, Baron Marshall von Biberstein, who brought to the
Embassy of Pera the prestige of a former Secretary of State
of the Wilhelmstrasse; in spite of the enormous sums in *baksheesh* paid out to the Sultan's new favourite Izzet Bey, the
concession for the vital stretch of railway from Konia to
Baghdad was still hanging fire. For the past twenty years
Abdul Hamid had adhered to a policy of neutrality based on
the principle of playing up one Power against the other, and
he was frightened of granting any concessions which might
involve him in a war. The situation in Africa, where the growing colonial rivalry between France and England had come
to a clash at Fashoda, made him particularly anxious to avoid
any move which might antagonise him with France or her
ally Russia. Also England's attitude was causing him concern,
for there was a certain trend in the English Press and Parliament to look upon German successes in Asia Minor and
Syria as a useful counterpoise to French and Russian ambitions.
Even for the sake of the Kaiser's friendship, Abdul Hamid had
no intention of assisting England's Imperial policy.

Once more he resorted to his favourite diplomatic weapon
of procrastination, loading his guests with gifts and compliments, committing himself no further on the subject of
concessions, than by leasing to the Directors of the Anatolian
Railways the Port of Haydar Pasha on the Bosphorus, from
where a ferry service could connect the railways of Europe and
of Asia. The official inauguration of the station in the presence
of the Emperors of the East and of the West, was one of the

many brilliant ceremonies with which Abdul Hamid tried to distract the Kaiser from the more vital issues.

Even the splendour of his reception, which out-vied that of the previous visit, (a French Embassy official estimated that the German Emperor's Eastern tour cost the Turkish Treasury thirty million francs of which six million francs were spent on presents alone) even the fraternal warmth of the Sultan's welcome could not distract William from the business in hand. He was no longer the eaglet feeling his wings, freed for the first time from Prince Bismarck's tutelage. The eaglet had grown into an eagle, representing in himself alone the destinies of the German people, and he had come to Constantinople for one purpose only—to charm, persuade, and, if necessary, coerce Abdul Hamid into granting him the Baghdad Railway concession.

Never had the Turks given a foreigner and a European such a warm and spontaneous welcome. With mixed feelings the various ambassadors saw the German Emperor, dressed in his glittering uniforms (it was rumoured that he had no less than one hundred all designed by himself), riding through the streets on a white horse acclaimed by cheering crowds. The English and the Austrians were benevolent, the Russians and French were aloof, and Monsieur Cambon commented with his usual sarcasm, 'The Kaiser delights in talking about Naval and Military matters and in parading his various uniforms, but he is neither a soldier nor a sailor, only a commercial traveller who has found in the Sultan the perfect milk cow.' Of all the hundreds of cartoons emanating from the French press, the cruellest of all, and one which even Izzet did not dare to show his master, depicted Turkey as a milk cow, with Britain, Russia, France and Italy painfully holding her by the legs, while Germany takes the milk.

In the 'Merasim' Kiosk, entirely redecorated in honour of their second visit, the German Emperor and Empress had only to express a wish to have it instantly fulfilled. The timid self-effacing Augusta, prematurely aged by the strain of coping with her ebullient husband, revelled once more in the atmosphere of the Arabian Nights, but William showed signs of impatience. Oriental diplomacy got on his nerves and, though he had a certain liking for Abdul Hamid, a liking mixed with envy at his unlimited power as Sultan and Caliph, he was beginning to suspect that 'the old spider' as he called him in private was deliberately holding up the Baghdad Railway Concession till he saw how France and England were going to settle their differences in Africa.

In spite of the constant exchange of compliments and presents, culminating in the Kaiser presenting the town of Constantinople with a particularly ugly fountain of his own design to be erected on the site of the ancient Hippodrome, there was an underlying tension in the air. Host and guest were not so much concentrated on one another as on what was happening in the regions of the Blue Nile. The telegraph wires of Yildiz were kept busy day and night bringing Abdul Hamid news of the latest moves of Kitchener and of Marchand. Would it end in war, with France and England dragging in the rest of Europe? Then Turkey, profiting by her neutrality, could take the opportunity of winning back Egypt, and of restoring her prestige among the Arabs of North Africa.

The Kaiser was equally interested, but for very different reasons, seeing himself with a free hand in Asia while France and England were quarrelling over Africa.

The Fashoda crisis was still at its height when the German Emperor and Empress embarked for Palestine on the afternoon of October 27. The outward signs of friendship had been pre-served, but the Kaiser had to leave without his concession and, in conversation with the Sultan's ministers, he made no attempt to hide his disappointment. Abdul Hamid affected to ignore the existence of these conversations and bade his guests good-bye at Dolmabagche Pier with an air of genuine affection, as if there had never been the slightest contretemps.

The sun was setting behind the mountains of Thrace as the SS. *Hohenzollern* put out to sea. The last rays of sunlight flashed across the roofs of Stamboul and the waters of the Bosphorus to break in shafts of gold against the windows of Scutari. In the evening light the Marmara became the purple sea of Byzantium, and standing on deck the Kaiser saw himself as another Barbarossa, while railway concessions and commercial treaties faded into the background.

It was getting dark as the Sultan drove back to Yildiz, and it was difficult to distinguish the faces of the crowds which lined the road. There was nothing he hated so much as driving in the dark, and the lanterns of his bodyguard, the occasional street lamps, only served to enhance the sinister appearance of the faces, till each one seemed that of a potential assassin. The fear of assassination, which was always with him, had been accentuated during the past weeks by the news of the tragic death of the beautiful Elizabeth of Austria, murdered by an Italian anarchist while she was on holiday in Geneva. The report of the trial, at which the murderer confessed he had no other grievance against the Empress beyond the fact she wore a crown and, on hearing the verdict, had cried out: 'Long live Anarchy,' reached Abdul Hamid at the time of the Kaiser's visit. From now on he always wore a shirt of mail under his clothes whenever he ventured out in public.

He was glad the visit was over, so that he could shut himself up again in his palace, which every year became more of a fortress. Workmen who were never allowed to see the plans on which they were working were kept constantly employed in strengthening the walls and in making secret passages and underground tunnels. In earlier years, privileged ambassadors like Henry Layard had been invited to the Sultan's private apartments, but now not even the Kaiser had been invited to those rooms, where every door was lined in steel and every room had its cage of parrots, a bird particularly cherished by Abdul Hamid, owing to its habit of screeching at the sight of strangers.

It was with relief that he now heard the gates of Yildiz close behind him, a relief mingled with a sense of emptiness, the same feeling he had known after the Kaiser's first visit, regretting the human companionship, the pleasure of associating with an intelligent man on equal terms. Had Izzet been waiting for him on his return from the Mabeyn, he might have been persuaded that very evening to sign the *irade* granting the Kaiser his coveted concessions. But in place of the subtle Izzet, grown rich on the *baksheesh* of the German Embassy and the favours of his master, was the honest, conscientious Sureya, a

Turk of the old school and fanatically opposed to any European alliance.

As first secretary of the Mabeyn it was Sureya's job to sort and classify the vast mass of correspondence which poured into Yildiz from the four corners of the world and which ranged from the dispatches of ministers and *valis* to the petitions of mendicant dervishes, from the reports of the Turkish Ambassadors abroad to the prognostications of Arabian astrologers. Nothing was too trivial to be brought to the Sultan's notice, for his chief failing, and one which grew worse with the years, was his inability to distinguish the important from the unimportant, and he even went so far as to accept it as a tribute to his fame when certain perverts in Germany and Switzerland wrote offering to have themselves castrated so as to serve in the Imperial harem.

Was it by accident or design that Sureya had placed on top of the pile of papers waiting for his scrutiny a report from one of the military authorities in Mesopotamia, stating that a group of German archaeologists, digging in the region of Mosul, had been discovered to be not archaeologists, but geologists surveying for oil? A mere glance at the report and all Abdul Hamid's underlying distrust of the Germans came to the surface. His friend the Kaiser was out to despoil him of his remaining assets and William's Eastern tour immediately became suspicious to him. His natural instinct had been to sabotage it, for he resented the idea of a foreign Emperor travelling through his dominions in regal state. He had already been irritated by the spontaneous cheers which had greeted the Kaiser in his capital, for he had been unable to ignore the fact that this time the cheering was not dictated by his orders, but by a feeling of genuine gratitude for the country which had helped the Turks to win the war against the Greeks. Personal jealousy also played a part, jealousy of William with his splendid physique and martial bearing, posturing in his shining uniforms in Jerusalem and Damascus, towns which added to the glory of his empire, but which he had never had the courage to visit himself.

If, at Izzet's suggestion, he had not only consented to the Kaiser's journey, but had expended vast sums in order to make it the most splendid and sensational journey any monarch had ever made in a foreign country, it was because he hoped that by parading the German alliance and William's enthusiasm for the East he might end by embroiling Germany with England, always on the watch for the safety of her India route. But to his irritation he found England's attitude to be one of indifference, even at times of actual benevolence. A special correspondent of *The Times* was assigned to accompany the Kaiser on his journey, which was made under the aegis of the English travel agents, Thomas Cook, and it was particularly annoying for Abdul Hamid to read in an English newspaper: 'The superb arrangements for the Emperor's journey to the Holy Land are a triumph of the ingenuity and organisation of Messrs. Cooks.'

All these smouldering grievances now came to the fore, mounting up into a case against Izzet, the prime promoter of the German alliance, whom his enemies did not hesitate to call a German spy. Dismissing Sureya, the Sultan sent for Izzet and the tone of his voice led the First Secretary to hope that this might bring about the disgrace of the hated Arab intruder.

Izzet, however, was as imperturbable as ever when Abdul Hamid confronted him with the proofs of German duplicity, accusing him of being in their pay and ordering him to countermand the arrangements made for the Kaiser's reception in Jerusalem. He was used to these scenes of hysteria and was a past-master at extricating himself out of difficult situations. Time after time he had been on the verge of disgrace, always saving himself by his ingenuity and understanding of the Sultan, whom in public he affected to adore, but whom he secretly despised. He had heard of the German activities in Mesopotamia and, while keeping the news from the Sultan, had made it his business to find out the results of the geologists' discoveries. These results were now in his pocket and, in view of Abdul Hamid's cupidity and greed, he knew his career was not only safe, but in the ascendant, as soon as he handed his master a copy of the report which stated: 'that a small area around Mosul offered far greater opportunities for profit than the whole of the Trans-Caucasian oilfields.' Watching the Sultan's anger turn to avid interest, Izzet ventured to suggest in his slow precise way, that it might be wiser before the concession hunters flocked like vultures to these regions, to take the whole area under His Majesty's divine protection, adding quietly that it could be included with the utmost discretion as part of His Majesty's private property, independent of His Majesty's Civil List.

The following day an Imperial *irade* announced that Izzet el Abit had been promoted to the rank of Pasha.

Meanwhile the Kaiser, unaware of the contretemps which had nearly wrecked his tour, was indulging to the full his art of showmanship. The people of Syria and of Palestine had never seen such a gorgeous caravanserai since the days at the beginning of the century when the unfortunate Caroline of England exposed her indiscretions to their eyes.

The Emperor was on show from the moment he landed at Haifa and the greater the number of journalists who crowded into the tent specially reserved for their reception, the better was he pleased. Escorted by twenty-seven of the highest officials of the Empire, guarded by six hundred soldiers, he made a triumphal progress from Jaffa to Jerusalem. The Turkish Crescent and the German Eagle mingled with the banners of Thomas Cook who had supplied the five hundred mules, the twenty-six sleeping tents, six reception tents and kitchens, as well as the numberless dragomans, cooks and water-carriers who provided for the comfort of the travelling court.

The Kaiser entered Jerusalem dressed in shining armour, in memory of the Crusader knights, but the white silk coat which protected him from the dust was fashioned with a pilgrim's cowl and he impressed the crowds with his piety by getting off his horse as soon as he reached the outskirts of the city and kneeling down to say his prayers in the middle of a dusty road. Whatever mockery it might arouse in certain sections of the world press, and the whole tour was irresistible material for the cartoonists, there is no denying that his emotional effects were superb. He was all things to all men, inaugurating the German Lutheran Church and at the same time buying the German Catholics a piece of land said to be the site of the house of the Virgin Mary; receiving delegations of Jews and Moslems; entertaining priests and rabbis, merchants and bankers, while proclaiming to be 'the knight of peace and labour, interested not in riches but in the healing of souls.' Altogether he was a success, and his very success was arousing the suspicions of those who, like the British Prime Minister, Lord Salisbury, had hitherto been benevolently inclined. It was beginning to look as if this 'knight of peace and labour' was planning to rob England of trade worth many millions.

The Sultan's hopes were at last materialising. A slight rift was beginning to show in the relations between the British Government and Queen Victoria's grandson. At the same time the latest news from Fashoda showed that the French were preparing to withdraw after the Russians had made it clear that they were not prepared to fight for them. With the English grip on Egypt stronger than ever and no hope of turning them out by his own efforts, the Sultan was ready to follow Izzet's advice and redouble his attentions for his friend the Kaiser. In Palestine William had taken on the roles of Paladin and Pilgrim; in Syria he adopted the headgear of a Bedouin Sheikh and even Prince Bulow was surprised when he insisted on laying a wreath on the grave of Saladin. His visit to Damascus was the climax of his visit when, in front of a vast crowd, he evoked the friendship of Haroun Al Rashid and of Charlemagne, declaring that His Imperial Majesty, Abdul Hamid, and the three hundred million Moslems who owed him allegiance as Caliph, had no better friend than the Emperor of Germany.

William was a gambler playing for high stakes and the speech which shocked some of his own subjects and startled Europe was acclaimed with enthusiasm throughout the Moslem world, while the Sultan responded by an effusion of gratitude. But the wheels of diplomacy move slowly in the East and no one believed more than Abdul Hamid in the old proverb that 'Haste is the Devil.' It was not until one year later on November 27, 1899, that Abdul Hamid finally announced his decision to award the Directors of the Deutsche Banke and of the Anatolian Railways the concession to construct the railway from Konia to Baghdad and the Persian Gulf.

Chapter XXX

A NEW CENTURY was born, coinciding with the Sultan's
Silver Jubilee. The hopes of the Turkish exiles living
in poverty in Paris, London and Geneva had not
materialised, for not only was Abdul Hamid still upon the
throne, but time had invested him with a legendary quality.
Anathematised by intellectuals and criticised by the Army, he
was, nevertheless, popular with a large section of his subjects.
To the poor of Constantinople he was the good father Hamid
who gave vast sums in charity and clothed and fed the victims
of the frequent fires which devastated the wooden houses of
Stamboul. Stories of his personal economy, the preference he
gave to the petitions of the humble, of the simplicity and piety
of his daily life were broadcast throughout the Empire and
now, in this year of jubilee, in an atmosphere of comparative
political calm, while England's interests were concentrated
in the Transvaal and Russia was adventuring in the Far East,
Abdul Hamid inaugurated what for every pious Moslem was
to be the crowning work of his life.

As Sultan and Caliph he announced to the faithful his decision to construct a railway from Damascus to the Holy
Cities of Mecca and Medina, thereby enabling those who had
hitherto been too old and weak to face the perils and hardships
of the pilgrimage to achieve the state of grace by visiting the
Prophet's tomb. No Christian was to be allowed to subscribe
to the building of the holy railway, which was to be entirely
financed out of the voluntary contributions of pious Moslems,
and the Sultan headed the subscription list with a donation of
£50,000.

The response to his appeal for funds was immediate. Indian
princes vied with him in their generosity and the humblest
of Moslems in the farthest Pacific island gave his mite. Lack of
trained technicians forced the Sultan to employ German and
Italian engineers in the actual construction of the railway, but

the bulk of the work was done by the Army and the Moslem peasantry, who worked with enthusiasm on a job which would ensure them a place in the Prophet's paradise. The success of the Hedjaz railway was to prove to the outside world that, given an impelling force, the Turks were capable on their own initiative of carrying out a successful enterprise entirely free from graft. In spite of the enormous difficulties encountered by the climate, the terrain and the raids of marauding Bedouins, work proceeded so smoothly and efficiently that only eight years after the Sultan had launched his first appeal for funds the railway had already reached the outskirts of Medina.

Credit for the idea has usually been given to Izzet Pasha, but in all probability it had been germinating in the Sultan's mind since the time when Queen Victoria wrote complaining of the unnecessary hardships suffered by her Moslem subjects on the Mecca pilgrimage. Those who knew him best asserted that Abdul Hamid was not religious at heart, that in the privacy of his apartments he neglected the prayers and ablutions prescribed by the Koran, but the motives behind the Hedjaz Railway were strategical and political rather than religious, and as Pan-Islamic propaganda it was enormously successful; so successful that it was beginning to worry the British authorities in Egypt, for the new railway ran perilously near to the disputed Sinai Peninsula. For the moment, however, the British Government had its hands full in the Transvaal and Abdul Hamid was able to launch his railway to a general chorus of approbation.

An Indian summer seemed about to dawn on his long and troubled reign. The Armenians were still staging demonstrations in England and America, but the small-scale massacres which occasionally took place in some remote village in Kurdestan attracted little attention in the world Press. Macedonia was in a constant state of ferment with Bulgars, Serbs and Albanians staking their various claims, committing every form of banditry and murder, while the reforms promised at the Treaty of Berlin still waited for the Sultan's sanction. It suited Abdul Hamid's policy to encourage the rivalries of the various Balkan princes and the European powers took little notice, so long as Austria and Russia, the two countries most directly concerned, were interested in preserving the *status quo* in the Balkans, and England, usually so ready to interfere, had her forces tied up in Africa.

For the first time in many years, the Sultan's frontiers were free from danger of attack, but this feeling gave no sense of security to his private life. The humble people worshipped him as a legend, but so long as his brother Murad lived he could still be called a usurper. Ali Suavi's revolt had only been the first of a series of abortive attempts to liberate the ex-Sultan, each of which had been dealt with more severely than the last. The Sheikh ul Islam on three occasions presented Abdul Hamid with *fetvas* giving him the power to have his brother put to death, but throughout his life he had a horror of signing a death warrant and this applied even to the brother whose continued existence haunted his days and nights. So Murad was allowed to live, while the dungeons of Yildiz were filled with young men accused of conspiring in his favour and contraband newspapers printed by political exiles abroad and smuggled into the country told the people that the ex-Sultan had recovered his sanity and was being kept in unlawful detention. All the efforts of Abdul Hamid's police were powerless to prevent their circulation, while the threats and protests of his ambassadors abroad were powerless to suppress the activities of his political opponents.

Among the exiles were many former friends and relatives, victims of his tyrannical rule. Even the long-suffering Mavroyeni had ended by falling into disgrace, accused of keeping a secret diary for future publication. The loss of the only doctor whom he trusted was disastrous to the Sultan's health as he resorted more and more to his own empirical knowledge of medicine, refusing to touch the prescriptions ordered by his physicians, or tossing the contents of twenty boxes of pills into a common bowl and taking one at random so as to lessen the risk of poison.

The Hungarian, Vambéry, whose friendship with the Sultan had survived many vicissitudes, became the object of his suspicions when he dared to suggest that philosophy and political economy should be included in the curriculum of the new University which was to be inaugurated in celebration of his

Jubilee. The Sultan declared that such knowledge would be dangerous for his people and would be like putting a sharp knife into the hands of a young and inexperienced child. In the end the whole plan was dropped, Vambéry left Constantinople for Europe and, by the irony of fate, the building intended for the University became the Parliament House of 1908.

Renegade Christians, Levantine adventurers and Arab riff-raff amassed vast fortunes and became Pashas overnight, while the Sultan's loyal subjects who tried to open his eyes to the peculations of his ministers were politely thanked for their information and sent to meditate on their grievances in some distant province.

Abdul Hamid was prepared to be robbed by his ministers and was even cynical enough to joke about it. He would discuss quite openly the peculations of the old Minister of Marine, who owed his continued office to the fact that he had reduced the Turkish Navy to such a state of neglect that there was no fear of it ever playing a part in a revolt against the Throne. On one occasion, when it was reported to Abdul Hamid that a certain conjuror had performed the extraordinary feat of swallowing some knives and forks, he remarked that he did not see anything so very miraculous about this, as his Minister of Naval Affairs swallowed big iron-clad frigates without doing any harm to himself.

European visitors were shocked by his dissimulation, the way he flattered his ministers and servants to their faces and described them as rogues and scoundrels the minute they had left the room: the way in which he encouraged them to spy upon each other and listened to each in turn. He deliberately encouraged the rivalry between Izzet and Abul Huda, the two creators and promoters of Pan-Islam, and it was largely thanks to Izzet's intrigues that Abul Huda never achieved the coveted position of Sheikh ul Islam. But the Sultan's superstitious belief in his prophetic powers still gave the old Sheikh an ascendancy at the Islamic Councils which met at Yildiz once a week to discuss the latest development of the Pan-Islam campaign and Abul Huda had the satisfaction of preventing Izzet from carrying out what would have been the financial *coup* of his career.

In the summer of 1896 the Zionist leader, Dr. Herzl, visited

Constantinople with a view to persuading the Sultan to lease a part of Palestine as a national home for the Jews. Under the auspices of a renegade Austrian, a certain Weiss Pasha, Herzl succeeded in penetrating the inner sanctum of the Palace Secretariat and the *baksheesh* offered and the sums involved were sufficiently tempting to interest both Izzet and his Imperial master. Thousands of acres of land in Palestine, including the orange groves of Jaffa and the port of Haifa, were incorporated in the Sultan's Civil List and he saw the opportunity, not only of filling his private exchequer, but, which was even more important, of gaining the goodwill of International Jewry and thereby facilitating the grant of future loans.

Dr. Herzl's hopes seemed bright until Abul Huda got wind of the scheme and, as the Sultan's religious adviser, impressed on him the immense harm it would do to his prestige throughout the Arab world. With the approach of his Jubilee, Abdul Hamid's spiritual ambitions got the better of his cupidity and Dr. Herzl left Constantinople with a jewelled snuff box as the only souvenir of a visit which might have altered history.

Abul Huda was not without rivals in the religious sphere. The Sultan was always susceptible to new influences and, for a time, the celebrated Persian Sheikh Djemaleddin El Afghani, as famous in the drawing rooms of London as in the mosques of Cairo, became the keeper of his religious conscience. Inspired by Djemaleddin, he envisaged the vast project of making peace between the two rival sects of Islam, the Sunni and the Shia, and of all of the visitors to Constantinople in the year of the Jubilee none was more welcome than the Shiite ruler, the Shah of Persia. But like so many other of these ambitious projects it came to nothing, lost in the vast pile of papers stacked high on the Sultan's desk.

While Abdul Hamid's energies were concentrated on strengthening his hold on his Asiatic possessions, his capital was rapidly becoming an international centre to which, three times a week, the Orient Express brought a fresh complement of speculators and financiers. The wildest gambling took place on the Constantinople Bourse where prices fluctuated to such a degree as to become known as 'bosphorescence'. Unfortunately it was usually the Turks who were the victims of these speculations. Having no proper business experience, they were easy dupes for the Greeks and Armenians—a factor which contributed to the already existing bitterness between Moslem and Christian. Very few of the Sultan's ministers had any idea of how to balance a budget. While the industries controlled by the European Council of the Ottoman Debt flourished, the finances of the Sublime Porte were in a state of continual chaos and, in spite of the Sultan's personal attempts at economy, the palace continued to be administered with a reckless extravagance.

Abdul Hamid was growing old, but every year more and more women were introduced into his harem. Female companionship and understanding were doubly necessary to him now that his physical powers were waning. Women became the companions of his work as well as of his leisure and it was not unusual to find a veiled figure, seated by the Sultan's desk, opening with gloved hands the letters and petitions he did not dare to touch for fear of contamination.

The breath of a new century was slowly penetrating the harem. Dressed in trailing tea-gowns from Paris and Vienna the Sultanas dined à la franca in rooms furnished with all the worst excrescences of European taste and discussed the newest novel of Paul de Kock or the latest diplomatic scandal with the wives and daughters of the Sultan's ministers. Abdul Hamid countenanced these visits from the outside world, for there was always a hope that prattling female tongues might provide him with some useful information on his ministers. Failing the information, he was amused by gossip. In his young days one of Flora Cordier's greatest assets had been her witty, unbridled tongue and the tedium of conversation in the harem was considerably relieved by a whiff of Pera's scandal.

Constantinople in the first months of the new century presented as many curious anomalies as the Imperial harem. While the new hotels in Pera and the Palace of Yildiz blazed with electric light, the rest of the town was so badly lit that it was dangerous to venture out after dark without an armed guard. It had needed all the ingenuity of a French electrical company to persuade Abdul Hamid that dynamos were not connected with dynamite and that there was no risk of his being blown up at night if he had electricity installed in his palace. But even so he refused to trust the ordinary citizen with such a dangerous innovation. Hotels were privileged only because he needed the tourist's money. But when it came to the telephone, not even the most enterprising of companies could persuade him to have one installed at Yildiz. Here his ministers and secretaries were partly to blame. Dreading the time when their indefatigable master would be able to telephone them at all times of the day and night they played on his fears by making him believe that it was an infernal machine, fraught with hidden dangers.

Those who attempted to make Constantinople into a modern European city found themselves continually obstructed by the Sultan's prejudices and suspicions. In his memoirs Sir Edgar Vincent, later Lord D'Abernon, describes some of the difficulties of transacting business with Abdul Hamid, his habit of postponing an Imperial *irade* for weeks or even months, so that all concerned should realise that his was the sanction that mattered. During these weeks, those interested in concessions had to pay interminable visits to the Sultan's private secretaries or to the leading chamberlains of the palace, wasting hours in ceremonial courtesy and the consumption of innumerable cups of coffee. It was part of the palace etiquette that all discussions should take place in the presence of any visitors who happened to be calling. These visitors sat round the room on divans and so heard all that was going on. As a third of the population of Constantinople was in the pay of one or other of the foreign Embassies there was little hope of keeping any transaction secret.

In spite of these obstructions, diplomats and business men continued to intrigue one against the other. The Americans had now joined in the race for concessions and the head of a philanthropic mission sent to organise Armenian relief was showing more interest in the oil-wells of Mesopotamia than in the reports of Armenian bishops. With a few exceptions the behaviour of the foreign diplomats fully justified Abdul Hamid's low opinion of human nature but the most unscrupulous were also the most useful. No one was more shameless in his transactions than the new French Ambassador, Monsieur Constans, who in his eagerness to secure concessions sacrificed all dignity and prestige. Monsieur Constans' connections with the barons of the *haute finance* were of considerable value to the Sultan in procuring him loans on the French Bourse, while his passion for business rather than diplomacy facilitated the task of the Deutsche Banke in obtaining the co-operation of French bankers in the financing of the Baghdad railway.

The railway was still the chief bone of contention among the rival Powers. A few months before the Germans secured the prize, a British group had attempted to get the concession by offering more favourable terms. The English were enjoying a brief spell of popularity at the Porte, owing to the charm of their new Ambassador, Sir Nicholas O'Connor, who seems to have exercised on the Sultan the same fascination as his compatriot and predecessor Lord Dufferin. But neither the British Government nor the City of London gave their full support to the scheme and six months later the outbreak of hostilities in the Transvaal left the field open to the Germans.

Fortunately for England there were a few far-sighted individuals ready to protect her interests. No sooner had it become known that the Germans had secured the concession, than that great imperialist, Lord Curzon, then Viceroy of India, became alarmed at the construction of a railway which would link the head of the Persian Gulf with the railways of Central Europe. Lord Curzon was not a man to write home for instructions. Acting on his own initiative he ordered the British Resident in the Persian Gulf area to proceed to Kuwait and negotiate with the Sheikh a clandestine agreement, by which the latter accepted the protection of the British Government and promised to enter into no international agreements without the consent of a British resident adviser. A few years later when a German technical commission visited Kuwait to negotiate for terminal and port facilities, they found the Sheikh curiously intractable. Complaints were made to the Sublime Porte and the Sultan immediately despatched an expedition to Kuwait to assert his sovereignty. But the British had forestalled him. The presence of a gun-boat flying the Union Jack in the harbour of Kuwait warned Abdul Hamid and his German ally that Great Britain regarded the Persian Gulf as her own particular sphere of influence and would brook no rival on those coasts.

Chapter XXXI

THOUSANDS OF COPIES of the Koran printed at the Sultan's expense were being distributed throughout the Moslem world; the Baghdad railway was crawling towards the outskirts of the Taurus, and new oil-wells were being drilled in Mesopotamia. But at the time when Abdul Hamid's energies were concentrated on the spiritual and material welfare of his Asiatic Empire came news of revolution on his European frontiers.

There had been trouble in Macedonia for nearly twenty-five years, ever since the statesmen at Berlin had given back to Turkey territory which the Russians, at San Stefano, had promised to the Bulgarians. Macedonia remained Turkish on the condition that the Sultan would carry out the necessary reforms, but a quarter of a century had elapsed without Abdul Hamid making any attempt to keep his promises. The administration was still as corrupt and inefficient as in the past; the traditionally hostile elements of Greeks, Bulgarians and Albanians were left to fight their own quarrels, while the Sultan exploited their rivalries, secretly favouring the Albanians who played in Macedonia the rule which the Kurds had played in Armenia, encroaching on their neighbours' land and raiding their cattle.

Abdul Hamid could afford to ignore the protests of Europe for so long as the Balkan Powers were at each other's throats and Austria's *Drang nach Osten* was directed to Salonika, so long as Russia and Bulgaria remained estranged and the Czar refused to recognise Ferdinand of Saxe-Coburg as ruler of the principality there was as little chance of the Powers agreeing over Macedonia as over Armenia. But the twentieth century had brought new orientations into the field of foreign politics and the death of Victoria of England marked the end of an era. England's war against the Boers had had a bad press in Europe and she was now in search of friends. No one was more versed in the art of making friends than her new King, and Edward VII's royal progresses from Ischl to Paris and from Paris to Reval were to have dangerous repercussions on Abdul Hamid and the policy of *Divide et Impera* which till now had served him so well.

The European Powers were settling their differences. A *rapprochement* between France and England was in the air; there were friendly overtures between France and Italy; Russia and Austria had agreed to co-operate in the Balkans, and the Czar had finally recognised Ferdinand of Saxe-Coburg as Prince of Bulgaria. However interested in maintaining the *status quo* in the Balkans and in preventing Macedonia from belonging to one or other of the rival principalities, neither Austria nor Russia could afford open anarchy on the frontiers of Europe. When the Bulgarian minority in Macedonia began to form secret committees based on the pattern of the *Carbonari* of Naples and revolution flared up from one end of Macedonia to the other, giving the Sultan the excuse to dispatch his hordes of Bashibazooks to stamp it out, Russia and Austria finally realised that they would have to put pressure on Abdul Hamid.

Once more the murder of a European consul—this time a Russian, stabbed by an Albanian at Monastir—forced the Powers to action and the so-called Murzteg Programme, drawn up by the Foreign Ministers of Austria and Russia, supported and one may say, inspired by England (who after being accused of piracy in Africa, was re-establishing her position as Governess of the Levant), called on Abdul Hamid to disband his Bashibazooks and to re-organise the Gendarmerie under the supervision of European officers.

Abdul Hamid made the usual promises and procrastinated as usual, while the Macedonian cauldron he had kept simmering for over twenty years boiled over without his making any attempt to put out the flame. Half measures calculated to save his face and appease the Powers only served to enrage the revolutionaries still further. Even the Herculean efforts of a handful of European officers who, after countless delays, were finally allowed to take up their posts, could not restore order to the bandit-ridden countryside. Thus, when the Powers began to disagree over the various sectors under their control and his friend the Kaiser refused to co-operate in the policing of Macedonia, Abdul Hamid had every reason to hope that this international police force would be as short lived as the military consuls Great Britain had despatched to Anatolia at the end of the Russian-Turkish war.

From 1903 to 1907 circumstances helped to foster his illusions. Russia's humiliating defeats in the Far East and her troubles at home distracted her attention from the Balkans and the Straits. Austria was secretly negotiating with Turkey for permission to construct a railway from Bosnia to the Sandjak of Novi-Bazaar, and a flourishing chain of brothels, under the patronage of her Consuls, was her chief contribution to the civilising of Macedonia, while France and Italy were both so immersed in the lucrative past-time of concession hunting that they could spare little time for the welfare of the Catholic minorities of whom they were supposed to be the protectors.

Old and worn, harassed and coerced, Abdul Hamid was still an adept in the game of diplomatic chess. His chief trouble as always was with the English and the personal charm of Sir Nicholas O'Connor could not mitigate the asperity of the notes in which the British Government pressed Abdul Hamid for financial and judicial reforms in Macedonia. England took the lead when the combined Powers, including Germany, drafted a collective note, demanding the appointment of an international Committee to control the finances of Macedonia. The Kaiser made haste to inform his friend that he was only interested in improving conditions for the benefit of the Turkish Treasury, but the Sultan's pride was outraged and for five months he stood out against what he regarded as an infringement of his sovereign rights.

This time the Concert of Europe remained firm, and in December 1905 the combined naval squadrons of four Powers occupied the Aegean island of Mytelene. The presence of foreign warships in Turkish waters, for whose presence he blamed England and England alone, cowed the Sultan to submission. But Abdul Hamid was never so dangerous as when he appeared to submit, and a few months later an anti-European riot in Alexandria, instigated by the Sultan's agents, followed by

Turkish movements on the Egyptian frontier and the occupation of a town in Egyptian territory showed the British in Egypt that they were to be made to pay for their country's energetic advocacy of Macedonian reform.

The so-called Akaba Crisis, during which the Sultan tried to bring the boundaries of Turkey near to the Suez Canal, was successfully dealt with by Lord Cromer. But the anti-British feeling it aroused in Egypt at the time, the violence of nationalist feeling in support of the Caliph, the ambiguous role played by certain German diplomats, in particular a brilliant young archaeologist by the name of Baron von Oppenheim whose frequent excursions to the railhead of the Hedjaz railway at Maan were giving anxiety to the British authorities, all went to show that Abdul Hamid in an unpleasant mood was still a dangerous force to be reckoned with.

He felt himself to be particularly strong at the moment, for his brother Murad had died in the spring of 1904 and, after a reign of nearly thirty years, he was at last free from the fear of being considered as a usurper. Two months after Murad's death a terrible earthquake shook Constantinople on the day of the Bairam Festival, when he was holding his yearly audience in the throne room of Dolmabagche. A diplomat who was present records that when a tremor shook the great palace from end to end, sending the four-ton crystal chandelier hurtling to the ground, and courtiers screamed and panicked, the Sultan was the only one present who remained completely calm and never left his throne.

Continually haunted by an assassin's knife, he astounded his chamberlains by his courage when a young officer made an unsuccessful attempt to stab him one day as he was coming out of his private theatre at Yildiz. The following year of 1905 saw another attempt at assassination when a carriage filled with dynamite exploded in the square outside the Hamidieh Mosque while the Sultan was at prayers. The bodies of the unfortunate victims of the outrage were removed before Abdul Hamid came out of the Mosque and the ceremony proceeded as usual with the Sultan driving his open phaeton at a trot up the hill while his Pashas in their heavy gold-embroidered uniforms ran panting behind on foot. But this time there was panic in Yildiz. Here was no isolated act of a madman but a deeply laid plot with ramifications abroad. The chief of the police put the blame on the Armenians, but it was all too convenient to blame the Armenians for every outrage committed in the town. Arrests and confessions under torture could not placate the Sultan, for there was no satisfactory explanation as to how the carriage, loaded with dynamite, had got past the guards. How far had disaffection spread among the Army? Were there traitors even among his aides-de-camp?

The reports of Munir Pasha, his Ambassador in Paris and chief source of information regarding the activities of Turkish exiles, held many disquieting references to the recent activities of the Young Turks and the existence of a secret society in their midst, known as the 'Committee of Union and Progress.' In spite of his army of spies and the large funds the Sultan had placed at his disposal, Munir had made little headway in discovering the identity of the men who controlled this movement.

Hundreds of innocent people were arrested throughout the Empire in an attempt to connect the Armenian bomb outrage with the Young Turks. The censorship laws were tightened, even the foreign mailbags were tampered with. But the *valis* and *kaimakams* who carried out the orders of Yildiz had grown old in a police state and failed to recognise the subtle breath of freedom which stirred the various cities of the Empire from Salonika to Baghdad.

Abdul Hamid was now reaping the consequences of the mistakes made both by him and his ancestors in banishing disaffected politicians to the provinces. Men like Midhat did not spend three years in Syria without disseminating their doctrines and ideals. Young officers who had dared to criticise the inefficiency of their superiors were not likely to become more loyal when banished to Macedonian barracks in brigand-infested areas.

Obrenovitch or Karageorge, Nicholas of Montenegro or Ferdinand of Bulgaria, Abdul Hamid was a match for them all. Druse emirs and Arab sheikhs were flattered and entwined in his net, but his failure lay in his ignorance of his own people, the Ottoman Turks. Wrapped in his dreams of Pan-Islam, he did not understand the new brand of nationalism which was being born in the back streets of Salonika. In this thriving port on the Aegean, where the Moslem Turk was in the minority, the young officers of the Third Army Corps sent to suppress the Christian rebels in the mountains came into contact with the Masonic Lodges which flourished in a town where one third of the population was of Jewish origin. The Sultan had always suspected the Masonic Lodges of subversive activities. His dislike of them dated from the time when his brother Murad accepted the Grand Mastership of the Turkish masons. But one of the most flourishing lodges of Salonika was under Italian protection. To suppress it would involve him in a quarrel with the Ambassador, Marchese Imperiali, whose country was only waiting for an opportunity to pounce on Tripoli.

It has never been fully ascertained as to how far the Turkish Revolutionary Movement depended on the 'Grand Orient', that vast secret organisation with its political tentacles all over Europe. Started by a small group of exiles in Paris and Geneva, the 'Committee of Union and Progress' was completely transformed in character when it finally took shape in Macedonia. In Paris the leaders were poets and idealists, wanting nothing more than the restoration of Midhat's constitution; in Macedonia they were angry and embittered men of action, humiliated by the continual intervention of Europe and the presence of European officers in the Gendarmerie, infuriated by the way in which a pack of Arab adventurers were selling their country to foreign capitalists. While their own salaries remained unpaid, the Ottoman Treasury had found the money to guarantee the Germans nearly twenty thousand francs (£800) for every kilometre of the railway which was to cross the Taurus mountains to Baghdad. 'Turkey for the Turks' was the new slogan in the barracks of Resna and of Monastir, though the brains of the new movement were mostly of Jewish or Albanian origin.

Political events at the beginning of 1908 brought matters to a head. Italy staged a naval demonstration off Tripoli, on the excuse of protecting her nationals from the attacks of Senussi tribesmen. The Powers withdrew their garrisons from Crete, an ominous indication of its future union with Greece. In England a Liberal Government had come into power, and several of its members belonged to the Balkan Committee which for the past years had been pressing for a stronger line with the Turks in Macedonia. But all these events were dwarfed by the greatest diplomatic coup of the century. Cruising in northern waters, King Edward VII and his nephew, the Czar Nicholas II, signed a Treaty of Friendship, destroying overnight the pivot of the Sultan's foreign policy which revolved round the rivalry of England and Russia. But however great the Sultan's consternation and fury at the news, it was nothing compared to the indignation of the young officers in the tumble-down barracks of Macedonia.

The high officials who accompanied Their Majesties to Reval were said to have spent most of their time in discussing the Macedonian problem and it was rumoured that an elaborate scheme for the pacification of the whole region was shortly to be published by the British Foreign Office. In the eyes of the 'Committee of Union and Progress' the Sultan Hamid's policy was mainly responsible for having brought Russia and England together. It was all very well for his Foreign Minister to inform the European Ambassadors that they could expect no further concession in Macedonia, but the news from Reval was evidence that Macedonia would be stolen from Turkey just as Eastern Rumelia, Egypt and Tunis had been stolen in the past.

Political exiles were gradually drifting back to Turkey, smuggled in on tramp steamers and *caiques*, disguised as priests and stevedores, in Albanian *fustanella* or the rags of wandering dervishes. Members of the 'Committee of Union and Progress' had left Salonika to propagate their doctrines in the barracks of Syria and of Asia Minor. The word 'Constitution', forgotten and forbidden for the past thirty years, was again in circulation.

Whether the Sultan's Ministers were aware of the seriousness of the movement and were unable to suppress it, or whether the spies were too frightened to tell the truth, Abdul Hamid appeared to have been left in ignorance of the gravity of the situation. He was still corresponding with Munir Pasha in

Paris, pressing for the extradition of such Young Turks as were known to him, when the principal men in the movement were already back in Turkey.

Even as late as July 2, 1908, when the news came through from Salonika that an infantry major by the name of Niyazi Bey had looted four thousand medjidiehs from the battalion treasure-chest and led his men into the mountains to raise the standard of revolt on behalf of both Moslems and Christians—even when Enver Bey, one of the most brilliant graduates of the Military Staff College had deserted from Resna with one hundred and fifty men and taken to the mountains above Lake Ochrida—even then Abdul Hamid failed to recognise the danger.

There had always been trouble in Macedonia and a handful of revolutionaries were now taking the opportunity to stir up more trouble. He had only to send a battalion of his loyal Asiatics and they would soon be made to regret the foolhardiness of their actions. Meanwhile he reverted to his usual tactics by trying to divide the leaders among themselves. While Niyazi was declared an outlaw, Enver was recalled to Constantinople and bribed with offers of promotion. But Abdul Hamid had many shocks in store for him and the first was when Enver sent no answer to His Imperial Majesty's most gracious invitation. On July 8, the Commander-in-Chief of the forces in Northern Macedonia, one of the Sultan's most trusted generals, was assassinated at Monastir and from all over Macedonia came news of Turkish garrisons and Christian insurgents throwing in their lot with the mutineers. The whole of the Third Army Corps was in revolt before the Sultan could put his hands on any of the leaders, and the final shock came when the first battalion of Anatolian soldiers landed in Salonika and, instead of firing on their comrades, threw down their arms and joined in the cry, 'Liberty, progress and equality.'

On July 23, 1908, a formal ultimatum, signed by the Central Committee of Union and Progress in Monastir, informed His Imperial Majesty that unless the Constitution was restored within twenty-four hours the Second and Third Army Corps would march on the capital.

Chapter XXXII

THE HUNDRED CLOCKS of Yildiz Kiosk were ticking away momentous hours. Strains of light music played by someone, whose thoughts were not concentrated on the music, drifted through open windows. The Sultan had retired to the Little Mabeyn and the look on his face, as he crossed the threshold, was such as to make even the Chief Eunuch shake in his embroidered shoes.

In the courtyards and gardens chamberlains and equerries gathered round with anxious faces, whispering to one another the latest news from the capital. Something had gone wrong with the Army—an unpopular pasha had been shot—Government spies were being beaten to death, others did not dare to show themselves in the street—crowds were reported to be marching on Yildiz, shouting for the Constitution without any interference from the police.

The whispers died away as the slight, bearded figure of Izzet Pasha passed by on his way to an audience with the Sultan. The news which Izzet was bringing to his master was not of a pleasant nature. The Macedonian ultimatum heralded a general revolution. From all over the Empire, *valis* and *kaimakams* were throwing in their lot with the Young Turks and the Sultan's spies and agents were being murdered, not only in Salonika and Constantinople, but in Baghdad and Erzerum.

Abdul Hamid's position was not enviable. He had either to fight or to restore the Constitution, in which case he would be signing his own death warrant, for the Young Turks had never forgiven him his betrayal of Midhat. But would he have the energy and courage to resist? Izzet had his doubts, listening to the sound of music played by a hand which had lost control. He knew his master so well and recognised the piano playing as an ominous sign that his nerves were at breaking point and that at any moment he might give way to a violent fit of hysteria. The piano playing had stopped before the Chief Eunuch dared to usher him into the royal presence. Outwardly the Sultan appeared to be quite calm and rational, but the very calm made Izzet feel the hopelessness of his cause. How could he convince this tired old man who looked as if he had not got the strength to drag himself out into the garden that he might have to fight to preserve his throne.

'Force must be met with force. Your Majesty must deal with the Young Turks as your Great Ancestor Mahmud dealt with the Janissaries. Open your gates to the crowds now marching on your palace and go out among them, speak to them as your children, denounce the Young Turks as traitors and within an hour they will be shouting for their Padishah louder than they are now shouting for the Constitution.'

All the eloquence of his Arab forebears, the sophistry of his Jesuit education, went into Izzet's words which were those of a gambler putting on his last stake. He was under no illusion as to what awaited him at the hands of the Young Turks and had made his plans accordingly. He had bank deposits in London, Paris and Berlin, and a ship of the Khedivial line had been chartered to take him and his family to safety in the event of an emergency. But tonight he felt a curious reluctance to part from the master whose thoughts he had interpreted and whose policy he had directed for the past fifteen years, whom he despised and yet admired, hated and yet loved.

'I am an old man, and my empire is disintegrating.' There was infinite weariness in the Sultan's voice. 'But so long as I live, it shall never be said that I caused civil war among my people. You are young, Izzet, and the world is open to you.' With these words Abdul Hamid took up a pen and put his signature to a paper lying on the desk, which he handed to Izzet, adding, 'Here is a *firman*, authorising you to travel to whatever part of Europe you wish. When you return to Constantinople as an old man you will find many changes. Turkey will be a country, not an empire. Democracy will have taken the place of religion, and I doubt whether my people will be any happier than now.'

There were tears in Izzet's eyes as he kissed his master's hand for the last time. All his eloquence had deserted him, his words choked in his throat and already he felt the bitterness of the exile.

Izzet had gone, and for the first time in his life Abdul Hamid felt lost and helpless. The three thousand inhabitants of Yildiz waited on his wishes, but he had never felt so lonely as tonight. In the whole of his capital was there no one he could trust? Or was this the punishment of Allah, for having opened out his country to foreign concessionaires and allied himself with a Christian emperor. He had no illusions about the Kaiser. So long as the kilometric guarantees for the Baghdad railway were regularly paid it did not matter to William of Hohenzollern whether he or his brother Reshad sat on the Throne of Osman. In the end it might have been wiser to have come to terms with England and let her police his Empire. Kutchuk Said was probably right when, during the Armenian Massacres, he warned him not to quarrel with the one Power whose foreign policy was based on the preservation of the Ottoman Empire. At the time Said had been banished for his presumption, but tonight Abdul Hamid remembered him as the only minister he had trusted in over thirty years.

All the most constructive acts of his reign, the administration for the Ottoman debt, the École Civile for the training of Civil Servants, the Military College at Pangalti and the Medical Establishment at Scutari were associated with Said. He liked to think that he had been lenient with him in his exile. When the old man fell ill he had let him come back to Constantinople, to live in retirement in his house at Nishantash. And tonight he found himself wondering why he had kept him in retirement for so long when his integrity and courage might have helped where the subtleness and trickiness of an Izzet could only fail.

Dawn was rising behind the hills of Asia, stealing over the minarets of Scutari to wake the sleeping *muezzin*, when Kutchuk Said, still struggling with the buttons of his court uniform, was driven at a gallop through the gates of Yildiz. The younger guards failed to recognise the once so familiar face with the truculent mouth, the neat square beard grown grey in the intervening years. But the older ones stood stiff to attention, for if Said Pasha was back at the palace it could only be in the capacity of Grand Vizir. How often in moments of crisis he had trod these garden paths at hours when even the wild animals in the Sultan's menagerie were asleep and the drowsy slaves on duty in the courtyards had to be stirred to life. But tonight the whole palace shared in the Sultan's vigil and drops of sweat, the sweat of a man frightened for his life, hung on the pendulous cheeks of the Chief Eunuch.

Abdul Hamid was waiting for him in his study with a map of Macedonia spread out on a table in front of him. In his loose white *entari*, with his huge fez pushed back on his high narrow forehead and the light falling on his beak-like nose, the first impression was that of a great white bird hovering over his prey.

Then he looked up and Said saw the cavernous eyes and twitching mouth of a man who had not known sleep for days.

'What have you got for me, Said, in your Portfolio?' The questioner seemed already to know the answer and unhesitatingly Said replied 'Sire, I bring you the Constitution.' At first he did not know whether these words would cost him his life or make him for the sixth time Grand Vizir. He saw the Sultan rear his head—the vulture about to strike—and a hand stretch towards the table where a small jewelled pistol was lying beside a *tesbieh*. For a second the fingers appeared to hover, then they clutched at the amber beads, and the moments passed while Abdul Hamid remained engrossed in thought, with the beads slipping through his nervous fingers. Morning crept in through the windows. From the distant city and the nearby mosque came the muezzin's cry—'God is great. I bear witness there is no God but God . . . .' But even Said who knew his master so well and was familiar with all his arts of dissimulation was not prepared for the sudden *volte face*, when, speaking in a voice which gathered strength with every word, the Sultan said, ' I am wholeheartedly in favour of a Constitution which it was always my intention to restore as soon as my people were ready for it. Let it be proclaimed immediately together with full amnesty for all political prisoners.'

Prostrating himself to the ground in a low *salaam*, Said paid homage both to God's Vice-regent upon Earth and to the greatest actor of his age.

The *irade* proclaiming the Constitution was published in the morning papers of Friday, July 24, and Constantinople gave itself up to a frenzy of rejoicing, unequalled even in those brief halcyon days of 1876. Not in Constantinople alone, but in Salonika and Monastir, where the 'Committee of Union and Progress' had not even waited for the publication of the Sultan's *irade*; in Damascus and Baghdad, in Van and Trabzon, the restoration of the Constitution was hailed as the dawn of a new era.

Eyewitnesses in Constantinople described the amazing scenes which took place in the square of Aya Sofia and Galata Bridge, when Greeks and Bulgars, Kurds and Armenians embraced one another as brothers and Young Turk officers harangued the crowds, telling them that Jews, Christians and Moslems were no longer divided, but all working together for the glory of the Ottoman nation. Caught on the swelling tide of enthusiasm, *softas* and *mollas* were seen wearing the red-and-white cockade of liberty. Even the shopkeepers, leaving their shops wide open, and the guild of butchers in their white overalls joined in with the crowds which surged round the Sublime Porte, cheering for the Sultan and the Constitution.

There was one great difference, however, between the celebrations in Salonika and those in Constantinople. In the capital it was still the Sultan, 'Good old Baba Hamid', who was given credit for the wisdom of his edict, and the anger and resentment of those who had suffered under the Hamidian régime was largely directed against the palace *camarilla* who, by lies and deceit, had kept their Padishah away from his loyal subjects. But it was another matter in Salonika. Here it was the young majors of the Committee who were hailed as the heroes of the revolution, and there was hardly a cheer for the Sultan when Enver Bey, so handsome and dashing in his new uniform, drove in triumph through the streets escorted by a regiment of artillery and a band playing the *Marseillaise*. The officers of the Second and Third Army Corps who, till yesterday, had been ready to march on the capital, had now sworn to support the Sultan and the Constitution. But their oath to the Sultan was probably as hollow as when Abdul Hamid swore to support the Constitution on the Sunday of July 26, when sixty thousand of his loyal subjects broke into the courtyards of his palace to give him an unexpected, and probably unwanted, ovation.

In the past years his people had only glimpsed him through a double hedge of bayonets, sitting far back in his carriage, or standing for a brief second on the steps of the Mosque. But now he appeared before them on the balcony—a rather pathetic, shabby little figure, blinking at them in the July sunlight, asking rather sadly what it was they wanted from him. And all the propaganda of the Young Turks, the legends of the 'Ogre of Yildiz,' were forgotten in a wave of emotion which swept through the crowd as one of them cried out, 'We only want to see Your Majesty in good health. For thirty-two years your presence has been denied us by traitors. Thank God you have shown yourself to us. Long live the Padishah.' Perhaps Abdul Hamid was touched by this demonstration. But few clear-sighted politicians can have believed in his sincerity when he replied, 'It is true that traitors have separated me from you but these times are passed.' (Only the day before a deputation from the 'Committee of Union and Progress' had caused him to sign an *irade* dismissing his First and Second Secretaries, his Commander-in-Chief and Minister of Marine.) He went on: 'At the beginning of my reign I granted a Constitution to my country, but I had to withdraw it, for the people were not yet ready for it. Now I proclaim it indefinitely and I am determined it shall be carried into effect.' Summoning the Sheikh ul Islam, who was standing at the back of the balcony, he solemnly swore in his presence to protect and preserve the Constitution.

This was Abdul Hamid's first public appearance in the role of democratic monarch and by now he had already experienced several nasty shocks. In spite of the veneration in which he was held by the populace, or perhaps because of it, the Young Turks were determined to make themselves as politely unpleasant as possible. No one dared openly challenge the

authority of the Sultan-Caliph, but he could be attacked through
his entourage and the accounts of the swindles and robberies of
the palace pashas, which now appeared in the daily Press, were
not calculated to enhance his reputation. People were bound to
be influenced, when they saw hitherto privileged beings like
Abul Huda stripped of their possessions and unceremoniously
bundled off to prison to await the judgment of the 'Committee
of Union and Progress', who though not yet officially in power
made it quite clear they were only ready to tolerate a Government subservient to their wishes. The one man whom the
Committee would have liked to lay their hands on, had
evaded them. By the morning of August 2, Izzet Pasha,
together with his family and dependants, was safely on his way
to Europe, where he was to become a familiar figure on the
promenades of Brighton and Boulogne.

Abdul Hamid had neither time nor sympathy to spare for
the vicissitudes of his former favourites. He was relieved to
hear that Izzet had escaped, chiefly because he had used him
in certain financial transactions which he did not want the
Committee to hear of. His expropriation of the richest of
the Mesopotamian oil fields and his negotiations both with the
Deutsche Banke and certain American oil companies were not
matters to be made public. Not content with depriving him of
some of his most intimate counsellors, the Committee were
beginning to interfere with the provisions of his Civil List.
Before a month was over his private theatre at Yildiz had
been closed and his three hundred musicians reduced to a quarter
of that number; his two hundred and ninety aides-de-camp
whittled down to a mere thirty, and his famous Arab stud-
farm taken over by the State. None of these economies affected
him personally, for his pleasures were of the simplest; pottering
about his carpentry shop and having the latest adventures of
Sherlock Holmes read aloud to him at night were his principal
relaxations, nevertheless these restrictions and forced economies were galling to his pride and those who were familiar with
his hysterical rages marvelled at his self-control.

He did not even demur when the Young Turks got rid of
Kutchuk Said for having drawn up an Imperial Rescript re-
serving to the Sultan the right to appoint the Sheikh ul Islam

and the Ministers of War and Marine. Public opinion in Constantinople would have been prepared to accept this but Salonika protested in a manner which left no doubt as to the intentions of the Army. So the most loyal of his ministers was made to resign in favour of the veteran Kiamil Pasha whose reputation as an anglophile was for the moment useful to the Committee. By now the Sultan had realised that it did not matter whether Said, or Kiamil or any other greybeard was Grand Vizir. It was those steely-eyed young majors, with their Prussian bearing (all the more irritating since it was he who was responsible for their German training), and those intellectual revolutionaries newly returned from exile who had to be placated. And because he was determined at all costs to keep his Throne Abdul Hamid set himself out to counter unpleasantness by charm and force by acquiescence. Four hundred thousand pounds from his private revenues was graciously handed over as a gift to the State. The palace he had intended for a University was presented to the people for their new Parliament House and it was here, on December 17, 1908, that he faced the greatest ordeal of all, his formal abdication as an autocrat.

It took five months for the elections to be held and the new Parliament to assemble, and by December the first ardours for the joys of democracy were dying down. Once more it was Turkey's fate to find that in spite of the enthusiasm which the events of July 24 evoked in the world Press, the support of Europe was as usual confined to words. No troops were mobilised when Austro-Hungary, acting in direct violation of the Treaty of Berlin, annexed the Province of Bosnia-Herzegovina where she had been in military occupation since 1878. Not even the German Kaiser spoke out for his Turkish ally when Ferdinand of Bulgaria returned from a visit to Vienna where he was treated with Royal honours, and formally announced the independence of his country and his assumption of the title of Czar.

These two events, closely connected with one another, had enormous repercussions throughout the Turkish Empire. There was an unofficial boycott of Austrian goods, while the brotherly love between Moslem and Christian, preached by the Young Turks, gave way to the old rivalry and fear of a Greater Bulgaria encompassing Macedonia. Nevertheless there was still sufficient goodwill and hope for the future, as well as a genuine patriotism among the delegates assembled in the square of Aya Sofia on the morning of December 17, to make the inauguration of the new Parliament a moving and at the same time a triumphal occasion.

New-washed from the recent snow, Constantinople shone in the winter sun and the scarlet banners of the Star and Crescent fluttered against the brilliant sky. The whole population was out in the streets to cheer no matter what: whether it was the troops or the delegates, the green-turbaned zouaves and white-skirted Albanians, or the long-robed deputies from the Hedjaz and the forty turbaned or mitred priests, representing every race and religious denomination of the Empire. Never since the days of the Moslem conquest had Aya Sofia seen so many resplendent uniforms, such a glittering show of polished swords and *yataghans* and gold embroidery. Only the dogs were not impressed, lying curled up in the sunlight, those dogs whom the Young Turks had already condemned as unprogressive, but who refused to move when the Macedonian soldiers tried to kick them out of the way, for they were part of the tradition of the city and therefore safe so long as good Baba Hamid was on the throne.

Inside the Parliament House, the deputies were waiting for their sovereign, but not all of them were animated with friendly feelings towards him, for some of them had known the inside of his prisons and suffered years of exile for their beliefs. In the Diplomatic Tribune sat the foreign ambassadors, polite, jaded and inclined to be sceptical over the birth of a nation. Whispering to one another in French, they noted the appearance of the three men whom they knew to be the most important figures in the room. Over there in the corner sitting next to a Druse emir was Enver Bey, the modest young hero of the Revolution whose photograph was sold by hundreds in the streets and whose neat features and air of quiet distinction belied the fact that his origins were of the humblest. What link could there be between Enver with his perfumed moustaches and manicured hands and the swarthy, thick-wristed

Tallaat with the gipsy eyes who was said to be the dominating brain of the Committee. The ambitious young staff officer and ex-post office official were a strange combination and, to complete the trio, there was Djemal Bey, with a reputation for having started life as a pasha's darling page boy, but whose gallantries were now a public by-word both in Salonika and Constantinople—a curious trio to nurse a nation through the birth pangs of democracy. Small wonder if the Ambassadors were inclined to be sceptical, recognising the hand of the Grand Orient manipulating the puppets on the stage and they were even more sceptical when they heard the frenzied cheering of the crowds outside at the approach of their Padishah.

Neither Mahomet the Conqueror, nor Suleyman the Magnificent nor his own grandfather Mahmud had ever received a more rapturous ovation than Abdul Hamid as he drove through the streets of his capital on the way to confront the forces which were out to destroy him.

'A living corpse' was how he was described by those who saw him shuffling into the Royal Box under the glare of the acetylene lamp, saluting the Assembly with a tired gesture of a white-gloved hand, barely listening as a secretary read aloud his inaugural address. It was only when the deputy from Mecca intoned a prayer and the words of the Koran drifted across the silent room that the ghostly figure suddenly came to life, rising from his throne and extending his hands in a simple, child-like gesture, with the palms turned upwards as if to gather the blessings falling from heaven. There was something so moving, so apparently spontaneous about this gesture, that even the most cynical were touched and Jews and Freemasons, Atheists and Christians, prayed with the Caliph of Islam.

Chapter XXXIII

FIVE MONTHS HAD passed and to all outward appearances Abdul Hamid had settled down to the role of a constitutional monarch, overcoming his fears (or perhaps because those fears were partly eliminated now that he felt himself to be protected by the nation) he showed himself more frequently in public and attended prayers in the great mosques of Stamboul. A banquet at Yildiz in honour of the people's representives ended as a personal triumph for the Sultan and one saw the strange sight of the ex-school master, Ahmet Riza, who had spent years in exile editing a paper which had indulged in the most vitriolic language against his sovereign, now sitting at his right hand, pouring into his apparently sympathetic ear the account of those lean years in Paris when he had been so poor he had had to cook his own food. Even the most violent of revolutionaries kissed the Sultan's hand on leaving and, with tears in his eyes, Abdul Hamid assured them that he had never been so happy as now that he had regained the confidence of his people.

With his cynical humour Abdul Hamid may have derived a certain pleasure from these scenes. The most ironical of all was when he received a deputation of English Liberals, representatives of the hated Balkan Committee which had been a thorn in his flesh for the past year. Now he set out to charm the disciples of the late Mr. Gladstone, listening attentively to their views on Macedonia, their praise of the Young Turks. But even entertaining the Balkan Committee was better than having nothing to do and the 'Committee of Union and Progress' was determined that the Sultan should be given as little opportunity as possible of interfering in the affairs of the nation. After working incessantly from daybreak to midnight, he had now hours of unwanted leisure on his hands, hours in which to play the piano, gossip with his women and fondle his long-haired angora cats and, what was particularly dangerous for his enemies, hours in which to indulge his passion for intrigue. The Young Turks could deprive him of his twenty thousand accredited spies, they could dismiss and imprison his intimates, but they could not prevent the palace servants from going in and out of Stamboul or the holy men of Islam from paying homage to their Caliph.

It delighted the Sultan to hear of the mistakes which the apostles of freedom were making in the name of progress. After coming into power on the slogan of 'Turkey for the Turks' and 'Throw off the Frankish yoke', they had had to call in a whole new lot of foreigners to help in the re-organisation of the Empire. There was a Frenchman at the Treasury, an Englishman at the Customs, another Englishman in charge of the neglected Navy, where he had been horrified to find officers growing vegetables on the decks of battleships. There was a German at the Chamber of Commerce, an Italian as Inspector of Gendarmerie and all this sweeping and cleaning up and wholesale dismissals were making the Young Turks unpopular with quite a large number of people. Even the army was beginning to grumble. A disaffected regiment stationed at Yildiz was exiled to the deserts of Arabia in quite as summary a fashion as under the old régime. But the disaffection of a small minority was beginning to spread and by their arrogance and anti-religious sentiments the Young Turk officers added fuel to the flames. In their mania for efficiency they drilled the soldiers till they had no time left for the *keyf* so beloved by the oriental, and before long they were complaining they had not even the time for the prayers and ablutions prescribed by the Koran.

Abdul Hamid watched and waited, signing innumerable *irades* for legislation over which he was not consulted and which he knew was bound to encounter bitter opposition. The projected girls' school at Kandilli was a case in point. He himself had nothing against it. Many years ago he had discussed the idea with Lady Layard, but, like so many other plans, he had put it aside the moment he had sensed the antagonism of the religious orders. And now a rumour went round the capital, to add to all the other rumours already in circulation, that the country was being run by heathens determined to corrupt the daughters of respectable Moslems. The fires of religious fanaticism were relighted and in the back streets of Stamboul and the courts of the *medreses* a counter-revolutionary movement gathered force. By the early spring a group of reactionaries, of religious fanatics and out-of-work spies, of degraded officers and discontented pashas had formed themselves into an organisation known as the Mahommedan Brotherhood, pledged to protect the Sheriat from being violated by the Jews and Free-masons of Salonika.

Cut off from the capital, the 'Committee of Union and Progress' did not sense the growing hostility. Fearing the responsibilities of office, they continued to function as a secret society advising, but more often threatening, the Government in power. There was one particularly stormy session of Parliament when old Kiamil Pasha dared to defy the Committee and Enver and his friends asserted their authority by brandishing their revolvers in the faces of the frightened deputies. The following day Kiamil was dismissed and Hilmi Pasha, a former Inspector-General of Macedonia and now entirely subservient to the Committee, put in his place.

The murder of a notorious journalist who had attacked both the Committee and the reactionaries brought matters to a head. The murderer, who was said to have been wearing the uniform of a Young Turk officer, had escaped and the Government was accused of not having made any attempt to discover his identity. Feelings ran high and the funeral of a man who in life had been the most scurrilous of blackmailers, brought the reactionaries out in force. There were cries of 'Long live the Sheriat' and 'Death to the Committee'—cries so loudly voiced that even the police did not dare to interfere.

The following morning, Constantinople woke to the sound of gunfire; those who were brave enough to venture out into the streets found troops in possession of all the principal squares and buildings, but they were undisciplined, leaderless troops whose officers had either fled or been beaten-up and imprisoned. Mutiny had broken out during the night when N.C.O.'s and men from the Taxim Barracks rose against their officers and sent messages to their comrades in other barracks, calling on them to join in safeguarding their religion against the atheists of Salonika. In a few hours the greater part of the Constantinople garrison had joined in the revolt. Thirty-six officers had been killed and fifty others wounded, without the mutineers encountering any serious opposition. By mid-day the city was in the hands of non-commissioned officers, and the Parliament Building in the square of Aya Sofia was sur-rounded by a seething mass of soldiers shouting in their raucous voices for a government which would respect the Holy Law. Only sixty out of five hundred deputies had put in an appearance and they had every reason to regret their foolhardiness when a young Druse emir, deputy for Lattakia, was seized by the crowd and torn to pieces on leaving the build-ing, having been mistaken for the editor of a progressive news-paper which had advocated the emancipation of women.

The whole of the 'Committee of Union and Progress' had gone underground and their nominee, Hilmi Pasha, handed in his resignation. By evening the excitement had mounted to a frenzy. Policemen discarded their modern helmets (one of the recent innovations) and replaced them with the fez. Soldiers, chanting religious hymns, fired shots at random in the air and panic spread through the Christian quarters when the black flag of the Mahdi, symbol of religious warfare, was hoisted on Galata Bridge.

An eye-witness describes the terror inspired by these fanatical men, with their strained faces, their violent staccato utterances of curses and of slogans—simple men with one-track minds, who had been worked upon by agitators and neglected by their officers and who now imagined that all they held dear was in danger.

The part Abdul Hamid played in these events is a question which has been asked time and again. After his arrest, the Second Eunuch, Nadir Aga, asserted that the orders for the counter-revolution emanated from Yildiz, that a few days previously the Sultan had drawn two million Turkish pounds out of a foreign bank and that his son, Burhaneddin, had been engaged in distributing money to the mutineers. But the con-fessions of men frightened for their skins cannot be regarded as reliable evidence and both Said and Kiamil, who are far more respected and reputable witnesses, deny Abdul Hamid's connection with the mutiny, saying that he was broken in health and spirits and more frightened than anyone else when the revolt broke out.

From first to last the Sultan's behaviour was ambiguous. Had he acted with courage on the evening of April 13, when the crowds were shouting outside his palace gates, proclaiming their loyalty to their Padishah, it might have been in his power to dissolve the Constitution and re-establish his dictatorship. But he sought refuge in half-measures. He came out on to the balcony and asked the mutineers to be good children and return to their barracks, promising them a full amnesty and conceding to most of their demands—most but not all, for when they demonstrated for the reinstatement of Kiamil as Grand Vizir, he temporised. To appoint an enemy of the Committee was too much in the nature of defiance and he refused to commit himself until he knew the reactions of Salonika. The appointment of Tevfik Pasha, a former diplomat not incriminated with either party, was a deliberate act of procrastination and the first act of the new Vizir, which must have been prompted by Yildiz rather than by the Sublime Porte, was to get into communication with Salonika and assure the Committee that the Constitution was not in danger. At the same time Abdul Hamid appears to have made no attempt to put a stop to disorders. His courtiers describe him as white with terror when the crew of one of his battleships appeared at Yildiz and called him out to show him the trussed-up body of their captain, caught, so they said, in the very act of training his guns on the palace. Hating the sight of blood, the Sultan hurried indoors before the wretched man was trampled to death in the courtyard. But it was not until forty-eight hours later that he signed the *irade* authorising the leading *ulema* to visit the barracks and preach against assassination. Perhaps he hoped that the worse the disorders, the sooner Europe would understand what came of Constitutions in countries that were not ready for them.

But if the Sultan's behaviour was ambiguous, so was that of the Young Turks. Had the Commander-in-Chief of the Constantinople garrison acted with firmness at the beginning, he could have prevented the mutineers at Taxim from invading

Stamboul. But he had strict orders to do nothing and by noon the situation had grown so out of hand that he barely escaped with his life. The subalterns who fell before the fanatical fury of their men may have been as much the victims of their own party as of the propaganda of the Mahommedan Brotherhood. For, if the Sultan hoped that the disorders would force Europe to intervene in his favour, the Young Turks were ready to welcome any disorders which would give them an excuse to get rid of Abdul Hamid.

The panic which spread through the Sultan's European provinces at the news of the counter-revolution found no echo in the Committee headquarters in Salonika. Here at last was the opportunity the leaders had been waiting for. They were not impressed by the new Government's assurances that the Constitution was not in danger. A government at the mercy of thirty thousand leaderless troops and a mob of half-starved theological students was not in a position to give assurances. The stories of the first refugees from the capital all pointed to the Sultan being in connivance with the mutineers, and, on April 16, a laconic message from Salonika informed the Sublime Porte that the Third Army Corps under the command of the famous Arab general, Mahmud Shevket, was marching on the capital to restore order. But so great was the mythical prestige of the secluded being in Yildiz Kiosk that not even the most ruthless member of the Committee, not even Shevket himself, dared to suggest that he was marching against the Sultan. Even when his armies were only thirty miles from the city, Shevket still cried 'Long Live the Sultan' and, in the same way as the general did not dare to act openly against Abdul Hamid, so Abdul Hamid did not dare to show his apprehension at the approach of the Salonikans. A message from Yildiz, transmitted by the Grand Vizir, announced that 'His Sublime Majesty awaits benevolently the arrival of the so-called Constitutionalist Army. He has nothing to lose or gain or fear, since His Sublimity is for the constitution and is its supreme guardian.'

The reactionary forces controlled the city for ten days and, though there were comparatively few excesses committed after the first twenty-four hours, business remained at a standstill and the meetings of the National Assembly were attended by only a handful of deputies. The news of the approach of the Macedonian armies had a further paralysing effect on the city's life. Half the population was in hiding, the embassies were crowded with refugees, while the Christian inhabitants lived in terror of the reactionaries arming the Kurdish forces, as at the time of the Armenian rising. Reports of fresh massacres in Southern Turkey, where Adana was a scene of horrors on the scale of those enacted twelve years previously at Urfa and at Van, brought panic to the Armenian quarters. Would the Salonikans arrive in time? No one could foresee that an expedition, which the European strategists estimated would take three weeks, would be carried out in six days.

In Yildiz Kiosk the Sultan waited on events. Two days after the mutiny he made his first public appearance at the Friday *selamlik*, which was chiefly remarkable for the complete absence of officers. The Sultan was described as looking 'particularly cheerful' as he drove to the Mosque surrounded by a guard of soldiers and non-commissioned officers. Dervishes, *hodjas* and *softas* were predominant among the wildly cheering crowds, and one of the *ulema* added a new note by praying aloud for the Caliph.

If only Abdul Hamid could have come out into the open instead of intriguing in the shadows so much might have been different. Said and Kiamil were probably right in describing him as a man sick in mind and body, obsessed by one idea, that of preserving his throne. There were thirty thousand troops in Constantinople waiting for a leader, but he frittered away his days in intrigue and in bribing those who were ready to turn on him at the first change of fortune. Vast sums out of his private funds were spent in preventing the advance of the Salonikans. Soldiers, *hodjas, imams*, all were bribed to stir up trouble in their ranks, but only a small percentage of the money reached the pockets of those for whom it was intended. Most of it remained in the hands of the two chief palace eunuchs, Djafer Aga and Nadir Aga, and in those fateful days between April 16 and 23, these two sinister figures, the one monstrously fat, the other slim and delicate as a girl, appeared to be the Sultan's principal counsellors. There was neither love, nor trust, nor friendship in the palace which he had made a prison. Even his favourite son, Burhaneddin, had proved himself to be a man of straw. The charming, talented boy whom he used to show off in front of his foreign guests had grown up as weak and as ineffectual as his brothers and his uncles. By becoming a member of the Mahomedan Brotherhood, he had made a pathetic attempt to play a part in politics, whether on his own initiative or on his father's orders has never been revealed, but the large sums which passed through his hands leads one to suspect the latter. Now he was the first of the rats to leave the sinking ship and the Salonikans had not reached the outskirts of Constantinople before Burhaneddin Effendi fled from his father's palace.

Without discipline or leadership, the mutineers had no concerted plan of defence and once the *feux de joie* had been exhausted many of them began to wonder why they had mutinied in the first place. The Salonikans, on the contrary, were superbly organised under a first-class general gifted with a profound knowledge of the psychology of his men. 'They were not marching,' he said, 'in the interests of the Committee but of the Ottoman Army to wipe out the stain on its honour caused by the excesses of the mutineers.' Masonic influences and anti-religious tendencies were not encouraged among his troops and the C.U.P., realising the antagonism their methods had aroused in Constantinople, remained for the moment in the background. Enver and Niyazi, the two heroes of the July revolution, were both serving under Shevket and on his staff was a pale young man with cold, transparent eyes, whom the world was to hear of later, by the name of Mustafa Kemal.

Chapter XXXIV

BEHIND THE CLOSED lattices of the old Phanar quarter and the shuttered blinds of the bazaars; in the dusty offices of the Sublime Porte and the counting houses of Galata; in the docks where the ships were waiting to unload and the Customs Building where no one knew who was in control, the inhabitants of Constantinople waited in uncertainty and fear. The impossible had been accomplished and in less than six days the Salonikans were encamped at San Stefano, only seven miles from the capital. The gutter Press, which in the early days of the counter-revolution had been violently anti-Committee, began to change its tune and for the first time to voice what no one had dared to suggest before, that the Sultan might have to go.

But the real proof that the legend of his inviolability was crumbling came with the first exodus from the neighbourhood of Yildiz. In terror of bombardment, pashas and peasants were packing their belongings and taking to the roads. The panic spread to the inhabitants of Yildiz itself and, to calm his frightened servants and safeguard his position, Abdul Hamid announced that he himself had summoned the Third Army Corps to restore order in the capital.

Supplies of mutton and of goat's cheese, a gift from their generous Padishah, awaited the troops at San Stefano and, together with the provisions, came a delegation from the Sultan with authority to negotiate an agreement. But were Abdul Hamid's assurances to be believed, any more than Shevket was to be believed when he issued a proclamation promising a free pardon to all mutineers who submitted to his orders, accusing the agitators of having spread the false rumour that he had come to dethrone the Sultan when the power to do so rested only with Parliament and the Sheikh ul Islam?

Meanwhile the operations proceeded with a relentless efficiency. All the Sultan's attempts to impede the advance by mediation failed, and in the early hours of Friday, April 23, the Salonikans reached Kiathane at the furthermost end of the Golden Horn. Abdul Hamid heard the news as he was dressing for the Friday *selamlik*. But whereas on other mornings, he had woken a prey to his imaginary fears, needing drugs and restoratives before he could face the short five-minute drive to the Mosque, today, when a hostile army was encircling the town, he gave an impression of almost superhuman calm. Years ago an old gipsy had prophesied that he would only reign so long as he drank of the waters of Kiathane. The old gipsy may have been right, for the Arab guards, who had deserted during the night to join the invading army, and the street dogs of Stamboul, howling at the approach of strangers, seemed to sense a coming change. But in spite of his gloomy presentiments, traditions had still to be preserved, and, with crowds held back a little further than usual, the *selamlik* took place with the same pomp as if he were still the Shadow of God on Earth. For the last time the people of Constantinople saw that small, hunched figure driving past in an open carriage and for the last time Abdul Hamid heard the raucous cries of the troops shouting 'Padishahim chok yasha.' But when he turned to salute the Diplomatic Tribune he noted that, for the first time, no Ambassadors were present. They too had sensed a coming change.

Through the clear spring air came the sound of gunfire. The big barracks outside the Adrianople Gate was capitulating to the Salonikans. Shevket's troops were penetrating the city from three sides, and so little were the counter-revolutionaries prepared, that many of the soldiers surrendered without firing a shot. Stamboul and the Sublime Porte were captured within an hour and artillery was only needed in the assault on Taxim Barracks, in the centre of the town, where a garrison had dug themselves in in preparation for a siege. Fighting was bitter here on both sides and for the first time the battle lust of the Salonikans was fully aroused. Enver was in command on this section of the front and with superb *panache* stormed the barricades under heavy shell-fire. A four-hour battle resulted in victory for the Salonikans and by evening three-quarters of the city was in their hands. Never had a town been captured in which greater courtesy was shown to non-combatants. Soldiers helped old ladies on and off the horse-trams; military cadets mounted guard outside the foreign embassies and within an hour of the battle excited crowds were filling the coffee-houses discussing the day's events. But even now no one really knew what was going to happen to the Sultan, though the soldiers were beginning to whisper among themselves that it seemed as if old Baba Hamid was done for.

Meanwhile senators and deputies had been invited to the Macedonian headquarters at San Stefano to decide the Sultan's fate. The German Ambassador was known to be exerting pressure in his favour, but the 'Committee of Union and Progress' had prepared such an overwhelming case against him that there were those who considered that death, not merely deposition, should be the penalty. As President of the Senate, Said Pasha presided over the meeting, a pathetic task for one who had served his master so faithfully and so long. Yet in spite of the fact that the building was surrounded by troops in the pay of the Committee; in spite of the sudden and dramatic arrival of Enver, who, dirty and unshaven, in his battle-stained uniform, burst into the Assembly and demanded the Sultan's death, only a small majority actually voted in favour of his deposition. And it was still left for the Sheikh ul Islam to make the final decision, for even the most violent revolutionaries did not dare to break with a tradition which went back to the days of Suleyman the Magnificent.

Did Abdul Hamid know that his fate was in the balance on that Friday night when the firing had died away and the only sounds which reached him from the city were the faint echoes of soldiers singing and street dogs barking at the moon? Yildiz was now cut off from communication by land and sea. Even the Imperial Yacht, which for the past few days had been lying off Dolmabagche, had disappeared and no one dared tell Abdul Hamid that it had joined the rest of the fleet, which had gone over to the Salonikans. No one dared to tell him, but neither did he ask, for what struck chamberlains and eunuchs the most was his apparent indifference to outside events. The master whom they had seen reduced to terror by the threat of some mad Armenian was so unmoved by the Salonikan victories as to make them wonder what plots might still be hatching in his twisted machiavellian brain. But for once the brain was empty of ideas. Faced by a crisis, he was no more than a sick old man, seeking refuge in the legend of his semi-divinity—a legend which no longer existed. When the whole world was speculating on his future and the telegraph wires were kept humming with the latest communiqués from San Stefano, when the Salonikans were encamped barely a mile from Yildiz, he spent most of the night lying on a divan with a shawl across his knees while one of his chamberlains read aloud to him the latest adventures of Sherlock Holmes.

The next morning the Salonikans opened up with an assault on the last remaining garrison of Yildiz and Scutari, and woken by the gunfire, the Second Eunuch, Nadir Aga, went to knock at his master's door; the Sultan came out in his dressing gown to enquire what was happening. 'Your Majesty's loyal soldiers are crushing the rebels,' was the answer, for no one in the palace dared to suggest that the Macedonian troops were hostile to the Sultan, and throughout that day Abdul Hamid continued to behave as if the petty squabbles of his armies were none of his concern. Only yesterday he had sent further emissaries to the Macedonian Headquarters renewing the suggestion that the so-called Constitutional Forces should consider themselves his guests. But the reverberation of the guns had so far been his only reply.

For the whole of that morning Abdul Hamid kept to his normal routine, going from the baths to his study, reading reports from the provinces, most of which had been piling up during the past weeks and bore no relation to present events. By midday the guns were silenced, the two battalions stationed at Yildiz had either surrendered or fled and the Macedonian troops were closing in on the palace. So superb was their discipline, that not a single soldier dared to trespass in the park till he received his orders from Headquarters. And it was not until the following evening of Sunday, April 25, that the Sheikh ul Islam gave his answer to the fateful question.

'If an *Imam* of the Moslems appropriates public monies; if after killing, imprisoning and exiling his subjects unjustly, he swears to amend his ways and then perjures himself . . . if he causes civil war and bloodshed among his own people; if it is shown that his country will gain peace by his removal, and if it is considered by those who have power, that this *Imam* should abdicate or be deposed, is it lawful that one of these alternatives should be adopted?'

In his white and gold robes and yellow turban the Sheikh ul Islam represented the highest dignity of the Mahomedan faith, but he knew himself to be as much in the power of the Committee as the Sultan he was called upon to depose and the answer came:

'It is permissible.'

In the years to come, Abdul Hamid often thought back of what he might have done in those days. He might have appealed to the judgement of Europe and played on the rivalries of the Powers as he had played in the past, or he might have crossed over to Asia and, as Caliph of Islam, proclaimed a Holy War against the infidels of Salonika. There was so much he might have done if he had not been sunk in a deep apathetic gloom which robbed him of all initiative. By Saturday night the humblest inhabitants of Yildiz, the cooks and the scullions, the carpenters and the electricians were in flight and only a few hundred remained where formerly there had been thousands. The fires went out and the electricity failed and the Sultanas were reduced to eating the cold remains of food, salvaged by the eunuchs from the deserted larders. For the first time in thirty-three years Abdul Hamid ate a meal which had not been prepared in his private kitchen and was too preoccupied to consider the possibility of poison.

To cheer his spirits and those of his dependants he called for more lights and music, but, typical of the inefficiency of the palace purveyors, no one had thought of laying in a stock of candles. There had been a time when the palace band numbered over three hundred musicians, but the economy cuts of the Young Turks had reduced it to less than fifty and of these over half had already fled. The few who were left set out to play in a mechanical fashion what had always been the Sultan's favourite tunes. But the strains of *Madame Angot* and *La Belle*

Hélène could not keep at bay that dark insidious fear which invaded every corner of Yildiz so that even the Sultan's pet angora cats stood with arched backs and bristling hair staring into the shadows.

That night Abdul Hamid could no longer listen to detective stories, for he kept waiting with taut nerves in the same way as his women, his eunuchs, his cats, and every other living thing in Yildiz were waiting for the approach of the invisible enemy. By Sunday the last of the palace guards had deserted and for twenty-four hours, before the Macedonian troops moved in, Yildiz with its secrets remained open to the world. Anyone with a grievance against the Sultan, and Constantinople was full of such men, could have wandered into the park and dropped a bomb or fired a shot which would have made him the hero of the Young Turks. But the very terror of its inhabitants seems to have created a protective wall of fear around the palace and the sturdy Macedonian soldiers, encamped on the neighbouring hillside, spent sleepless nights listening to the strange sounds emanating from the haunted park.

Lions in the menagerie waiting to be fed roared with hunger; apes and zebras, dogs and cats, chattered and brayed, yelped and mewed; owls hooted, parrots screeched, while other cries, half bestial and half human, of women and eunuchs giving way to tears and hysteria, sent cold shivers down the spines of the bravest soldiers.

Pursued by the ghosts of the past, harrowed by present terrors, the Sultan wandered from house to house, from room to room, through the labyrinth of twisted corridors and subterranean passages which had so often been replanned and reinforced that even he had difficulty in finding the way. Possessions, most of them useless, cluttered the rooms; golden keys opened safes full of the most priceless treasures. But what had it helped him to possess some of the largest diamonds in existence, rubies and emeralds as large as hens' eggs, when they had not been able to buy him either the loyalty or the affection of his subjects?

Memories he would willingly have dismissed crowded into the foreground: the big hospital up at Shishli, where hundreds of children were cured every year at his expense, could not compensate for the life of the little slave girl he had shot inadvertently when he found her playing with a jewelled pistol he had left lying on a table. Young men had languished for years in the dungeons of Yildiz for no other reason than because they had been denounced by spies. Six months ago the Young Turks had opened the prisons, but the ghosts had remained behind, giving shape to the shadows in the dimly lit rooms, drifting across moonlit lawns, so that it was almost a relief when the Macedonian troops moved in and the familiar tramp of soldiers' feet brought sanity back to Yildiz.

To calm his dependants, Abdul Hamid assured them that the troops had been summoned for his protection. But from the Chief Eunuch to the youngest of the odalisques, all were asking the same question; what was going to happen to the Sultan? And what was going to happen to them? The eunuchs were full of foreboding. Loathed for their arrogance and cruelty, they had nothing to expect but prison or the gallows, or at the best a life of beggary. But some of the younger women, particularly those who had never been summoned to the royal bed, were secretly elated by the coming of the Macedonians. The Sultan himself was under no illusions as to the future. Whatever might be the decision of the Sheikh ul Islam he knew he was in the Committee's power at last, caught like a rat in the trap of the Constitution. And when, on the morning of April 27, his Chief Secretary, a young man comparatively new to his post, informed him that a deputation of four parliamentarians was outside he realised his fate was sealed and for the last time availed himself of the privilege of allowing his visitors to wait.

Of the four men chosen to inform the Sultan of his deposition not one was of purely Turkish blood. They included Greeks, Jews and Armenians, and all of them, with the exception of their leader, General Essad, were prominent members of the C.U.P. One of them, a Greek-Jewish lawyer by the name of Carasso, should never have been included in the deputation. A man of somewhat unsavoury reputation, he owed his position to the fact that he was a prominent member of the Masonic Lodge, *Macedonia Risorta*, which was housed in

Italian property. Owing to the capitulations, this property was immune from the attentions of Abdul Hamid's police and two years before the outbreak of the July Revolution Carasso had obtained permission for the newly formed 'Committee of Union and Progress' to hold meetings in his Lodge. In this way members of the Committee became Masons while Carasso established himself in the inner councils of the C.U.P. Whether the Committee, who had now assumed complete control in Constantinople, were out to humiliate the Sultan, or whether no Turk had volunteered for the task, a deputation consisting entirely of Levantines was hardly qualified to depose the ruler of a vast Asiatic Empire.

They were uneasy, rather than triumphant, as they waited in the reception room of the Little Mabeyn which gave out onto the garden. Thirty eunuchs mounted guard, their frightened faces reflected in the mirrors which were placed at every angle of the room, so that from wherever one was sitting, one could see who was coming in at the door and who was going out. The Sultan was invisible, but his presence filled the room. His medicine bottle was on the table, his galoshes behind the stove. For all they knew, he might be watching them from behind that large Japanese screen in the corner and the thought was scarcely reassuring, for His Majesty was known always to carry a revolver and never known to miss. No one spoke. Next door a parrot chattered away in Arabic and a cuckoo clock ticked away the minutes which seemed like hours. Then the door opened and silently, almost unobtrusively, Abdul Hamid walked into the room accompanied by his seventeen-year-old son, Abdurrahman. Of the four deputies, General Essad was the only one who had ever seen the Sultan at close quarters, and he was even smaller than they had imagined, while the military great-coat, which hung so loosely from his shoulders, emphasised his almost skeleton thinness. He waited for the ceremonial greetings to be over before he asked in a voice, which sounded surprisingly deep coming from that fragile body, 'What do you want? What has happened?' and in his blunt, soldierly fashion Essad replied, 'In conformity with a *fetva*, which has been pronounced, the Nation has deposed you. The National Assembly charges itself with your personal security and that of your family. You have nothing to fear.'

For a moment it seemed as if the Sultan had not heard. It was an old trick perfected by long practice. Then realising that subterfuge was useless, he submitted, saying as his uncle had said in the same circumstances, 'This is *Kismet*.'

Up to now he had inspired a respect amounting to awe, but fear gained once more the upper hand, and in pitiable tones, he begged for his life, asking the deputies to swear that he was safe. He was not a criminal, he told them. History would record how he had worked for the good of his country. He was an old man and if the nation wished to depose him, they should allow him to end his days in Cheragan where he had let his brother Murad live in peace for over twenty-five years.

Essad promised to submit his request to Parliament. It was not his business to tell the Sultan that the nation had already decided on Salonika as his place of exile.

With punctilious courtesy the deputation was about to leave, when a look of concentrated fury came over the Sultan's face and raising his voice, he cried, 'May God punish those responsible for this calamity,' whereupon the Greek Carasso answered, 'God is just and will punish those who are responsible,' and on hearing these words young Abdurrahman burst into a flood of tears.

It was almost nine o'clock in the evening when the officers arrived who were to escort the ex-Sultan into exile. This time he was waiting for them, surrounded by his eunuchs and the few courtiers who had remained with him. Ceremony was dispensed with and, coming straight to the point, the general in charge informed him that his brother Reshad had ascended the throne under the name of Mahommed V, and the nation, having decided that two Sultans could not remain in the same place, had appointed him to escort His Majesty to Salonika. The shock of hearing that Salonika, the town that had ruined him, was to be his place of exile, proved too much for Abdul Hamid's nerves. He stammered, faltered, as if to make a last appeal, then fainted into the arms of the Chief Eunuch, who, feeling the rope already round his neck, was wishing himself a thousand miles away. The officers were embarrassed, particularly so as a rustling and weeping from behind a screen denoted the presence of women, and the general waited for the Sultan to recover before reading out his orders. Three *kadins*, four concubines, two princes, four eunuchs and fourteen servants were to accompany the ex-Sultan to Salonika. They were to take with them only the barest personal necessities. The rest of the luggage was to follow later. All His Majesty's wishes would be attended to, provided he complied with these orders. But Abdul Hamid was too stunned to remonstrate or argue. An eyewitness recalls that he stood staring at his hands, which he kept opening and closing as if his reflexes had been slowed down by shock.

Drained of all emotion he moved as if in a trance, his farewell to his foster-mother, who was too old and ill to travel, was as cold and as formal as if he were saying goodbye to a stranger, his eunuchs were dismissed with a nod and the only time he showed any feeling was in worrying as to who would feed his pet angora cats.

Midnight had struck by the time the carriages were loaded and a white-faced, tottering old man stood for the last time on the threshold of the palace from where he had ruled an Empire for thirty-three years. The soldiers who were now his gaolers presented arms, women sobbed, eunuchs grovelled at his feet, kissing the hem of his coat, and from somewhere in the palace came a parrot's mocking cry, 'Long Live the Padishah.'

Epilogue

THE VILLA ALLATINI, to which Abdul Hamid was brought in the first days of his exile, was the largest and most luxurious villa in Salonika. The property of a Jewish banker, it had been leased for the past two years to the Italian General in command of the Gendarmerie, Count Robillant Pasha. The General had always been on excellent terms with Abdul Hamid who had gone out of his way to charm him with presents of thoroughbreds for his stables and jewelled orders for his wife and, no sooner had he heard of the difficulties the authorities were having in finding suitable accommodation for the ex-Sultan, than he gallantly offered to vacate his own villa.

His daughters still remember the excitement of the sudden departure for Italy, the hurried packing and their mother's distress at leaving her pretty chintzes and mahogany furniture to the dubious care of the harem ladies. But when Abdul Hamid arrived late in the evening, after a journey of over twenty hours, the Villa Allatini seemed to him to be lacking in every comfort. There were European bathrooms but no *hamman*; the beds provided did not please his women, and the escorting officers, who had orders to comply with all his wishes within reason, forced a furniture store in the town to open and supply all that was wanted, in spite of the lateness of the hour.

No reigning monarch could have been treated with greater consideration than Abdul Hamid in the first weeks of exile. The railway journey from Constantinople to Salonika had been made in the royal coach, which the Oriental Railway Company had presented to him twenty years before and which he had never used until now. The Mayor of Salonika had been on the platform to receive him on arrival and the two young officers who acted as his guards behaved more like his aides-de-camp. When Abdul Hamid complained that the eggs and milk in Salonika were not fresh, a Government official made a special journey from Constantinople to bring him fifty pedigree fowls and two white cows from his farm at Yildiz. Encouraged by these attentions, he gave free rein to his whims. First it was his pet angora cats, then it was a giant St. Bernard, and as the weeks passed and he became bored with the familiar faces of his women he asked for more and younger odalisques, as well as two more eunuchs. But no sooner had they arrived, cats and dogs, eunuchs and odalisques, than he took no more notice of them than if they had been there for years.

All this generosity and pandering to his whims had a motive. The ex-Sultan was known to possess a large fortune abroad which the Young Turks were anxious to lay their hands on. In order to save his skin and to avoid the fate of the Kizlar Agasi, who had been publicly hanged and exposed on Galata Bridge, the Second Eunuch, Nadir 'Aga, had turned King's evidence and, after accusing Abdul Hamid of having instigated the counter-revolution, offered to reveal the secrets of his palace. It was he who showed the officers of the special committee, appointed to make an inventory of the ex-Sultan's possessions, the complicated mechanism which opened out the treasure vaults of Yildiz. But the eleven sacks full of golden coins, totalling over half a million Turkish pounds, the piles of precious stones and packets of railway shares discovered in these vaults, did not satisfy the commission. A small notebook left behind by the ex-Sultan in the hurry of departure, or perhaps on purpose, revealed that the greater part of his fortune was in foreign banks. So long as he was in possession of these funds, which could not be handed over without his consent, Abdul Hamid was still in a position to make trouble. Izzet, his ablest henchman, had escaped to Europe and the day could come when yet another revolution was financed by the ex-Sultan's gold.

To get hold of this money it was necessary to win Abdul Hamid's confidence, and the two young officers in charge at the Villa Allatini were instructed to play on his patriotism and to hint that, if he made a magnanimous gesture and helped the new state, his exile might not be permanent. Their task was not an easy one, for on arrival the ex-Sultan was in such a state of apathetic gloom that he hardly spoke to anyone, and spent most of the time sitting by a window staring at the sea. But gradually his health and spirits revived, the fine spring weather and fresh breezes from the Aegean tempted him out of doors and he began to enjoy his walks in the garden, where the roses were almost as beautiful as those at Yildiz. He was gracious with his guards, tender with his women who, apart from regretting their jewellery which had been confiscated by the State, settled down quite happily to life at the Villa Allatini. As his interest in life revived, so his interest in politics revived, but the newspapers he perused so avidly held little to his liking.

To compensate for the fact that the blessings of democracy were slow in materialising, the Young Turks were indulging in a campaign of vituperation against the Hamidian régime. While the elongated corpses of the Palace favourites were suspended from Galata Bridge, Yildiz itself, divested of its treasures, was thrown open to the public. Every gutter-journalist was invited to inspect the trap-doors and subterranean passages which led to the ogre's lair. Nothing was sacred, even to the late Sultan's wardrobes showing his two thousand shirts. And the kindly sixty-year-old dotard now sitting on the Throne was powerless to prevent the hitherto carefully preserved prestige of majesty from being destroyed.

In the first weeks of exile Abdul Hamid read of the breaking up and dispersal of his harem. With hundreds of unwanted women on their hands to feed and clothe for the rest of their lives, the Young Turks had the ingenuous idea of sending circulars to various villages in Circassia and the Balkans, inviting anyone who in the past had had a daughter or sister bought or kidnapped by the purveyors of the Imperial harem to visit Constantinople at the Government's expense and claim their long-lost relatives. The whole idea was so absurd that Abdul Hamid had no hesitation in ridiculing it in front of his women—as if the pampered beauties of his Court would ever resign themselves to the lives of beasts of burden. But the chance remark of one of his *kadins*, a quickly suppressed sigh of regret, was sufficient to arouse his fears, leaving him to suspect that the gaiety shown in his presence was only assumed and that the day might come when the last of his women would desert him, leaving him alone in a hostile town.

As he pondered over his loneliness, his tenderness towards his women gave way to irascibility, while he became almost obsequious when speaking to his guards, who recognising his fears were quick to reassure him that one disinterested gesture on his part was all that the Government needed in order to change their policy towards him. The new state was poor and Turkey's enemies were profiting from their poverty. By helping her now His Majesty would find that his country was not ungrateful. Abdul Hamid listened and was not convinced, but as day succeeded day and week succeeded week and the future seemed ever more hopeless, he began to contemplate a last desperate gamble, alien to his whole character. Of what use was a fortune locked in foreign banks while he remained a prisoner in Salonika, but as a basis for bargaining with the Young Turks it might procure him what he wanted most of all—his freedom.

Things were not going well with the new régime. There were dissensions among the leaders. The C.U.P. had not yet committed itself to govern and one cabinet of greybeards had succeeded the other. The departure of European officers from Macedonia had resulted in more rioting and bloodshed and the dispatch of fresh troops to the disaffected areas. The Wahabites were in revolt in Arabia and the massacres of Armenians in Adana had brought French warships to Alexandretta. The Treasury was empty and in spite of the enthusiasm of English Liberals, the Young Turks had not succeeded in raising a fresh loan in the City of London. Reading of the difficulties which confronted his enemies, Abdul Hamid began to feel that, given his freedom, all things were possible. The young officers were clever enough to foster his dreams, but there were times when he was more prosaic, demanding guarantees for the future. If he handed over his money how did he know that he and his family might not be left to starve. The Ottoman State was magnanimous, they assured him, and generosity would be met with generosity. Parliament would guarantee a monthly allowance of one thousand Turkish pounds to be paid to him and his heirs. Still he hesitated, till boredom and frustration forced his hand and, one day in June 1909, he handed over to the younger of his gaolers, Fethi Bey, two letters addressed to the Credit Lyonnais and to the Deutsche Banke instructing them to send all securities held in his name to their branches in Salonika.

The best financial brain of the C.U.P., a converted Jew by the name of Djavid, paid a special visit to the Villa Allatini to receive in the name of the Turkish Government the steel-bound chests containing sixteen thousand railway shares and other securities, totalling in all one million, eighty thousand pounds. There were compliments and speeches and for the space of an afternoon, Abdul Hamid basked in the adulation of former days. He did not hear the sceptical remarks of the Bank Managers, the congratulations of Djavid to his guards, who shortly afterwards were promoted to more important posts. But it did not take him long to discover that he had been duped by the Young Turks, that far from giving him his freedom, they now planned to guard him more strictly than before. His monthly allowance was regularly paid, but his letters to the Government received politely evasive replies. Realising his helplessness, he fell into pathetic impotent rages which frightened no one but his women and after his rages had spent themselves, tears of self-pity would pour down the wrinkled cheeks he no longer took the trouble to rouge.

Strangest of all was that this frail, old man, who in the past had been so often near to death, was destined to live another nine years and to witness with dismay the tribulations of his country. Events were shaping very differently to the way in which they had been envisaged by the Young Turks. In 1911 Italy seized the propitious moment to lay claim to Tripoli and neither the reckless bravery of an Enver nor the brilliance of a young staff officer, Mustafa Kemal, who organised the Arabs so well that the enemy made little headway on land, could compensate for the fact that Italy had the sea power.

In the end Turkey was forced to lose, not only her last remaining African possessions, but also the Aegean islands of the Dodecanese. Tragic but inevitable, the Tripolitanian War was soon overshadowed by the events of the following year when circumstances in the shape of the first Balkan War brought

Abdul Hamid back to Constantinople. Salonika was about to become a battlefield, coveted in turn by all three allies, Ferdinand of Bulgaria, George of Greece and Peter of Serbia, the most unnatural allies history ever brought together. And to add to the trio was the King of the Black Mountain, Nicholas of Montenegro, with his passion for gambling on the Vienna Stock Exchange.

Abdul Hamid may have been right in saying that if it had not been for the arrogance and chauvinism of the Young Turks these four men would never have got together. But perhaps he underestimated the activity of a Cretan lawyer, Eleftheros Venizelos, who was the principal architect of the Balkan Alliance.

It was a sad homecoming after three years of exile. Whether as a courtesy towards a former friend, or to oblige the Young Turks, whose shipping in the Aegean was being harried by the Greeks, the Kaiser sent the Embassy Stationnaire ship *Lorelei* to bring Abdul Hamid back from Salonika. Among the officers on board was Sherif Pasha, a former aide-de-camp, now married to one of the royal princesses. With Sherif the ex-Sultan was willing to talk, forgetting his own troubles in his anxiety to hear the latest news from the battlefront, where Turkey had suffered a series of humiliating defeats, culminating in the complete rout of her army by the Bulgarians at Lule Bourgas.

The failure of supplies; the failure of the wretched conscript, brought from the burning suns of Tripolitania and Arabia, to adapt himself to the cold of Thrace; above all the failure of von der Goltz's vaunted fortresses, all contributed to one of the worst defeats in history. Thousands died on the battlefield, but thousands more died in the camps and on the roadside, stricken with the most deadly form of cholera. There were neither field hospitals nor medical supplies and the diseased and the wounded were left to freeze to death in the mud of the Thracian plains.

Two weeks after the battle of Lule Bourgas, Turkey had lost almost all of her European possessions, the Serbs had captured Uskub and Monastir, the Greeks had proclaimed the union with Crete and won the race for Salonika, the Bulgarians had invested Adrianople. Small wonder if in conversation with

Sherif, the old Sultan said with sadness, 'All this would never have happened if I had been on the throne.'

To keep the various races of the Balkans at loggerheads with one another had been one of the keystones of his foreign policy, but what did these young men of the Committee understand of the finer arts of diplomacy? They could only blunder and bluster and make cheap theatrical gestures which the country could ill afford.

In the days when Abdul Hamid was brought back to Constantinople to be lodged, or rather imprisoned, at Beylerbey on the Asiatic shore, the Bulgarians were launching an offensive against the last defence lines of the capital. And in the chancelleries of Europe they were already questioning as to who would have Constantinople. Would Russia, or Germany, or England ever allow one country to secure the coveted prize, or would it become an international port open to all? No one spoke any longer of maintaining the *status quo* in the Balkans and no one asked the opinion of the melancholy old man brooding over the ruins of his empire.

All that Abdul Hamid asked for on his arrival at Beylerbey was to be given a small backroom so as to be spared the view of Stamboul and Dolmabagche and his former palace on the hill. For six years he lingered on, a silent and helpless witness to the tragedies which overtook his country. For a brief moment fortune favoured the Turks, when quarrels broke out among the jackals of the Balkans, robbing them of their prey, and Enver, staging a *coup d'état*, dismissed the Cabinet, shot dead the Commander-in-Chief and swept into power on a wave of popular enthusiasm culminating with the recapture of Adrianople. But this short period of triumph only heralded greater disasters. With Enver and his party in power, Turkey was irretrievably harnessed to Germany's war chariot. Whereas Abdul Hamid had flattered and been cajoled without ever allowing himself to be definitely committed, the Young Turks plunged headlong into a military alliance with Germany, till there came that fateful day in the late autumn of 1914, when the two German battleships the *Goeben* and the *Breslau* escorted by a squadron of Turkish destroyers, steamed out of the Bosphorus to attack Russian shipping in the Black Sea.

No one knew better than Abdul Hamid how little his country stood to gain by war, how much she stood to lose. In one mad gamble.the Young Turks had jeopardised all his hopes and ambitions for the future of his empire, the riches of the Mesopotamian oil-fields, Turkey's leadership of the people of Islam. His life's work was in ruins but the death he had so often dreaded in the past, and would now so readily have welcomed, kept him waiting another four years. Little is known of those last years except that his fears were realised when some of the younger women of his small harem asked and received permission to leave him. Only one of his *kadins*, Mushfike Sultana, remained with him to the end, nursing him in his failing health, reading to him for hours on end from the newspapers which were his only literature. Yet he had probably never been so close to his people as now when his own personal fears were merged in his fears for his country's future, when the guns from Gallipoli echoed across the Straits and British submarines penetrating into the Marmara brought panic and chaos to the capital. As disaster followed upon disaster, men began to speak in whispers of the good old days when Baba Hamid was on the throne. He lingered on until January 1918, when the doctors were summoned to his bedside, and the Sultan who had feared assassination all his life died peacefully in the arms of his *kadin*. Allah, who is merciful, spared him the sight of the long line of Allied warships which nine months later anchored in the Golden Horn.

Glossary

Entari A loose garment worn indoors

Bostandji A gardener—The Imperial Bostandjis took part in the royal processions

Dairé An apartment

Feradje A woman's cloak

Fetva A decree issued by the Sheikh ul Islam

Firman A written decree

Hatti Humayan Imperial rescript

Haseki Sultana The mother of a royal prince

Irade A personal decree issued by the Sultan

Jehad A holy war

Kadin One of the four principal sultanas

Kahvedji Bashi The chief coffee maker

Kaimakam High Sheriff

Keyf Rest, contemplation

Kizlar Agasi The Chief Eunuch

Konak A large house

Lala A eunuch personally attached to the prince's service on attaining adolescence

Medrese A religious school usually attached to the mosque

Sheikh ul Islam Chief religious dignitary among the Mohammedans

Sheriat Sacred Law

Softas Theological student

Tekke A meeting place for a religious sect

Tesbieh A rosary

Turbe A mausoleum

Ulema A doctor of Sacred Law

Vali A governor of a province

Yali A house usually of wood built directly over the water

Bibliography

Histoire de l'empire Ottoman (18 Vols.), von Hammer, (French Edition), 1839

Stratford Canning (2 Vols.), Lane Poole, London

The Invasion of the Crimea, Kinglake, London, 1863

Gladstone (2 Vols.) Lord Morley, London

The Life of Robert, Marquis of Salisbury (Vol. II) Lady Gwendoline Cecil, 1921

Disraeli (Vol. VI), Moneypenny and Buckle, 1910-1912

The Story of My Struggles (2 Vols.) Arminius Vambéry, 1904

Personal recollections of Abdul Hamid and his court, Arminius Vambéry, Nineteenth Century, 1909

The Future of Constitutional Turkey, Arminius Vambéry, Nineteenth Century, March, 1909

Bismarck, His Reflections and Reminiscences (2 Vols.), London, 1898

My Memoirs, Henri de Blowitz, London, 1903

The Diary of an Idle Woman in Constantinople, Frances Elliot, Tauchnitz, Leipzig, 1893

The War in Bulgaria (2 Vols.), Lieut.-General Valentine Baker Pasha, London, 1879

Sir William White, His Life and Correspondence, H. Sutherland Edwards

The Making of Modern Turkey, Sir Henry Luke, London, 1936

Turkey in Europe, 'Odysseus' (Sir Charles Eliot), London, 1900

The Life of Midhat Pasha, Ali Haydar Midhat, London, 1903

Modern Egypt (Vol. I), Earl of Cromer, London, 1908

Kaiser Wilhelm, Emil Ludwig, London, 1926

La Renovation de l'empire Ottoman, Paul Imbert, Paris, 1909

Armenian Atrocities, The Murder of a Nation, Arnold Toynbee, with a Preface delivered by Lord Bryce, London

Abdul Hamid II und die reformen in der Turkei, Karl Kuntzner, Dresden, 1897

Sultan Murad V, Djemaleddin Bey, London, 1895
Le Sultan, L'Islam et les puissances, Victor Berard, Paris, 1907
La Macédoine, Victor Berard, Paris, 1897
La Politique du Sultan, Victor Berard, Paris, 1897
La Revolution turque, Victor Berard, Paris, 1909
Turkey, the Great Powers and the Baghdad Railway, Meade Earle, New York, 1923
Von Mittelmeer Zum Persiches Golfe, Baron von Oppenheim, 1899
Memoirs, Halidé (Edib.), London, 1926
The Twelve Years Reign of H.M. Abdul Hamid II, Princess Annie de Lusignan, London, 1887
Histoire de l'empire Ottoman des origines à nos jours, de la Jonguiere, Paris, 1914
Question d'orient, Driault, Paris, 1917
The Eastern Question, Marriott, London, 1917
The Harem, Penzer, London, 1936
Behind the Sublime Porte, Miller, 1931
History of the Ottoman Empire, Miller, 1917
Lettres de la Turquie, Ubicini, Paris, 1856
The Old Diplomacy (Vol. I), Lord Hardinge of Penshurst, 1947
Forty Years in Constantinople, Edwin Pears, London, 1907
Abdul Hamid, Edwin Pears, London, 1917
The Fall of Abdul Hamid, MacCullagh, London, 1916
Abdul Hamid, the Shadow of God, Alma Wittlin, (English Edition), London, 1940
The Last of the Dragomans, Andrew Ryan
Memoirs, von Beust, 1870
Memoirs, von Bülow, 1930–1931
The Awakening of Turkey, E. Knight, London, 1909
Portraits and Appreciations, Viscount D'Abernon, London, 1931
The Turkish Problem, Count Leon Ostrorog (translated by Winifred Stevens), London, 1915
Correspondence 1870–1924 (Vol. I) Paul Cambon, Paris, 1925
Abdul Hamid intime, Georges Dorys, Paris, 1902
Lord Carnock, Harold Nicolson, London, 1930
Abdul Hamid Le Sultan Rouge, Gilles Roy, Paris, 1936

Aus Dem Leben des General Feld-Marschalls Freiherr von der Goltz Pasha, nach Briefen an seinen Freund, Bernhard von Schmiterlow, Berlin, 1926

Letters from Constantinople, Mrs. Max Muller, London, 1897

The Structure of the Ottoman Dynasty, A. D. Alderson, Oxford, 1956

Europe in the Nineteenth and Twentieth Century, A. Lipson & C. Black

Constantinople aux derniers jours d'Abdul Hamid, Fesch, Paris, 1900

Gallipoli, Alan Moorehead, London, 1957

Storm Centres in the Near East, Robert Graves, London

Turkey in Revolution, Charles Buxton, London, 1909

Ben Kedim, Aubrey Herbert, London, 1922

Aux pays d'Espionage, Paul Regla, Paris, 1897

Les Secrets de Yildiz, Paul Regla, Paris, 1897

Rise of Napoleon III, Simpson, London, 1909

Napoleon. The Recovery of France, Simpson, London, 1923

Turkey Old and New. Telford Waugh, 1930

La Turquie sous Abdul Aziz, Osman Bey, 1868

Mourad V, Comte E de Keratry, Paris

Le Palais de Yildiz et La Sublime Porte, Mourad Bey, Paris, 1897

Secrets of the Bosphorus, Henry Morgenthau, 1918

The Sultan and his Subjects (2 Vols.), Richard Davey, 1897

England's responsibility towards Armenia, Rev. Malcolm Maccoll, 1895

La Ruine d'un Empire, G. Gaulis, 1913

Scenes of the 30 days War between Greece and Turkey, Henry Nevinson, 1898

La Turquie agonisante, Pierre Loti, 1913

Persia (2 Vols.), Lord Curzon

Letters of Queen Victoria (2 Vols.), Viscount Esher, 1907

Victoria of England, Edith Sitwell

Tages Buch, Theodor Herzl (2 Vols.)

Modern Turkey, Toynbee

Islamic Civilisation and the West, Harold Bowen and Gibbs, Oxford

The Koran, Edited and translated, Sale, new edition, 1908

Memoirs of Tahsin Pasha (in Turkish) Istanbul

Golden Horn, Francis Yeats-Brown, London, 1932

Layard Papers (Vols. IV–VIII), British Museum

Ford Papers – Letters and Journals, unpublished

Max Muller. Letters to his parents (from Constantinople 1894—unpublished)

Public Record Office, Foreign Office records, 4078, 2462

La Cérémonie du Biat, description taken from *La Turquie*, August 30, 1876, published in Constantinople

Illustrated London News, 1867, 1876, 1909

Punch, July, 1867, 1896, 1909

The Last Sultan of Turkey, Chryssaphides and Rene Lara, *Nineteenth Century*, June, 1909

Manchester Courier, 1892

Daily Mail, June, 1909

The Times, 1896, 1898, 1908, 1909

Encyclopaedia Britannica, 'Armenia'

Islamic Encyclopaedia

Index